BHAGAVAD GĪTĀ

BHAGAVAD GĪTĀ

(The Scripture of Mankind)

The Text in Devanagari with Transliteration in Roman letters and Translation

Transliterated & Translated
by
Swāmī Tapasyānanda

Sri Ramakrishna Math
Mylapore, Chennai - 600 004

Published by :
Adhyaksha
Sri Ramakrishna Math
Mylapore, Chennai - 4

First Published on 8 August 2010
Swami Ramakrishnananda Jayanti

II-3M 3C-1-2012
ISBN 978-81-7823-544-8

Printed in India at
Sri Ramakrishna Math Printing Press
Mylapore, Chennai - 4

Introduction

This pocket edition of the Bhagavad Gītā will be useful for those who want to carry a great scripture even to their work spot in order to seek holy company in the midst of work.

Though put in the context of a battle scene, the object of the Gītā is not war-mongering but exhorting man to do his duty, whatever it be, in a spirit of detachment and dedication. Such an attitude can be sustained only if a man has unreserved faith in God and in His supremacy over the destiny of man individually and of the cosmos as a whole. So beginning with and exhortation to action, the Gītā gives in substantiation of that teaching a universal theology without any sectarian or dogmatic stance, which would be found congenial by all who are not in the grip of those narrow loyalties. For this reason we have designated it as the scripture of mankind.

A study of this small Text of seven hundred verses will convince any one that such an encomium of the wisdom contained in it is not a misplaced over-estimate.

Key to Pronunciation

Sounds like	
a	o in son
ā	a in master
i	i in if
ī	ee in feel
u	u in full
ū	oo in boot
ṛ	somewhat between r and ri
e	ay in May
ai	y in my
o	o in oh
au	ow in now
k	k in keen
kh	ckh in blockhead
g	g (hard) in go

gh	gh in log-hut
ṅ	ng in singer
c	ch (not k) in chain
ch	chh in catch him
j	j in judge
jh	dgeh in hedgehog
ñ	n (somewhat) as in French
ṭ	t in ten
ṭh	th in ant-hill
ḍ	d in den
ḍh	dh in godhood
ṇ	n in under
t	t in French
th	th in thumb
d	th in then
dh	th in breathe
n	n in not

p	p in pen
ph	ph in loop-hole
b	b in bag
bh	bh in abhor
m	m in mother
y	y in yard
r	r in run
l	l in luck
v	v in avert
ś	sh in reich (German)
ṣ	sh in show
s	s in sun
h	in hot
ṁ	m in sum
ḥ	h in half

Contents

Meditation on the Gītā

ॐ पार्थाय प्रतिबोधितां भगवता नारायणेन स्वयं
व्यासेन ग्रथितां पुराणमुनिना मध्ये महाभारतम् ।
अद्वैतामृतवर्षिणीं भगवतीम् अष्टादशाध्यायिनीम्
अम्ब त्वामनुसन्दधामि भगवद्गीते भवद्वेषिणीम् ।।

Om pārthāya pratibodhitāṁ
bhagavatā Nārāyaṇena svayaṁ
vyāsena grathitāṁ purāṇamuninā
madhye mahābhāratam /
advaitāmṛta varṣiṇīṁ bhagavatīm
aṣṭādaśā'dhyāyinīm
amba tvām anusandadhāmi
bhagavad-gīte bhavadveṣiṇīm //

Om! O Blessed Mother Bhagavad-Gītā, Thou Goddess!

Who was imparted to Arjuna by Nārāyaṇa Himself, who was recorded amidst the Mahābhārata by Vyāsa the ancient sage, who showers the nectar of Advaita, who is composed of eighteen chapters—I meditate on Thee, the destroyer of Samsāra!

नमोऽस्तु ते व्यास विशालबुद्धे फुल्लारविन्दायतपत्रनेत्र ।
येन त्वया भारततैलपूर्णः प्रज्वालितो ज्ञानमयः प्रदीपः ॥

Namo' stu te Vyāsa viśāla-buddhe
phullāravindā'yata-patra-netra /
yena tvayā bhārata-taila-pūrṇaḥ
prajvālito jñāna-mayaḥ pradīpaḥ //

Salutations to Thee, O Vyāsa of mighty intellect, Thou whose eyes are large like the petals of a full-blown lotus! It was Thou who lit the wisdom-lamp which brims with the oil that is the Mahābhārata.

प्रपन्नपारिजाताय तोत्रवेत्रैकपाणये ।
ज्ञानमुद्राय कृष्णाय गीतामृतदुहे नमः ॥

Prapanna-pārijātāya
totra-vetra'ika-pāṇaye /
jñāna-mudrāya kṛṣṇāya
gītāmṛta duhe namaḥ //

Salutations to Thee kṛṣṇa, who art a veritable wish-yielding tree to all surrendered ones, whose one hand holds a cane to drive cattle while the other is held in the jñāna-pose, and who is famous as the milker of the nectarine milk that is the Bhagavad-Gītā.

सर्वोपनिषदो गावो दोग्धा गोपालनन्दनः
पार्थो वत्सः सुधीर्भोक्ता दुग्धं गीतामृतं महत् ॥

Sarvo'paniṣado gāvo
dogdhā Gopāla-nandanaḥ /
pārtho vatsaḥ sudhīr-bhoktā
dugdhaṁ gītāmṛtaṁ mahat //

All the Upaniṣads are the cows; the cowherd's son Kṛṣṇa is the milker; Pārtha (Arjuna) is the calf; the nectarine Gītā is the milk; and the pure-minded are the drinkers of it.

वसुदेवसुतं देवं कंसचाणूरमर्दनम् ।
देवकीपरमानन्दं कृष्णं वन्दे जगद्गुरुम् ॥

Vasudeva-sutaṁ devaṁ
kaṁsa-Cāṇūra-mardanam /
Devakī-paramānandaṁ
kṛṣṇaṁ vande jagadgurum //

I salute Lord Kṛṣṇa, the son of Vasudeva, the bestower of supreme delight to Devaki, the destroyer of Kamsa and Cāṇūra, and the teacher of the world.

भीष्मद्रोणतटा जयद्रथजला गान्धारनीलोत्पला
शल्यग्राहवती कृपेण वहनी कर्णेन वेलाकुला ।
अश्वत्थामविकर्णघोरमकरा दुर्योधनावर्तिनी
सोत्तीर्णा खलु पाण्डवै रणनदी कैवर्तकः केशवः ॥

Bhīṣma-droṇa-taṭā jayadratha-
jalā Gāndhāra-nīlotpalā
Śalya-grāhavatī Kṛpeṇa
vahanī Karṇena velākulā /

Aśvatthāma-vikarṇa-ghora-
makarā Duryodhanā'vartinī
s'ottīrṇā khalu pāṇḍavai
raṇa-nadī kaivartakaḥ
Keśavaḥ //

Lo! The battle-river of Kurukṣetra, with Bhīṣma and Droṇa as the banks; with Jayadratha as the water; with the prince of Gāndhāra as the blue water lily; with Śalya as the crocodile; with Kṛpa as the current; with Karṇa as the high wave; with Aśvatthāma and Vikarṇa as terrible sharks; and with Duryodhana as the whirl-pool—was crossed by the Pāṇḍavas because they had Kṛṣṇa as the ferry-man.

पाराशर्यवचः सरोजममलं गीतार्थगन्धोत्कटं
नानाख्यानककेसरं हरिकथासम्बोधनाबोधितम् ।
लोके सज्जनषट्पदैरहरहः पेपीयमानं मुदा
भूयाद्भारतपङ्कजं कलिमलप्रध्वंसिनः श्रेयसे ॥

Pārāśarya-vacaḥ-sarojam
amalaṁ gītārtha-gandhotkaṭaṁ
nānā'khyānaka-kesaraṁ Harikathā-
saṁbodhanā-bodhitam /
loke sajjana-ṣatpadair
aharahaḥ pepīyamānaṁ mudā
bhūyād bhārata-paṅkajaṁ
kalimala-pradhvaṁsinaḥ
śreyase //

May the stainless lotus of Mahābhārata, which was born on the waters of the words of Vyāsa, the son of Parāśara, which has the message of the Gītā for its overpowering fragrance, which contains numerous narratives proclaiming the glory of Hari as its stamens, and which is sucked again and again in great joy every day by the honey-suckers of virtuous men—may it prevail for the good of all who want to be cleansed of the taint of the age of Kali!

मूकं करोति वाचालं पङ्गुं लङ्घयते गिरिम् ।
यत्कृपा तमहं वन्दे परमानन्दमाधवम् ॥

Mūkaṁ karoti vācālaṁ
paṅguṁ laṅghayate girim /
yat kṛpā tam ahaṁ vande
paramānanda-mādhavam //

I salute Mādhava (Lord Kṛṣṇa), the Supremely Blissful One, by whose grace a dumb man can become eloquent, and a lame person cross over mountains.

यं ब्रह्मा वरुणेन्द्ररुद्रमरुतः स्तुन्वन्ति दिव्यैः स्तवै-
र्वेदैः साङ्गपदक्रमोपनिषदैर्गायन्ति यं सामगाः ।
ध्यानावस्थिततद्गतेन मनसा पश्यन्ति यं योगिनो
यस्यान्तं न विदुः सुरासुरगणा देवाय तस्मै नमः ॥

Yaṁ Brahmā-Varuṇe'ndra-Rudra-
Marutaḥ stunvanti divyaiḥ stavaiḥ
vedaiḥ sāṅga-pada kramo'paniṣadaiḥ
gāyanti yaṁ sāmagāḥ /
dhyānā'vasthita-tad-gatena
manasā paśyanti yaṁ yogino

yasyāntaṁ na viduḥ surāsura-
gaṇā devāya tasmai namaḥ //

My salutations to that Supreme Being, whom Brahmā, Varuṇa, Indra and Rudra glorify by divine hymns; whom singers of Sāman praise by chanting the Veda with all the complementary parts, sections and Upaniṣads; whom Yogins intuit with minds concentrated in meditation; and whose limit neither the hosts of Devas nor of Asuras know.

1. Arjuna's Conversion

'Kṛṣṇa! My limbs are giving way, my mouth is parching.' (*Śloka* 29)

Chapter-1

Arjuna's Conversion

धृतराष्ट्र उवाच —

धर्मक्षेत्रे कुरुक्षेत्रे समवेता युयुत्सवः ।
मामकाः पाण्डवाश्चैव किमकुर्वत सञ्जय ।।

Dhṛtarāṣṭra Uvāca:
Dharma-kṣetre kuru-kṣetre
samavetā yuyutsavaḥ /
māmakāḥ pāṇḍavāścaiva
kim akurvata, Sañjaya // 1 //

Dhṛtarāṣṭra said:

O Sañjaya! What indeed did my people and the followers of the Pāṇḍavas do after having assembled in the holy land of Kurukṣetra, eager to join battle?

सञ्जय उवाच —

दृष्ट्वा तु पाण्डवानीकं व्यूढं दुर्योधनस्तदा ।
आचार्यमुपसङ्गम्य राजा वचनमब्रवीत् ।।

Sañjaya uvāca:

Dṛṣṭvā tu pāṇḍavānīkaṁ
vyūḍhaṁ duryodhanas tadā /
ācāryam upasaṅgamya
rājā vacanam abravīt // 2 //

Sañjaya said:

Then seeing the army of the Pāṇḍavas arrayed in battle order, King Duryodhana for his part approached the teacher Droṇa and spoke to him the following words:

पश्यैतां पाण्डुपुत्राणामाचार्य महतीं चमूम् ।
व्यूढां द्रुपदपुत्रेण तव शिष्येण धीमता ।।

Paśyaitāṁ pāṇḍu-putrāṇām
ācārya mahatīṁ camūm /
vyūḍhāṁ drupada-putreṇa
tava śiṣyeṇa dhīmatā // 3 //

O Teacher! Behold this great army of the sons of Pāṇḍu, arrayed in battle order by your talented disciple, the son of Drupada.

अत्र शूरा महेष्वासा भीमार्जुनसमा युधि।
युयुधानो विराटश्च द्रुपदश्च महारथः॥

Atra śūrā maheṣvāsā
Bhīmārjuna-samā yudhi /
Yuyudhāno Virāṭaśca
Drupadaś ca mahā-rathaḥ // 4 //

Here (in that army) are many brave bow-men of note who are equal to Bhīma and Arjuna in battle—great car-warriors like Yuyudhāna, Virāṭa and Drupada;

धृष्टकेतुश्चेकितानः काशिराजश्च वीर्यवान् ।
पुरुजित्कुन्तिभोजश्च शैब्यश्च नरपुङ्गवः ॥

Dhṛṣṭaketuś Cekitānaḥ
Kāśi-rājaś ca vīryavān /
Purujit Kuntibhojaś ca
Śaibyaś ca nara-puṅgavaḥ // 5 //

Dhṛṣṭaketu, Cekitāna and the brave king of Kāśi; Purujit, Kuntibhoja and Śaibya the best of men;

युधामन्युश्च विक्रान्त उत्तमौजाश्च वीर्यवान् ।
सौभद्रो द्रौपदेयाश्च सर्व एव महारथाः ।।

Yudhāmanyuś ca vikrānta
Uttamaujāś ca vīryavān /
Saubhadro Draupadeyāś ca
sarva eva mahā rathāḥ // 6 //

The powerful Yudhāmanyu, the brave Uttamauja, the son of Subhadrā, and the sons of Draupadi—all these are indeed noted car-warriors.

अस्माकं तु विशिष्टा ये तान्निबोध द्विजोत्तम ।
नायका मम सैन्यस्य संज्ञार्थं तान्ब्रवीमि ते ।।

Asmākaṁ tu viśiṣṭā ye
tān nibodha dvij'ottama /
nāyakā mama sainyasya
saṁjñ'ārthaṁ tān bravīmi te // 7 //

O best of Brāhmaṇas, I shall mention for your information the names of the distinguished leaders of our army.

भवान् भीष्मश्च कर्णश्च कृपश्च समितिञ्जयः ।
अश्वत्थामा विकर्णश्च सौमदत्तिर्जयद्रथः ।।

Bhavān Bhīṣmaś ca Karṇaś ca
Kṛpaś ca samitiñ-jayaḥ /
Aśvatthāmā Vikarṇaś ca
Saumadattir Jayadrathaḥ // 8 //

Yourself, Bhīṣma and Karṇa, the victorious Kṛpa. Aswatthāmā, Vikarṇa and Jayadratha the son of Somadatta.

अन्ये च बहवः शूरा मदर्थे त्यक्तजीविताः ।
नानाशस्त्रप्रहरणाः सर्वे युद्धविशारदाः ॥

Anye ca bahavaḥ śūrā
mad-arthe tyakta-Jīvitāḥ /
nānā śastra praharaṇāḥ
sarve yuddha-viśaradāḥ // 9 //

These and many more brave men, who are ready to lay down their lives for my sake and who fight with various types of weapons, are present here. All of them are seasoned warriors.

अपर्याप्तं तदस्माकं बलं भीष्माभिरक्षितम् ।
पर्याप्तं त्विदमेतेषां बलं भीमाभिरक्षितम् ।।

Aparyāptaṁ tad asmākaṁ
balaṁ Bhīṣm'ābhirakṣitam /
paryāptaṁ tv idam eteṣāṁ
balaṁ Bhīm'ābhirakṣitam // 10 //

Though numerically superior, inadequate is the army of ours defended by Bhīṣma, while theirs guarded by Bhīma is adequate.

अयनेषु च सर्वेषु यथाभागमवस्थिताः ।
भीष्ममेवाभिरक्षन्तु भवन्तः सर्व एव हि ।।

Ayaneṣu ca sarveṣu
yathā-bhāgam avasthitāḥ /
Bhīṣmam evābhirakṣantu
bhavantaḥ sarva eva hi // 11 //

Therefore do ye all protect Bhīṣma remaining in appropriate positions in your respective divisions.

तस्य सञ्जनयन् हर्षं कुरुवृद्धः पितामहः ।
सिंहनादं विनद्योच्चैः शङ्खं दध्मौ प्रतापवान् ।।

Tasya sañjanayan harṣaṁ
Kuru-vṛddhaḥ pitāmahaḥ /
siṁha-nādaṁ vinady'occaiḥ
śaṅkhaṁ dadhmau
pratāpavān // 12 //

Cheering him up, the valiant grandfather Bhīṣma, the oldest of the Kurus, sounded a lion-roar loudly and blew his conch-shell horn.

ततः शङ्खाश्च भेर्यश्च पणवानकगोमुखाः ।
सहसैवाभ्यहन्यन्त स शब्दस्तुमुलोऽभवत् ।।

Tataḥ śaṅkhāś ca bheryaś ca
paṇav'ānaka-gomukhāḥ /
sahas'aiv'ābhyahanyanta
sa śabdas tumulo' bhavat // 13 //

Thereupon, conchs, kettle-drums, tabors, trumpets, and cowhorns all blared out suddenly causing a tremendous sound.

ततः श्वेतैर्हयैर्युक्ते महति स्यन्दने स्थितौ ।
माधवः पाण्डवश्चैव दिव्यौ शङ्खौ प्रदध्मतुः ।।

Tataḥ śvetair hayair yukte
mahati syandane sthitau /
Mādhavaḥ Pāṇḍavaś c'aiva
divyau śaṅkhau
pradadhmatuḥ // 14 //

Then Śrī Kṛṣṇa and Arjuna, seated in a great chariot with white horses yoked to it, blew their celestial conch-shell horns.

पाञ्चजन्यं हृषीकेशो देवदत्तं धनञ्जयः ।
पौण्ड्रं दध्मौ महाशङ्खं भीमकर्मा वृकोदरः ॥

Pāñcajanyaṁ Hṛṣīkeśo
Devadattaṁ Dhanañjayaḥ /
Pauṇḍraṁ dadhmau mahā-
śaṅkham
bhīma-karmā Vṛk'odaraḥ // *15* //

Śrī Kṛṣṇa blew his conch Pāñcajanya, Arjuna blew Devadatta, and Bhīma of terrible deeds sounded his great conch Pauṇḍra.

अनन्तविजयं राजा कुन्तीपुत्रो युधिष्ठिरः ।
नकुलः सहदेवश्च सुघोषमणिपुष्पकौ ।।

Anantavijayaṁ rājā
Kuntī-putro Yudhiṣṭhiraḥ /
Nakulaḥ Sahadevaś ca
Sughoṣa-Maṇipuṣpakau // 16 //

Raja Yudhiṣṭhira, the son of Kuntī, blew his conch Anantavijaya, and Nakula and Sahadeva, Sughoṣa and Maṇipuṣpaka respectively.

काश्यश्च परमेष्वासः शिखण्डी च महारथः ।
धृष्टद्युम्नो विराटश्च सात्यकिश्चापराजितः ॥

Kāśyaś ca param'eṣvāsaḥ
Śikhaṇḍī ca mahā-rathaḥ /
Dhṛṣṭadyumno Virātaś ca
Sātyakiś c'āparājitaḥ // 17 //

The great archer, king of Kāśi, the mighty car-warrior Śikhaṇḍī and Dhṛṣṭadyumna and invincible Sātyaki;

द्रुपदो द्रौपदेयाश्च सर्वशः पृथिवीपते।
सौभद्रश्च महाबाहुः शङ्खान् दध्मुः पृथक् पृथक् ॥

Drupado Draupadeyāś ca
sarvaśaḥ pṛthivī-pate /
Saubhadraś ca mahā-bāhuḥ
śaṅkhān dadhmuḥ pṛthak
pṛthak // 18 //

The king of Drupada, the sons of Draupadī, the mighty armed son of Subhadrā—all these, O king, sounded their conchshell horns again and again everywhere.

स घोषो धार्तराष्ट्राणां हृदयानि व्यदारयत् ।
नभश्च पृथिवीं चैव तुमुलो व्यनुनादयन् ।।

Sa ghoṣo Dhārtarāṣṭrāṇāṁ
hṛdayāni vyadārayat /
nabhaś ca pṛthivīṁ c'aiva
tumulo vyanunādayan // 19 //

That tumultuous uproar, resounding in the sky and over the land, pierced the hearts of the followers of Dhṛtarāṣṭra.

अथ व्यवस्थितान्दृष्ट्वा धार्तराष्ट्रान् कपिध्वजः ।
प्रवृत्ते शस्त्रसम्पाते धनुरुद्यम्य पाण्डवः ।।
हृषीकेशं तदा वाक्यमिदमाह महीपते ।

Atha vyavasthitān dṛṣṭvā
Dhārtarāṣṭrān kapi-dhvajaḥ /
pravṛtte śastra-sampāte
dhanur udyamya
Pāṇḍavaḥ // 20 //
Hṛṣīkeśaṁ tadā vākyam
idam āha mahīpate /

O King! Arjuna, the Pāṇḍava-leader with the banner crest of a monkey, on seeing the followers of Dhṛtarāṣṭra arrayed for battle and the clash of weapons about to start, held up his bow and said the following words to Śrī Kṛṣṇa:

अर्जुन उवाच —
सेनयोरुभयोर्मध्ये रथं स्थापय मेऽच्युत ।।
यावदेतान्निरीक्षेऽहं योद्धुकामानवस्थितान् ।
कैर्मया सह योद्धव्यमस्मिन् रणसमुद्यमे ।।

Arjuna uvāca:
Senayor ubhayor madhye
rathaṁ sthāpaya me' cyuta // 21 //

yāvad etān nirīkṣe' haṁ
yoddhu-kāmān avasthitān /
kair mayā saha yoddhavyam
asmin raṇa-samudyame // 22 //

Arjuna said:

O Acyuta! Please station my chariot between the two armies so that I may have a view, on the eve of this battle, of all those standing ready to fight, and learn who all are the persons with whom I have to contend.

योत्स्यमानानवेक्षेऽहं य एतेऽत्र समागताः ।
धार्तराष्ट्रस्य दुर्बुद्धेर्युद्धे प्रियचिकीर्षवः ।।

Yotsyamānān avekṣe' ham
ya ete' tra samāgatāḥ /
Dhārtarāṣṭrasya durbuddher
yuddhe priyacikīrṣavaḥ // 23 //

Let me see all those who have arrived to favour the evil-minded son of Dhṛtarāṣṭra in war and are standing ready to join battle.

सञ्जय उवाच —

एवमुक्तो हृषीकेशो गुडाकेशेन भारत ।
सेनयोरुभयोर्मध्ये स्थापयित्वा रथोत्तमम् ।।
भीष्मद्रोणप्रमुखतः सर्वेषां च महीक्षिताम् ।
उवाच पार्थ पश्यैतान् समवेतान् कुरूनिति ।।

Sañjaya uvāca:
Evam ukto Hṛṣīkeśo
Guḍākeśena Bhārata /
senayor ubhayor madhye
sthāpayitvā rath'ottamam //24//
Bhīṣma-Droṇa pramukhataḥ
sarveṣāṁ ca mahī-kṣitām
uvāca Pārtha paśy'aitān
samavetān Kurūn iti //25//

Sañjaya said:

O King Dhṛtarāṣṭra! Śrī Kṛṣṇa, to whom Arjuna addressed these words, stationed that most splendid of chariots at a place, between the two armies, confronting Bhīṣma, Droṇa and all those chiefs, and said: 'O Arjuna! See these men of the Kuru horde assembled for battle.'

तत्रापश्यत्स्थितान्पार्थः पितॄनथ पितामहान् ।
आचार्यान् मातुलान् भ्रातॄन् पुत्रान् पौत्रान् सखींस्तथा ।।
श्वशुरान् सुहृदश्चैव सेनयोरुभयोरपि ।
तान् समीक्ष्य स कौन्तेयः सर्वान् बन्धूनवस्थितान् ।।
कृपया परयाविष्टो विषीदन्निदमब्रवीत् ।

Tatr'āpaśyat sthitān Pārthaḥ
pitṛn atha pitāmahān /
ācāryān mātulān bhrātṛn
putrān pautrān sakhīṁstathā //26//

Śvaśurān suhṛdaś caiva
senayor ubhayor api /
tān samīkṣya sa Kaunteyaḥ
sarvān bandhūn avasthitān //27//

kṛpayā paray'āviṣṭo
viṣīdann idam abravīt /

There he saw standing in both the armies—fathers, grand-fathers, uncles, brothers, sons, grandsons, comrades, fathers-in-law and bosom friends. Seeing all these kinsmen arrayed, Arjuna was overcome with great pity, and said sorrowing:

अर्जुन उवाच —
दृष्ट्वेमं स्वजनं कृष्ण युयुत्सुं समुपस्थितम् ।।
सीदन्ति मम गात्राणि मुखं च परिशुष्यति ।
वेपथुश्च शरीरे मे रोमहर्षश्च जायते ।।

Arjuna uvāca:
Dṛṣṭvemaṁ svajanaṁ Kṛṣṇa
yuyutsuṁ samupasthitam // 28 //
Sīdanti mama gātrāṇi
mukhaṁ ca pariśuṣyati /
vepathuś ca śarīre me
roma-harṣaś ca jāyate // 29 //

Arjuna said:

Seeing these relatives standing eager to join battle, my limbs are giving way, my mouth is parching. I get trembling of the body and horripilations.

गाण्डीवं स्त्रंसते हस्तात्त्वक्चैव परिदह्यते ।
न च शक्नोम्यवस्थातुं भ्रमतीव च मे मनः ।।

Gāṇḍīvaṁ sraṁsate hastāt
tvakc'aiva paridahyate
na ca śaknomy avasthātuṁ
bhramatī'va ca me manaḥ // 30 //

My bow Gāṇḍīva is slipping from my hand. My skin too is burning. I find it impossible to stand firm, and my mind is, as it were, reeling.

निमित्तानि च पश्यामि विपरीतानि केशव ।
न च श्रेयोऽनुपश्यामि हत्वा स्वजनमाहवे ॥

Nimittāni ca paśyāmi
viparītāni Keśava /
na ca śreyo' nupaśyāmi
hatvā svajanam āhave // 31 //

O Keśava! I see adverse omens. I do not feel that any good will come by killing all one's kinsmen in battle.

न काङ्क्षे विजयं कृष्ण न च राज्यं सुखानि च ।
किं नो राज्येन गोविन्द किं भोगैर्जीवितेन वा ।।

Na kāṅkṣe vijayaṁ Kṛṣṇa
na ca rājyaṁ sukhāni ca /
kiṁ no rājyena Govinda
kiṁ bhogair jīvitena vā // 32 //

O Kṛṣṇa! I do not long for victory, or kingdom, or enjoyments. O Govinda! Of what use is kingdom, enjoyments or even life itself?

येषामर्थे काङ्क्षितं नो राज्यं भोगाः सुखानि च ।
त इमेऽवस्थिता युद्धे प्राणांस्त्यक्त्वा धनानि च ।।

आचार्याः पितरः पुत्रास्तथैव च पितामहाः ।
मातुलाः श्वशुराः पौत्राः श्यालाः सम्बन्धिनस्तथा ।।

Yeṣām arthe kāṅkṣitaṁ no
rājyaṁ bhogāḥ sukhāni ca /
ta ime' vasthitā yuddhe
prāṇāṁs tyaktvā dhanāni
ca // 33 //

Ācāryāḥ pitaraḥ putrāḥ
tathaiva ca pitāmahāḥ /
mātulāḥ śvaśurāḥ pautrāḥ
śyālāḥ sambandhinas
tathā // 34 //

Those for whose sake kingdoms, enjoyments, and pleasures are desired—those very teachers, fathers and sons, as also grandfathers, uncles, fathers-in-law and other relatives are here stationed in battle ready to give up their lives and possessions.

एतान्न हन्तुमिच्छामि घ्नतोऽपि मधुसूदन ।
अपि त्रैलोक्यराज्यस्य हेतोः किं नु महीकृते ।।

Etān na hantum icchāmi
ghnato' pi Madhusūdana /
api trailokya-rājyasya
hetoḥ kiṁ nu mahīkṛte // 35 //

Even for the sovereignty of the three worlds, I do not desire to kill them, though myself killed—how much less then for this earthly kingdom!

निहत्य धार्तराष्ट्रान्नः का प्रीतिः स्याज्जनार्दन ।
पापमेवाश्रयेदस्मान् हत्वैतानाततायिनः ॥

Nihatya Dhārtarāṣṭrān naḥ
kā prītiḥ syāj Janārdana /
pāpam ev'āśrayed asmān
hatv'aitān ātatāyinaḥ // 36 //

What joy can there be for us by killing these sons of Dhṛtarāṣṭra? Though they are murderous villains, only sin will accrue to us by killing them.

तस्मान्नार्हा वयं हन्तुं धार्तराष्ट्रान् स्वबान्धवान् ।
स्वजनं हि कथं हत्वा सुखिनः स्याम माधव ।।

Tasmān n'ārhā vayaṁ hantuṁ
Dhārtarāṣṭrān svabāndhavān /
svajanaṁ hi kathaṁ hatvā
sukhinaḥ syāma
Mādhava // 37 //

Therefore, O Mādhava! it is not befitting that we kill our relations, the sons of Dhṛtarāṣṭra. How could one be happy by the slaughter of one's own kinsmen?

यद्यप्येते न पश्यन्ति लोभोपहतचेतसः ।
कुलक्षयकृतं दोषं मित्रद्रोहे च पातकम् ।।
कथं न ज्ञेयमस्माभिः पापादस्मान्निवर्तितुम् ।
कुलक्षयकृतं दोषं प्रपश्यद्भिर्जनार्दन ।।

Yady apy ete na paśyanti
lobh'opahata-cetasaḥ /
kula-kṣaya-kṛtaṁ doṣaṁ
mitra-drohe ca pātakam //38//

Kathaṁ na jñeyam asmābhiḥ
pāpād asmān nivartitum
kula-kṣaya-kṛtaṁ doṣam
prapaśyadbhir
Janārdana //39//

O Janārdana! Even if these people with their intelligence overpowered by greed, do not see any evil in the decay of families and any sin in the persecution of friends, why should not we, who are aware of the evil of such decay of families, learn to desist from that sin?

कुलक्षये प्रणश्यन्ति कुलधर्माः सनातनाः ।
धर्मे नष्टे कुलं कृत्स्नमधर्मोऽभिभवत्युत ।।

Kula-kṣaye praṇaśyanti
kula-dharmāḥ sanātanāḥ
dharme naṣṭe kulaṁ kṛtsnam
adharmo' bhibhavatyuta // 40 //

When a clan becomes decadent, its ancient traditions (laws) perish. When traditions perish, the entire clan is indeed overcome by lawlessness.

अधर्माभिभवात् कृष्ण प्रदुष्यन्ति कुलस्त्रियः ।
स्त्रीषु दुष्टासु वार्ष्णेय जायते वर्णसङ्करः ॥

Adharm'ābhibhavāt Kṛṣṇa
praduṣyanti kula-striyaḥ /
strīṣu duṣṭāsu Vārṣṇeya
jāyate varṇa-saṅkaraḥ // 41 //

O Kṛṣṇa! When lawlessness prevails, the women of the clans become corrupt. O scion of the Vṛṣṇis! When women are corrupted, mixture of classes (promiscuity) prevails.

सङ्करो नरकायैव कुलघ्नानां कुलस्य च ।
पतन्ति पितरो ह्येषां लुप्तपिण्डोदकक्रियाः ॥

Saṅkaro narakāy'aiva
kula-ghnānāṁ kulasya ca
patanti pitaro hy eṣāṁ
lupta-piṇḍ'odaka-kriyāḥ // 42 //

Promiscuity results only in hell to those destroyers of the clans, as also to the members of the clan. For (being without legitimate progeny to perform obsequies), the spirits of their ancestors fall, deprived of the offerings of rice ball and water.

दोषैरेतैः कुलघ्नानां वर्णसङ्करकारकैः ।
उत्साद्यन्ते जातिधर्माः कुलधर्माश्च शाश्वताः ॥

Doṣair etaiḥ kula-ghnānāṁ
varṇa-saṅkara-kārakaiḥ /
utsādyante jāti-dharmāḥ
kula-dharmāś ca
śāśvatāḥ // *43* //

By the misdeeds of these ruiners of clans and promoters of promiscuity, the immemorial traditions of the communities and clans are uprooted.

उत्सन्नकुलधर्माणां मनुष्याणां जनार्दन ।
नरके नियतं वासो भवतीत्यनुशुश्रुम ।।

Utsanna-kula-dharmāṇāṁ
manuṣyāṇāṁ Janārdana /
narake niyataṁ vāso
bhavatī'ty anuśuśruma // 44 //

O Janārdana! We have heard that residence in hell awaits men, the religious traditions of whose clans have been destroyed.

अहो बत महत्पापं कर्तुं व्यवसिता वयम् ।
यद्राज्यसुखलोभेन हन्तुं स्वजनमुद्यताः ।।

Aho bata mahat pāpaṁ
kartuṁ vyavasitā vayam /
yad rājya-sukha-lobhena
hantuṁ svajanam
udyatāḥ // 45 //

Alas! What great sin have we resolved to commit when we prepared ourselves to destroy our kinsmen out of greed for the pleasures of a kingdom!

यदि मामप्रतीकारमशस्त्रं शस्त्रपाणयः ।
धार्तराष्ट्रा रणे हन्युस्तन्मे क्षेमतरं भवेत् ॥

Yadi mām apratīkāram
aśastraṁ śastra-pāṇayaḥ /
Dhārtarāṣṭrā raṇe hanyuḥ
tan me kṣemataraṁ
bhavet // 46 //

Far better would it be for me if the sons of Dhṛtarāṣṭra, with weapons in hand, kill me in battle, unarmed and unresisting!

सञ्जय उवाच —

एवमुक्त्वार्जुनः सङ्ख्ये रथोपस्थ उपाविशत् ।
विसृज्य सशरं चापं शोकसंविग्नमानसः ॥

Sañjaya uvāca:
Evam uktvārjunaḥ saṅkhye
rathopastha upāviśat /
visṛjya saśaraṁ cāpaṁ
śoka-saṁvigna-mānasaḥ // 47 //

Sañjaya said:

So saying, Arjuna, with his mind overwhelmed with sorrow, abandoned his bow and arrows and sat down on the chariot seat.

2. Yoga of Knowledge

'On attaining tranquillity all one's sorrows come to an end.' (65)

Chapter 2

Yoga of Knowledge

सञ्जय उवाच —

तं तथा कृपयाऽऽविष्टम् अश्रुपूर्णाकुलेक्षणम् ।
विषीदन्तमिदं वाक्यम् उवाच मधुसूदनः ॥

Sañjaya uvāca:

Taṁ tathā kṛpayā' viṣṭam
aśru-pūrṇākul'ekṣaṇam /
viṣīdantam idaṁ vākyam
uvāca Madhusūdanaḥ // 1 //

Sañjaya said:

To him who was thus overcome with pity and whose eyes were full of tears and bore a bewildered look, Śrī Kṛṣṇa spoke as follows:

श्रीभगवानुवाच —

कुतस्त्वा कश्मलमिदं विषमे समुपस्थितम् ।
अनार्यजुष्टमस्वर्ग्यम् अकीर्तिकरमर्जुन ।।

Śrī Bhagavān uvāca:

Kutas tvā kaśmalam idaṁ
viṣame samupasthitam /
anārya-justam asvargyam
akīrtikaram Arjuna // 2 //

The Blessed Lord said:

O Arjuna! Whence has this loathsome stupidity come upon you in this crisis? It (this attitude) is unworthy of a noble personage; it is a bar to heaven and a cause of much disrepute.

क्लैब्यं मा स्म गमः पार्थ नैतत्त्वय्युपपद्यते ।
क्षुद्रं हृदयदौर्बल्यं त्यक्त्वोत्तिष्ठ परन्तप ।।

Klaibyaṁ mā sma gamaḥ Pārtha
naitat tvayy upapadyate!
kṣudraṁ hṛdaya-daurbalyaṁ
tyaktv'ottiṣṭha parantapa // 3 //

O Pārtha! Yield not to unmanliness! It befits thee not. Abandoning this base faint-heartedness, rise up, O dreaded hero!

अर्जुन उवाच —

कथं भीष्ममहं सङ्ख्ये द्रोणं च मधुसूदन ।
इषुभिः प्रतियोत्स्यामि पूजार्हावरिसूदन ॥

Arjuna uvāca:

Kathaṁ Bhīṣmam ahaṁ saṅkhye
Droṇaṁ ca Madhusudana /
iṣubhiḥ pratiyotsyāmi
puj'ārhāv arisūdana // 4 //

Arjuna said:

O Kṛṣṇa! How can I attack Bhīṣma and Droṇa in battle with my arrows? They are, indeed worthy of worship, O destroyer of foes!

गुरूनहत्वा हि महानुभावान्
श्रेयो भोक्तुं भैक्ष्यमपीह लोके ।
हत्वाऽर्थकामांस्तु गुरूनिहैव
भुञ्जीय भोगान् रुधिरप्रदिग्धान् ॥

Gurūn ahatvā-hi mahā'nubhāvān
śreyo bhoktuṁ bhaikṣyamapīha loke /
hatvā' rtha kāmāṁs tu gurūn ih'aiva
bhuñjīya bhogān rudhirapradigdhān // 5 //

It is indeed better to live here in this world on a beggar's fare than to prosper by killing these venerable teachers. The enjoyment of pleasure and power obtained through the slaughter of these teachers and elders will surely be bloodstained.

न चैतद्विद्मः कतरन्नो गरीयो
यद्वा जयेम यदि वा नो जयेयुः ।
यानेव हत्वा न जिजीविषाम-
स्तेऽवस्थिताः प्रमुखे धार्तराष्ट्राः ॥

Na c'aitad vidmaḥ kataran no garīyo
yad vā jayema yadi vāno jayeyuḥ /
yān eva hatvā na jijīviṣamas
te' vasthitāḥ pramukhe
Dhārtarāṣṭrāḥ // 6 //

We do not know which of the two (alternatives) will be the better—the one that we should conquer them or the other that they should conquer us. The men on the side of Dhritrāṣṭra standing arrayed against us, are the very people after killing whom we should not care to live.

कार्पण्यदोषोपहतस्वभावः
पृच्छामि त्वां धर्मसम्मूढचेताः ।
यच्छ्रेयः स्यान्निश्चितं ब्रूहि तन्मे
शिष्यस्तेऽहं शाधि मां त्वां प्रपन्नम् ॥

Kārpaṇya-doṣ'opahata-svabhāvaḥ
pṛcchāmi tvāṁ-dharma
sammūḍhacetāḥ
yac chreyaḥ syān niścitam brūhi tan me
siṣyas te' haṁ śādhi māṁ tvāṁ
prapannam // 7 //

My natural disposition is vitiated by a sense of pity, and my mind is in utter confusion regarding my duty. Lord, I beg Thee: tell me with certainty what will lead to my good. I am Thy disciple. Instruct me, who have taken refuge in Thee.

न हि प्रपश्यामि ममापनुद्या-
द्यच्छोकमुच्छोषणमिन्द्रियाणाम् ।
अवाप्य भूमावसपत्नमृद्धं
राज्यं सुराणामपि चाधिपत्यम् ॥

na hi prapaśyāmi mam'āpanudyād
yac chokam ucchoṣaṇam
indriyāṇām /
avāpya bhūmāu asapatnam ṛddhaṁ
rājyaṁ surāṇām api
c'ādhipatyam // 8 //

I do not find anything that can assuage this grief which numbs my senses. Neither the unchallenged lordship over a prosperous kingdom, nor even the overlordship of all the Devas can do so.

सञ्जय उवाच —

एवमुक्त्वा हृषीकेशं गुडाकेशः परन्तपः ।
न योत्स्य इति गोविन्दमुक्त्वा तूष्णीं बभूव ह ।।

Sañjaya uvāca:
Evam uktvā hṛṣīkeśaṁ
guḍākeśaḥ parantapaḥ /
na yotsya iti Govindam
uktvā tūṣṇīṁ babhūva ha // 9 //

Sañjaya said:

Addressing Śrī Kṛṣṇa, the master of the senses, Arjuna, though valorous and vigilant, said, 'I will not fight' and sat silent.

तमुवाच हृषीकेशः प्रहसन्निव भारत ।
सेनयोरुभयोर्मध्ये विषीदन्तमिदं वचः ।।

Tam uvāca hṛṣīkeśaḥ
prahasan iva Bhārata /
senayor ubhayor madhye
viṣīdantam idaṁ vacaḥ // 10 //

O King! To him who was thus sitting grief-stricken between the two armies (instead of fighting), Śrī Kṛṣṇa said as if by way of ridicule.

श्रीभगवानुवाच —
अशोच्यानन्वशोचस्त्वं प्रज्ञावादांश्च भाषसे ।
गतासूनगतासूंश्च नानुशोचन्ति पण्डिताः ॥

Śrī Bhagavān uvāca

aśocyān anvaśocas tvaṁ
prajñā-vādāṁś ca bhāṣase /
gat'āsūn agat'āsūṁś ca
n'ānuśocanti paṇḍitāḥ // 11 //

The Blessed Lord said:

You arc moaning for those who should not be moaned for. Yet you speak like a wise man. The truly wise never weep either for the dead or for the living.

न त्वेवाहं जातु नासं न त्वं नेमे जनाधिपाः ।
न चैव न भविष्यामः सर्वे वयमतः परम् ॥

Na tv'ev'āham jātu nāsaṁ
na tvaṁ n'eme jan'ādhipāḥ /
na c'aiva na bhaviṣyāmaḥ
satve vayam ataḥ param // *12* //

Never was there a time when I did not exist, nor you, nor these rulers of men. Nor shall all of us cease to be hereafter.

देहिनोऽस्मिन् यथा देहे कौमारं यौवनं जरा ।
तथा देहान्तरप्राप्तिर्धीरस्तत्र न मुह्यति ।।

Dehino' smin yathā dehe
kaumāram yauvanaṁ jarā /
tathā dehā'ntara prāptir-
dhīras tatra na muhyati // 13 //

Even as the attainment of childhood, youth and old age is to one in this physical life, so is the change to another body (at death) for the embodied soul. Wise men are not deluded by this.

मात्रास्पर्शास्तु कौन्तेय शीतोष्णसुखदुःखदाः ।
आगमापायिनोऽनित्यास्तांस्तितिक्षस्व भारत ॥

Mātrā-sparśās tu Kaunteya
śīt'oṣṇa-sukha-duḥkhadāḥ /
āgam'āpāyino' nityāḥ
tāṁs titikṣasva Bhārata // 14 //

Contact of the senses with their objects generates cold and heat, pleasure and pain. They come and go, being impermanent. Bear with them patiently, O scion of the Bharata race!

यं हि न व्यथयन्त्येते पुरुषं पुरुषर्षभ ।
समदुःखसुखं धीरं सोऽमृतत्वाय कल्पते ।।

Yaṁ hi na vyathayanty ete
puruṣaṁ puruṣ'arṣabha /
sama-duḥkha-sukhaṁ dhīraṁ
so' mṛtatvāya kalpate // 15 //

O leader of men! That enlightened one who is unpertubed alike in pleasure and pain, whom these do not distress—he indeed is worthy of immortality.

नासतो विद्यते भावो नाभावो विद्यते सतः ।
उभयोरपि दृष्टोऽन्तस्त्वनयोस्तत्वदर्शिभिः ।।

N'āsato vidyate bhāvo
n'ābhāvo vidyate sataḥ /
ubhayor api dṛṣṭo' ntas-
tv anayos tattva darśibhiḥ //16//

The unreal can never come into existence, and the real can never cease to be. The wise philosophers have known the truth about these categories (of the real and the unreal).

अविनाशि तु तद्विद्धि येन सर्वमिदं ततम् ।
विनाशमव्ययस्यास्य न कश्चित् कर्तुमर्हति ।।

Avināśi tu tad viddhi
yena sarvam idaṁ tatam /
vināśam avyayasy'āsya
na kaścit kartum arhati // 17 //

Know that Reality, by which everything is pervaded, to be indestructible. No one can cause the destruction of this immutable Being.

अन्तवन्त इमे देहा नित्यस्योक्ताः शरीरिणः ।
अनाशिनोऽप्रमेयस्य तस्माद्युध्यस्व भारत ॥

Antavanta ime dehā
nityasyo'ktāḥ śarīriṇaḥ /
anāśino' prameyasya
tasmād yudhyasva
Bhārata // 18 //

What is said to perish are these bodies, in which the imperishable and unlimited Spirit is embodied. Therefore fight, O scion of the Bharata race!

य एनं वेत्ति हन्तारं यश्चैनं मन्यते हतम् ।
उभौ तौ न विजानीतो नायं हन्ति न हन्यते ॥

Ya enaṁ vetti hantāraṁ
yaśc'ainaṁ manyate hatam /
ubhau tau na vijānīto
nāyaṁ hanti na hanyate // 19 //

He who thinks him (the Self) to be the killer, and who experiences him (the Self) as the killed—both of them know not. He (the Self) neither kills nor is killed.

न जायते म्रियते वा कदाचि-
न्नायं भूत्वा भविता वा न भूयः ।
अजो नित्यः शाश्वतोऽयं पुराणो
न हन्यते हन्यमाने शरीरे ॥

Na jāyate mriyate vā kadācin-
nāyaṁ bhūtvā bhavitā vā na bhūyaḥ /
ajo nityaḥ śāśvato' yaṁ purāṇo
na hanyate hanyamāne śarīre // 20 //

He (this Self) has neither birth nor death. Nor does he cease to be, having been in existence before; unborn, eternal, permanent and primeval, he is never killed when the body is killed.

वेदाविनाशिनं नित्यं य एनमजमव्ययम् ।
कथं स पुरुषः पार्थ कं घातयति हन्ति कम् ॥

Ved'āvināśinaṁ nityaṁ
ya enam ajam avyayam /
kathaṁ sa puruṣaḥ Pārtha
kaṁ ghātayati hanti kam // 21 //

O Arjuna! know this self to be eternal, undecaying, birthless and indestructible. A person who knows him to be so—whom can he slay or cause another to slay.

वासांसि जीर्णानि यथा विहाय
नवानि गृह्णाति नरोऽपराणि ।
तथा शरीराणि विहाय जीर्णा-
न्यन्यानि संयाति नवानि देही ॥

Vāsāṁsi jīrṇāni yathā vihāya
navāni gṛhṇāti naro' parāṇi
tathā śarīrāṇi vihāya jīrṇāny-
anyāni saṁyāti navāni
dehī // 22 //

Just as a man gives up old garments and puts on new ones, so the embodied self abandons decrepit bodies and assumes new ones.

नैनं छिन्दन्ति शस्त्राणि नैनं दहति पावकः ।
न चैनं क्लेदयन्त्यापो न शोषयति मारुतः ।।

Nainaṁ chindanti śastrāṇi
nainaṁ dahati pāvakaḥ /
na c'ainaṁ kledayanty āpo
na śoṣayati mārutaḥ // 23 //

Him the weapons cleave not; Him the fire burns not; Him the waters wet not; Him the wind dries not.

अच्छेद्योऽयमदाह्योऽयमक्लेद्योऽशोष्य एव च ।
नित्यः सर्वगतः स्थाणुरचलोऽयं सनातनः ।।

Acchedyo' yam adāhyo' yam
akledyo' śoṣya eva ca /
nityaḥ sarvagataḥ sthāṇuḥ
acalo' yaṁ sanātanaḥ // 24 //

He cannot be cut or burnt. He can neither be wetted nor dried. Eternal, all-pervading, immovable and motionless, He is the same for ever.

अव्यक्तोऽयमचिन्त्योऽयमविकार्योऽयमुच्यते ।
तस्मादेवं विदित्वैनं नानुशोचितुमर्हसि ।।

Avyakto' yam acintyo' yam
avikāryo' yam ucyate /
tasmād evaṁ viditv'ainaṁ
n'ānuśocitum arhasi // 25 //

Knowing Him (the Self) to be unmanifest, inconceivable, and unmodifiable, it is improper to mourn for Him.

अथ चैनं नित्यजातं नित्यं वा मन्यसे मृतम् ।
तथापि त्वं महाबाहो नैवं शोचितुमर्हसि ।।

Atha c'ainaṁ nitya-jātaṁ
nityaṁ vā manyase mṛtam /
tathāpi tvaṁ mahā-bāho
n'aivaṁ śocitum arhasi // 26 //

In the alternative, even if you hold him (the Self) to be subject to constant births and deaths, there is no justification, O mighty armed, for your mourning for him.

जातस्य हि ध्रुवो मृत्युर्ध्रुवं जन्म मृतस्य च ।
तस्मादपरिहार्येऽर्थे न त्वं शोचितुमर्हसि ॥

Jātasya hi dhruvo mṛtyuḥ
dhruvaṁ janma mṛtasya ca /
tasmād aparihārye' rthe
na tvaṁ śocitum arhasi // 27 //

For the born, death is unavoidable; and for the dead, birth is sure to take place. Therefore in a situation that is inevitable, there is no justification for you to grieve.

अव्यक्तादीनि भूतानि व्यक्तमध्यानि भारत ।
अव्यक्तनिधनान्येव तत्र का परिदेवना ।।

Avyakt'ādīni bhūtāni
vyakta-madhyāni Bhārata /
avyakta-nidhanāny eva
tatra kā paridevanā // 28 //

Mystery surrounds the origin of beings. Mysterious too is their end. Only in the interim, between birth and death, are they manifested clearly. Such being the case, what is there to grieve about?

आश्चर्यवत्पश्यति कश्चिदेनम्
आश्चर्यवद्वदति तथैव चान्यः ।
आश्चर्यवच्चैनमन्यः शृणोति
श्रुत्वाप्येनं वेद न चैव कश्चित् ॥

Āścaryavat paśyati kaścit enam
āścaryavad vadati tath'aiva c'ānyaḥ
āścaryavad c'ainam anyaḥ śṛṇoti
śrutvā'py enaṁ veda na c'aiva kaścit // 29 //

Some have a glimpse of Him as a marvel, some speak of Him as a marvel, and yet others hear of Him as a marvel. Yet none understands Him in truth, in spite of (seeing, speaking and) hearing about Him.

देही नित्यमवध्योऽयं देहे सर्वस्य भारत ।
तस्मात् सर्वाणि भूतानि न त्वं शोचितुमर्हसि ।।

Dehī nityam avadhyo' yaṁ
dehe sarvasya Bhārata
tasmāt sarvāṇi bhūtāni
na tvaṁ śocitum arhasi // 30 //

At no time can the Spirit embodied in all beings be slain. Therefore there is no reason for you to grieve for any one.

स्वधर्ममपि चावेक्ष्य न विकम्पितुमर्हसि ।
धर्म्याद्धि युद्धाच्छ्रेयोऽन्यत् क्षत्रियस्य न विद्यते ।।

Svadharmam api c'āvekṣya
na vikampitum arhasi
dharmyād dhi yuddācchreyo' nyat
kṣatriyasya na vidyate || 31 ||

Further, even from the point of view of one's own duty, you ought not to falter. There is no greater good for a Kṣatriya than what a righteous war offers.

यदृच्छया चोपपन्नं स्वर्गद्वारमपावृतम् ।
सुखिनः क्षत्रियाः पार्थ लभन्ते युद्धमीदृशम् ।।

Yadṛcchayā c'opapannaṁ
svarga-dvāram apāvṛtam /
sukhinaḥ kṣatriyāḥ Pārtha
labhante yuddham
īdṛśam // 32 //

O Arjuna! That Kṣatriya must indeed be a happy man to whom comes unsought a war like this, which is an open gate to heaven.

अथ चेत्वमिमं धर्म्यं सङ्ग्रामं न करिष्यसि ।
ततः स्वधर्मं कीर्तिं च हित्वा पापमवाप्स्यसि ॥

Atha cet tvam imaṁ dharmyaṁ
saṅgrāmam na kariṣyasi /
tataḥ svadharmaṁ kīrtiṁ ca
hitvā pāpam avāpsyasi // 33 //

If you do not take part in this righteous war, you will incur sin, besides failing in your duty and forfeiting your reputation.

अकीर्तिं चापि भूतानि कथयिष्यन्ति तेऽव्ययाम् ।
सम्भावितस्य चाकीर्तिर्मरणादतिरिच्यते ।।

Akīrtiṁ c'āpi bhūtāni
kathayiṣyanti te' vyayām /
sambhāvitasya cākīrtir-
maraṇād atiricyate // 34 //

Besides, every one will speak ill of you for all time. More poignant than death is disrepute to a man accustomed to be honoured by all.

भयाद्रणादुपरतं मंस्यन्ते त्वां महारथाः ।
येषां च त्वं बहुमतो भूत्वा यास्यसि लाघवम् ॥

Bhayād raṇād uparatam
maṁsyante tvāṁ mahā-rathāḥ /
yeṣāṁ ca tvaṁ bahumato
bhūtvā yāsyasi lāghavam // 35 //

The great car-warriors will consider you as having fled from battle out of fear, and you who have been the object of their respect, will be despised by them hereafter.

अवाच्यवादांश्च बहून् वदिष्यन्ति तवाहिताः ।
निन्दन्तस्तव सामर्थ्यं ततो दुःखतरं नु किम् ॥

Avācya-vādāṁś ca bahūn
vadiṣyanti tav'āhitāḥ
nindantas tava sāmarthyaṁ
tato duḥkhataraṁ nu kim // 36 //

Your enemies will indulge in derogatory speeches against you, belittling your prowess. What is more painful than that?

अर्जुन उवाच —

स्थितप्रज्ञस्य का भाषा समाधिस्थस्य केशव ।
स्थितधीः किं प्रभाषेत किमासीत व्रजेत किम् ॥

Arjuna uvāca:

Sthita-prajñasya kā bhāṣā
samādhi-sthasya Keśava
sthita-dhīḥ kiṁ prabhāṣeta
kim āsīta vrajeta kim // 54 //

Arjuna said:

O Keśava! What are the signs of a person who has attained to steady wisdom and deep introspection? How does he speak? How does he sit? How does he walk? (How does he behave in life generally?)

श्रीभगवानुवाच —
प्रजहाति यदा कामान् सर्वान् पार्थ मनोगतान् ।
आत्मन्येवात्मना तुष्टः स्थितप्रज्ञस्तदोच्यते ।।

Śrī Bhagavān uvāca:
Prajahāti yadā kāmān
sarvān Pārtha mano-gatān /
ātmany'evā'tmanā tuṣṭaḥ
sthita-prajñas tado'cyate // 55 //

The Blessed Lord said:

O Son of Pṛthā! When all the desires of the heart have been abandoned, and the Spirit finds joyous satisfaction in Itself (without dependence on any external factor)—then is one spoken of as a person of steady wisdom.

दुःखेष्वनुद्विग्नमनाः सुखेषु विगतस्पृहः ।
वीतरागभयक्रोधः स्थितधीर्मुनिरुच्यते ।।

Duḥkheṣv anudvigna-manāḥ
sukheṣu vigata-spṛhaḥ /
vīta-rāga-bhaya-krodhaḥ
sthita-dhīr munir ucyate // 56 //

Whose mind is not agitated in adversity, who is free from desire, and who is devoid of attachments, fear and anger—such a person is called a sage of steady wisdom.

यः सर्वत्रानभिस्नेहस्तत्तत्प्राप्य शुभाशुभम् ।
नाभिनन्दति न द्वेष्टि तस्य प्रज्ञा प्रतिष्ठिता ।।

Yaḥ sarvatr'ānabhisnehas
tat-tat prāpya śubh'āśubham /
n'ābhinandati na dveṣṭi
tasya prajñā pratiṣṭhitā // 57 //

Whoever is without self-centred affection for anything, who rejoices not in favourable situations and hates not in unfavourable ones—such a person's wisdom is firmly set.

यदा संहरते चायं कूर्मोऽङ्गानीव सर्वशः ।
इन्द्रियाणीन्द्रियार्थेभ्यस्तस्य प्रज्ञा प्रतिष्ठिता ।।

Yadā saṁharate cāyaṁ
kūrmo' ṅgānī'va sarvaśaḥ /
indriyāṇī'ndriyārthebhyas-
tasya prajñā pratiṣṭhitā // 58 //

When a person can withdraw his senses from their objects just like the tortoise its limbs on all sides, his wisdom is firmly set.

विषया विनिवर्तन्ते निराहारस्य देहिनः ।
रसवर्जं रसोऽप्यस्य परं दृष्ट्वा निवर्तते ।।

Viṣayā vinivartante
nirāhārasya dehinaḥ /
rasa-varjam raso' py asya
paraṁ dṛṣṭvā nivartate // 59 //

From the abstinent soul sense objects fall away, but not the taste for them. When the Supreme Truth is realised, even the taste departs.

यततो ह्यपि कौन्तेय पुरुषस्य विपश्चितः ।
इन्द्रियाणि प्रमाथीनि हरन्ति प्रसभं मनः ।।

Yatato hy api Kaunteya
puruṣasya vipaścitaḥ /
indriyāṇi pramāthīni
haranti prasabhaṁ
manaḥ // 60 //

O son of Kuntī! The turbulent senses do violently draw away the mind of even a discerning person who is earnestly striving on the spiritual path.

तानि सर्वाणि संयम्य युक्त आसीत मत्परः ।
वशे हि यस्येन्द्रियाणि तस्य प्रज्ञा प्रतिष्ठिता ।।

Tāni sarvāṇi saṁyamya
yukta āsīta mat-paraḥ /
vaśe hi yaśy'endriyāṇi
tasya prajñā pratiṣṭhitā // 61 //

Having controlled them all, one should become entirely devoted to Me. He whose senses are under control, his wisdom is firmly set.

ध्यायतो विषयान् पुंसः सङ्गस्तेषूपजायते ।
सङ्गात् सञ्जायते कामः कामात्क्रोधोऽभिजायते ।।

Dhyāyato viṣayān puṁsaḥ
saṅgas teṣū'pajāyate /
saṅgāt sañjāyate kāmaḥ
kāmāt krodho' bhijāyate // 62 //

In one who dwells longingly on sense objects, an inclination towards them is generated. This inclination develops into desire, and desire begets anger.

क्रोधाद्भवति सम्मोहः सम्मोहात् स्मृतिविभ्रमः ।
स्मृतिभ्रंशाद् बुद्धिनाशो बुद्धिनाशात् प्रणश्यति ।।

Krodhād bhavati sammohaḥ
sammohāt smṛti-vibhramaḥ /
smṛti-bhraṁśād buddhi-nāśo
buddhi-nāśāt praṇaśyati // 63 //

Anger generates delusion, and delusion results in loss of memory. Loss of memory brings about the destruction of discriminative intelligence, and loss of discriminative intelligence spells ruin to a man.

रागद्वेषवियुक्तैस्तु विषयानिन्द्रियैश्चरन् ।
आत्मवश्यैर्विधेयात्मा प्रसादमधिगच्छति ॥

Rāga-dveṣa-viyuktais tu
viṣayān indriyaiś caran /
ātma-vaśyair vidhey'ātmā
prasādam adhigacchati // 64 //

A man of disciplined mind, who has his senses under control and who has neither attraction nor aversion for sense objects, attains tranquillity, though he may be moving amidst objects of the senses.

प्रसादे सर्वदुःखानां हानिरस्योपजायते ।
प्रसन्नचेतसो ह्याशु बुद्धिः पर्यवतिष्ठते ॥

Prasāde sarva-duḥkhānāṁ
hānir asyo'pajāyate /
prasanna-cetaso hy āśu
buddhiḥ paryavatiṣṭhate // 65 //

On attaining tranquillity all one's sorrows come to an end. For soon does the intellect of a tranquil person become steady.

नास्ति बुद्धिरयुक्तस्य न चायुक्तस्य भावना ।
न चाभावयतः शान्तिरशान्तस्य कुतः सुखम् ।।

Nāsti buddhir ayuktasya
na c'āyuktasya bhāvanā /
na c'ābhāvayataḥ śantir
aśāntasya kutaḥ
sukham // 66 //

A man of uncontrolled senses has no spiritual comprehension. He has no capacity for meditation either. For the unmeditative there is no peace. And where is happiness for one without peace of mind?

इन्द्रियाणां हि चरतां यन्मनोऽनुविधीयते ।
तदस्य हरति प्रज्ञां वायुर्नावमिवाम्भसि ॥

Indriyāṇāṁ hi caratāṁ
yan mano' nuvidhīyate /
tad asya harati prajñāṁ
vāyur nāvām ivāmbhasi // 67 //

The senses are naturally disposed to move towards their objects. Whichever of these senses the mind pursues, that sense carries away that mind as a gale does a ship on the high seas.

तस्माद्यस्य महाबाहो निगृहीतानि सर्वशः ।
इन्द्रियाणीन्द्रियार्थेभ्यस्तस्य प्रज्ञा प्रतिष्ठिता ।।

Tasmād yasya mahā-bāho
nigṛhītāni sarvaśaḥ /
indriyāṇ'īndriy'ārthebhyas-
tasya prajñā pratiṣṭhitā // 68 //

Therefore, O mighty Arjuna, he who can completely restrain his senses from pursuing their objects, has his wisdom firmly set.

या निशा सर्वभूतानां तस्यां जागर्ति संयमी ।
यस्यां जाग्रति भूतानि सा निशा पश्यतो मुनेः ।।

Yā niśā sarva-bhūtānāṁ
tasyāṁ jāgarti saṁyamī /
yasyāṁ jāgrati bhūtāni
sā niśā paśyato muneḥ // 69 //

What is like night to all ignorant beings, to that Ātman consciousness the self-controlled sage is awake; and the sensate life to which all ignorant beings are awake, that is like night to this illumined sage.

आपूर्यमाणमचलप्रतिष्ठं
समुद्रमापः प्रविशन्ति यद्वत् ।
तद्वत्कामा यं प्रविशन्ति सर्वे
स शान्तिमाप्नोति न कामकामी ।।

Āpūryamāṇam acala-pratiṣṭhaṁ
samudram āpaḥ praviśanti yadvat /
tadvat kāmā yaṁ praviśanti sarve
sa śāntim āpnoti na kāma-
kāmī // 70 //

He into whom objects of desire enter (unsought and causing no perturbation), even like the ocean that is ever being filled by the rivers but still remains steady within its bounds—such a person attains to peace, not he who runs madly after objects of desire.

विहाय कामान् यः सर्वान् पुमांश्चरति निःस्पृहः ।
निर्ममो निरहङ्कारः स शान्तिमधिगच्छति ।।

Vihāya kāmān yaḥ sarvān
pumāṁs carati niḥspṛhaḥ /
nirmamo nirahaṅkāraḥ
sa śāntim adhigacchati // 71 //

Whoever has abandoned desires, and moves about without attachments and the sense of 'I' and 'mine'—he attains to peace.

एषा ब्राह्मी स्थितिः पार्थ नैनां प्राप्य विमुह्यति ।
स्थित्वाऽस्यामन्तकालेऽपि ब्रह्मनिर्वाणमृच्छति ।।

Eṣā brāhmī sthitiḥ Pārtha
n'ainām prāpya vimuhyati /
sthitvā' syām antakāle' pi
brahma-nirvāṇam ṛcchati //72//

This, O son of Pṛthā, is the state of dwelling in Brahman. Having attained it, one is no more deluded. By abiding in that state even by the time of death, one is united with Brahman.

3. Yoga of Action

'Rain is born of sacrifice, and sacrifice originates from action.' (14)

Chapter 3

Yoga of Action

अर्जुन उवाच —

ज्यायसी चेत्कर्मणस्ते मता बुद्धिर्जनार्दन ।
तत्किं कर्मणि घोरे मां नियोजयसि केशव ॥

Arjuna uvāca:
Jyāyasī cet karmaṇas te
matā buddhir, Janārdana /
tat kiṁ karmaṇi ghore māṁ
niyojayasi, Keśava // 1 //

Arjuna said:

O Janārdana, if, according to Thee, discriminative insight is superior to action, why dost Thou enjoin on me this terrible action (of engagement in war)?

व्यामिश्रेणेव वाक्येन बुद्धिं मोहयसीव मे ।
तदेकं वद निश्चित्य येन श्रेयोऽहमाप्नुयाम् ।।

Vyāmiśreṇeva vākyena
buddhiṁ mohayasīva me /
tad ekaṁ vada niścitya
yena śreyo' ham āpnuyām // 2 //

By seemingly conflicting words, Thou art confusing my understanding. Speak to me only about that which will definitely lead to my highest good.

श्रीभगवानुवाच —
लोकेऽस्मिन्द्विविधा निष्ठा पुरा प्रोक्ता मयाऽनघ ।
ज्ञानयोगेन साङ्ख्यानां कर्मयोगेन योगिनाम् ॥

Śrī Bhagavān uvāca:
Loke' smin dvividhā niṣṭhā
purā proktā mayā' nagha /
jñāna yogena sāṅkhyānāṁ
karma yogena yogināṁ // 3 //

The Blessed Lord said:

In times of yore a twofold spiritual path was taught by me, O sinless one—that of knowledge for Sāṅkhyas (who are pure contemplatives), and that of action for Yogis (who combine detached work with devotion).

न कर्मणामनारम्भान्नैष्कर्म्यं पुरुषोऽश्नुते ।
न च सन्न्यसनादेव सिद्धिं समधिगच्छति ।।

Na karmaṇām anārambhān-
naiṣkarmyaṁ puruṣo' śnute /
na ca sannyasanād eva
siddhiṁ samādhigacchati // 4 //

By non-performance of action a man does not gain the state of spiritual passivity (or the state of egoless actionlessness called Naiṣkarmya). By mere external abandonment (Sannyasa), he does not attain to perfection.

न हि कश्चित् क्षणमपि जातु तिष्ठत्यकर्मकृत् ।
कार्यते ह्यवशः कर्म सर्वः प्रकृतिजैर्गुणैः ॥

Na hi kaścit kṣaṇam api
jātu tiṣṭhaty akarma-kṛt /
kāryate hy avaśaḥ karma
sarvaḥ prakṛtijair guṇaiḥ // 5 //

No man can ever remain even for a moment without performing any action. The impulses of nature deprive him of freedom in this respect and compel him to act.

कर्मेन्द्रियाणि संयम्य य आस्ते मनसा स्मरन् ।
इन्द्रियार्थान्विमूढात्मा मिथ्याचारः स उच्यते ।।

Karm'endriyāṇi saṁyamya
ya āste manasā smaran /
indriy'ārthān vimūḍhātmā
mithy'ācāraḥ sa ucyate // 6 //

He who restrains the organs of action but continues to brood in his mind over the objects of sensual desire (enjoyed through them)—such a deluded person is called a hypocrite.

यस्त्विन्द्रियाणि मनसा नियम्यारभतेऽर्जुन ।
कर्मेन्द्रियैः कर्मयोगमसक्तः स विशिष्यते ।।

Yas tv indriyāṇi manasā
niyamy'ārabhate' rjuna /
karm-endriyaiḥ karma yogam
asaktaḥ sa viśiṣyate // 7 //

But he who, controlling all sense organs (by the power of his will) and becoming non-attached, lives a life of communion through dedicated action such a person excels.

नियतं कुरु कर्म त्वं कर्म ज्यायो ह्यकर्मणः ।
शरीरयात्रापि च ते न प्रसिद्ध्येदकर्मणः ।।

Niyataṁ kuru karma tvaṁ
karma jyāyo hy akarmaṇaḥ /
śarīra-yatrā'pi ca te
na prasiddhyed akarmaṇaḥ // 8 //

Perform your prescribed duties. For, action is superior to inaction. If you are totally inactive, even the survival of the body would become impossible.

यज्ञार्थात्कर्मणोऽन्यत्र लोकोऽयं कर्मबन्धनः ।
तदर्थं कर्म कौन्तेय मुक्तसङ्गः समाचर ।।

Yajñ'ārthāt karmaṇo' nyatra
loko' yaṁ karma-bandhanaḥ /
tad-arthaṁ karma Kaunteya
mukta-saṅgaḥ samācara // 9 //

O son of Kuntī! In this world all actions, unless they are done as an offering to God (or as Yajña), become causes of bondage. Therefore, work for the sake of God without personal attachments.

सहयज्ञाः प्रजाः सृष्ट्वा पुरोवाच प्रजापतिः ।
अनेन प्रसविष्यध्वमेष वोऽस्त्विष्टकामधुक् ॥

Saha yajñāḥ prajāḥ sṛṣṭvā
puro'vāca Prajāpatiḥ /
anena prasaviṣyadhvam
eṣa vo' stva iṣṭa-kāmadhuk //10//

In the beginning Prajāpati, having created men together with Yajña (selfless work dedicated to God or Vedic sacrifice) as their duty, declared: 'By this shall you multiply. May this be to you the Cow of Plenty yielding all your wants!'

देवान्भावयतानेन ते देवा भावयन्तु वः ।
परस्परं भावयन्तः श्रेयः परमवाप्स्यथ ।।

Devān bhāvayat'ānena
te devā bhāvayantu vaḥ /
parasparaṁ bhāvayantaḥ
śreyaḥ param avāpsyatha // 11 //

You cherish the Devas with Yajña, and may the Devas in turn bless you (with rain and other desired gifts)! Thus, mutually cherishing, you shall attain the highest good.

इष्टान्भोगान्हि वो देवा दास्यन्ते यज्ञभाविताः ।
तैर्दत्तानप्रदायैभ्यो यो भुङ्क्ते स्तेन एव सः ।।

Iṣṭān bhogān hi vo devā
dāsyante yajña-bhāvitāḥ /
tair dattān apradāy'aibhyo
yo bhunkte stena eva saḥ // 12 //

Worshipped by sacrifices, the Devas will give you the desired objects of enjoyment. They are verily thieves who enjoy their gifts without giving their share in return.

यज्ञशिष्टाशिनः सन्तो मुच्यन्ते सर्वकिल्बिषैः ।
भुञ्जते ते त्वघं पापा ये पचन्त्यात्मकारणात् ॥

Yajña-śiṣṭ'āśinaḥ santo
mucyante sarva-kilbiṣaiḥ /
bhuñjate te tv aghaṁ pāpā
ye pacanty ātma kāraṇāt // 13 //

Those persons who eat what is left after sacrifice, are released from all sin. But those who cook food for the self alone (without sharing it with others), such degraded men eat sin.

अन्नाद्भवन्ति भूतानि पर्जन्यादन्नसम्भवः ।
यज्ञाद्भवति पर्जन्यो यज्ञः कर्मसमुद्भवः ॥

Annād bhavanti bhūtāni
parjanyād anna-sambhavaḥ /
yajñād bhavati parjanyo
yajñaḥ karma-
samudbhavaḥ // 14 //

From food (i.e., from reproductive power sustained by food) creatures are born. Food is produced by rain. Rain is born of sacrifice, and sacrifice originates from action.

कर्म ब्रह्मोद्भवं विद्धि ब्रह्माक्षरसमुद्भवम् ।
तस्मात्सर्वगतं ब्रह्म नित्यं यज्ञे प्रतिष्ठितम् ।।

Karma brahm'odbhavaṁ viddhi
brahmā'kṣara-samudbhavam /
tasmāt sarvagataṁ brahma
nityaṁ yajñe pratiṣṭhitam // 15 //

Works of sacrifice have their authority in the Veda. Veda has been revealed by the Supreme Being. Therefore the all-comprehending Veda is established in sacrifice (that is, has performance of sacrifice as its fundamental teaching).

एवं प्रवर्तितं चक्रं नानुवर्तयतीह यः ।
अघायुरिन्द्रियारामो मोघं पार्थ स जीवति ।।

Evaṁ pravartitaṁ cakraṁ
n'ānuvartayatī'ha yaḥ /
agh'āyur indriy'ārāmo
moghaṁ Pārtha sa jīvati // *16* //

Vain is the life of that sinful and sense-indulgent person who fails to fulfil his obligations in this cycle of mutual interdependence and service (which the law of sacrifice implies).

यस्त्वात्मरतिरेव स्यादात्मतृप्तश्च मानवः ।
आत्मन्येव च सन्तुष्टस्तस्य कार्यं न विद्यते ॥

Yas tv ātma-ratir eva syād
ātma-tṛptaś ca mānavaḥ /
ātmany eva ca santuṣṭas-
tasya kāryaṁ na vidyate // 17 //

But whoever delights in the Self (Spirit) alone, and is content and satisfied in the Self, for such a person there is no obligatory duty to discharge.

नैव तस्य कृतेनार्थो नाकृतेनेह कश्चन ।
न चास्य सर्वभूतेषु कश्चिदर्थव्यपाश्रयः ।।

N'aiva tasya kṛten'ārtho
n'ākṛten'eha kaścana /
na c'āsya sarva-bhūteṣu
kaścid artha-
vyapāśrayaḥ // 18 //

He has no object to gain here in this world by action. Nor does he lose anything by abstaining from action. For him, there is no dependence on any created being for any object of his.

तस्मादसक्तः सततं कार्यं कर्म समाचर ।
असक्तो ह्याचरन्कर्म परमाप्नोति पूरुषः ।।

Tasmād asaktaḥ satataṁ
kāryaṁ karma samācara /
asakto hy ācaran karma
param āpnoti pūruṣaḥ // 19 //

Therefore perform action always without attachment. For, by working without attachment a man attains the Supreme.

कर्मणैव हि संसिद्धिमास्थिता जनकादयः ।
लोकसङ्ग्रहमेवापि सम्पश्यन्कर्तुमर्हसि ॥

Karmaṇ'aiva hi saṁsiddhim
āsthitā Janakādayaḥ /
loka-saṅgraham evā'pi
sampaśyan kartum arhasi // 20 //

Men like Janaka verily attained to perfection by work alone. You ought to work for the good of the world (having their example in view).

यद्यदाचरति श्रेष्ठस्तत्तदेवेतरो जनः ।
स यत्प्रमाणं कुरुते लोकस्तदनुवर्तते ॥

Yad-yad ācarati śreṣṭhas-
tat-tad ev'etaro janaḥ /
sa yat pramāṇaṁ kurute
lokas tad anuvartate // 21 //

Whatever the noblest persons do, the ordinary man imitates. The standard they set, the ordinary men follow.

न मे पार्थास्ति कर्तव्यं त्रिषु लोकेषु किञ्चन ।
नानवाप्तमवाप्तव्यं वर्त एव च कर्मणि ।।

Na me Pārthā'sti kartavyaṁ
triṣu lokeṣu kiñcana /
n'ānavāptam avāptavyaṁ
varta eva ca karmaṇi // 22 //

In all the three worlds there is nothing, O son of Pṛtha, that is binding on Me as duty. Neither is there anything that I have to gain, nor anything that I cannot gain. Still I am always engaged in work.

यदि ह्यहं न वर्तेयं जातु कर्मण्यतन्द्रितः ।
मम वर्त्मानुवर्तन्ते मनुष्याः पार्थ सर्वशः ।।

Yadi hy ahaṁ na varteyaṁ
jātu karmaṇy atandritaḥ /
mama vartm'ānuvartante
manuṣyāḥ Pārtha
sarvaśaḥ // 23 //

O son of Pṛtha! If I did not ever continue in action unwearied, men all around would have followed My way.

उत्सीदेयुरिमे लोका न कुर्यां कर्म चेदहम् ।
सङ्करस्य च कर्ता स्यामुपहन्यामिमाः प्रजाः ॥

Utsīdeyur ime lokā
na kuryāṁ karma ced aham /
saṅkarasya ca kartā syām
upahanyām imāḥ prajāḥ // 24 //

If I were not to work, all these worlds would have perished. I would have been the cause of confusion among men and of their ultimate destruction.

सक्ताः कर्मण्यविद्वांसो यथा कुर्वन्ति भारत ।
कुर्याद्विद्वांस्तथाऽसक्तश्चिकीर्षुर्लोकसङ्ग्रहम् ॥

Saktāḥ karmaṇy avidvāṁso
yathā kurvanti Bhārata /
kuryād vidvāṁs tathā' saktaś
cikīrṣur loka-saṅgraham // 25 //

O scion of the Bharata race! Just as ignorant men do action out of attachment, so let enlightened ones perform the same unattached, with the good of the world in view.

न बुद्धिभेदं जनयेदज्ञानां कर्मसङ्गिनाम् ।
जोषयेत्सर्वकर्माणि विद्वान्युक्तः समाचरन् ॥

Na buddhi-bhedaṁ janayed
ajñānāṁ karma-saṅginām /
joṣayet sarva karmāṇi
vidvān yuktaḥ samācaran // 26 //

An enlightened man should not cause confusion in the minds of ignorant people (by his conduct). Himself working with equanimity, he should make them interested in all activities.

प्रकृतेः क्रियमाणानि गुणैः कर्माणि सर्वशः ।
अहङ्कारविमूढात्मा कर्ताहमिति मन्यते ।।

Prakṛteḥ kriyamāṇāni
guṇaiḥ karmāṇi sarvaśaḥ /
ahaṅkāra-vimūḍh'ātmā
kartā'ham iti manyate // 27 //

Everywhere the dispositions (powers) of Nature perform all works. But deluded by egoism, man thinks, 'I am the doer.'

तत्त्ववित्तु महाबाहो गुणकर्मविभागयोः ।
गुणा गुणेषु वर्तन्त इति मत्वा न सज्जते ।।

Tattva-vit tu mahā-bāho
guṇa-karma-vibhāgayoḥ /
guṇā guṇeṣu vartanta
iti matvā na sajjate // 28 //

But those who know the truth that the dispositions of Nature and the actions which spring from them are distinct from the Self, do not get attached, understanding that it is not the Self, but the dispositions of Nature as organs that settle on the respective objects which too are products of the same dispositions.

प्रकृतेर्गुणसम्मूढाः सज्जन्ते गुणकर्मसु ।
तानकृत्स्नविदो मन्दान्कृत्स्नविन्न विचालयेत् ।।

Prakrter guṇa-sammūḍhāḥ
sajjante guṇa-karmasu /
tān akṛtsna-vido mandān
kṛtsna-vin na vicālayet // 29 //

Men, deluded by the dispositions of Nature, get attached to work prompted by these dispositions. Those who know the whole Truth should not unsettle these dull-witted men of imperfect understanding.

मयि सर्वाणि कर्माणि सन्न्यस्याध्यात्मचेतसा ।
निराशीर्निर्ममो भूत्वा युध्यस्व विगतज्वरः ।।

Mayi sarvāṇi karmāṇi
sannyasy'ādhyātma-cetasā /
nirāśīr nirmamo bhūtvā
yudhyasva vigata-jvaraḥ // 30 //

Offering all your actions to Me, your mind in unison with the spirit and free from desires and egotism, you fight without the slightest touch of hatred or excitement.

ये मे मतमिदं नित्यमनुतिष्ठन्ति मानवाः ।
श्रद्धावन्तोऽनसूयन्तो मुच्यन्ते तेऽपि कर्मभिः ।।

Ye me matam idaṁ nityam
anutiṣṭhanti mānavāḥ /
śraddhāvanto' nasūyanto
mucyante te' pi
karmabhiḥ // 31 //

Whoever follow this teaching of mine, with their minds full of faith and free from disparagement, they also are released from the bondage of Karma.

ये त्वेतदभ्यसूयन्तो नानुतिष्ठन्ति मे मतम् ।
सर्वज्ञानविमूढांस्तान्विद्धि नष्टानचेतसः ।।

Ye tv etad abhyasūyanto
n'ānutiṣṭhanti me matam /
sarva-jñāna vimūḍhāṁs tān
viddhi naṣṭān acetasaḥ // 32 //

But those who disparage this doctrine of Mine and discard it, know such senseless men, blind to all wisdom, as lost.

सदृशं चेष्टते स्वस्याः प्रकृतेर्ज्ञानवानपि ।
प्रकृतिं यान्ति भूतानि निग्रहः किं करिष्यति ।।

Sadṛśaṁ ceṣṭate svasyāḥ
prakṛter jñānavān api /
prakṛtiṁ yānti bhūtāni
nigrahaḥ kiṁ kariṣyati // 33 //

Even a wise man acts in accordance with his nature. All beings follow their nature. What can repression do?

इन्द्रियस्येन्द्रियस्यार्थे रागद्वेषौ व्यवस्थितौ ।
तयोर्न वशमागच्छेत्तौ ह्यस्य परिपन्थिनौ ।।

Indriyasy'endriyasy'ārthe
rāgadveṣau vyavasthitau /
tayor na vaśam āgacchet
tau hy asya
paripanthinau // 34 //

It is natural for each organ to feel attraction or aversion in respect of objects pertaining to each sense. Do not come under their sway, for they are enemies (of all spiritual aspirants).

श्रेयान् स्वधर्मो विगुणः परधर्मात्स्वनुष्ठितात् ।
स्वधर्मे निधनं श्रेयः परधर्मो भयावहः ॥

Ṣreyān svadharmo viguṇaḥ
para-dharmāt svanuṣṭhitāt /
svadharme nidhanaṁ śreyaḥ
para-dharmo bhay'āvahaḥ // 35 //

One's own Dharma (duty), even though not glamorous, is better than duty alien to one's growth (Para-dharmaḥ), however well performed. For even death in doing one's duty leads to one's good, while a duty alien to one's growth is burdened with the fear of downfall.

अर्जुन उवाच —

अथ केन प्रयुक्तोऽयं पापं चरति पूरुषः ।

अनिच्छन्नपि वार्ष्णेय बलादिव नियोजितः ।।

Arjuna uvāca:

Atha kenaprayukto' yaṁ
pāpaṁ carati pūruṣaḥ /
anicchann api Vārṣṇeya
balād iva niyojitaḥ // 36 //

Arjuna said:

What is that, O scion of the Vṛṣṇi race, prompted by which a man is forced, as it were, to live a sinful life even against his will?

श्रीभगवानुवाच —

काम एष क्रोध एष रजोगुणसमुद्भवः ।
महाशनो महापाप्मा विद्ध्येनमिह वैरिणम् ।।

Śrī Bhagavān uvāca:
Kāma eṣa krodha eṣa
rajo-guṇa-samudbhavaḥ /
mah'āśano mahā-pāpmā
viddhy enam iha
vairiṇam // 37 //

The Blessed Lord said:

It is lust, it is anger, born of Rajoguṇa, insatiable and prompting man to great sin. Know this to be the enemy (in man's spiritual life).

धूमेनाव्रियते वह्निर्यथाऽदर्शो मलेन च ।
यथोल्बेनावृतो गर्भस्तथा तेनेदमावृतम् ॥

Dhumen'āvriyate vahnir
yathā' darśo malena ca /
yath'olben'āvṛto garbhas
tathā ten'edam āvṛtam // 38 //

As fire is enveloped by smoke, mirror by dust and the embryo by the placenta, so is knowledge overcast by lust.

आवृतं ज्ञानमेतेन ज्ञानिनो नित्यवैरिणा ।
कामरूपेण कौन्तेय दुष्पूरेणानलेन च ।।

Āvṛtaṁ jñānam etena
jñānino nitya-vairiṇā /
kāma-rūpeṇa Kaunteya
duṣpūreṇ'ānalena ca // 39 //

Knowledge, O Son of Kuntī, is covered up by this eternal foe of the aspirant after knowledge—the insatiable fire of lust.

इन्द्रियाणि मनो बुद्धिरस्याधिष्ठानमुच्यते ।
एतैर्विमोहयत्येष ज्ञानमावृत्य देहिनम् ।।

Indriyāṇi mano buddhir
asy'ādhiṣṭhānam ucyate /
etair vimohayaty eṣa
jñānam āvṛtya dehinam // 40 //

The senses, the mind and the Buddhi are said to be its seat. With these it veils knowledge and deludes the embodied spirit.

तस्मात्त्वमिन्द्रियाण्यादौ नियम्य भरतर्षभ ।
पाप्मानं प्रजहि ह्येनं ज्ञानविज्ञाननाशनम् ।।

Tasmāt tvam indriyāṇy ādau
niyamya bharatarṣabha /
pāpmānaṁ prajahi hy enaṁ
jñāna-vijñāna nāśanam // 41 //

Therefore, O scion of the Bharata race, controlling the senses at the beginning itself, slay this foul enemy, the destroyer of all knowledge and realisation.

इन्द्रियाणि पराण्याहुरिन्द्रियेभ्यः परं मनः ।
मनसस्तु परा बुद्धिर्यो बुद्धेः परतस्तु सः ।।

Indriyāṇi parāṇy āhur
indriyebhyaḥ paraṁ manaḥ /
manasas tu parā buddhir
yo buddheḥ paratas tu
saḥ // 42 //

The senses are great, they say. Superior to the senses is the mind, and superior even to the mind is the intellect. What is superior even to the intellect is He, the Ātman.

एवं बुद्धेः परं बुद्ध्वा संस्तभ्यात्मानमात्मना ।
जहि शत्रुं महाबाहो कामरूपं दुरासदम् ।।

Evaṁ buddheḥ paraṁ buddhvā
saṁstabhy'ātmānam-ātmanā /
jahi śatruṁ mahā-bāho
kāma-rūpaṁ durāsadam // 43 //

Thus knowing Him who is superior even to the Buddhi, and controlling the lower self with the higher, kill that tough enemy in the form of lust, O mighty-armed Arjuna!

4. Renunciation of Action in Knowledge

'Actions done in dedication to the Lord melt away with their very tendencies.' (23)

Chapter 4

Renunciation of Action in Knowledge

श्रीभगवानुवाच —

इमं विवस्वते योगं प्रोक्तवानहमव्ययम् ।
विवस्वान्मनवे प्राह मनुरिक्ष्वाकवेऽब्रवीत् ।।

Śrī Bhagavān uvāca:

Imaṁ Vivasvāte yogaṁ
proktavān aham avyayam /
Vivasvān Manave prāha
Manur Ikṣvākave' bravīt // 1 //

The Blessed Lord said:

I imparted this immortal Yoga to Vivasvān, Vivasvān to Manu, and Manu to Ikṣvāku.

एवं परम्पराप्राप्तमिमं राजर्षयो विदुः ।
स कालेनेह महता योगो नष्टः परन्तप ।।

Evaṁ paramparā-prāptam
imaṁ rāja'ṛṣyo viduḥ /
sa kālen'eha mahatā
yogo naṣṭaḥ Paraṅtapa // 2 //

O scorcher of foes! This Yoga handed down from teacher to disciple in succession, was known to the Rājarṣis (royal sages). But owing to long lapse of time, it was lost to the world.

स एवायं मया तेऽद्य योगः प्रोक्तः पुरातनः ।
भक्तोऽसि मे सखा चेति रहस्यं ह्येतदुत्तमम् ॥

Sa evāyaṁ mayā te' dya
yogaḥ proktaḥ purātanaḥ /
bhakto' si me sakhā c'eti
rahasyaṁ hy etad
uttamam // 3 //

You are My devotee and friend—thinking thus, I have today declared to you even that ancient Yoga. For, it is a noble secret (imparted by a teacher only to a worthy disciple).

अर्जुन उवाच —

अपरं भवतो जन्म परं जन्म विवस्वतः ।
कथमेतद्विजानीयां त्वमादौ प्रोक्तवानिति ।।

Arjuna uvāca:
Aparaṁ bhavato janma
paraṁ janma Vivasvataḥ /
katham etad vijānīyāṁ
tvam ādau proktavān iti // 4 //

Arjuna said:

Thy life-time is later, that of Vivasvān was much earlier. How then am I to understand that Thou didst impart this doctrine to him?

श्रीभगवानुवाच —
बहूनि मे व्यतीतानि जन्मानि तव चार्जुन ।
तान्यहं वेद सर्वाणि न त्वं वेत्थ परन्तप ।।

Śrī Bhagavān uvāca:
Bahūni me vyatītāni
janmāni tava c'ārjuna /
tāny ahaṁ veda sarvāṇi
na tvaṁ vettha
paraṅtapa // 5 //

The Blessed Lord said:

O Arjuna! You and I have passed through many births; I remember them all, but you do not, O scorcher of foes!

अजोऽपि सन्नव्ययात्मा भूतानामीश्वरोऽपि सन् ।
प्रकृतिं स्वामधिष्ठाय सम्भवाम्यात्ममायया ।।

Ajo' pi sann avyay'ātmā
bhūtānām īśvaro' pi san /
prakṛtiṁ svām adhiṣṭhāya
sambhavāmy ātma-
māyayā // 6 //

Though birthless and deathless, and the Lord of all beings as well, yet I (the Eternal Being) take birth by My inherent mysterious Power *[Ātmamāyayā)*, employing the pure or Sattva aspect of My material Nature (Prakṛti).

यदा यदा हि धर्मस्य ग्लानिर्भवति भारत ।
अभ्युत्थानमधर्मस्य तदात्मानं सृजाम्यहम् ।।

Yadā yadā hi dharmasya
glānir bhavati Bhārata /
abhyutthānam adharmasya
tad'ātmānaṁ sṛjāmy aham // 7 //

Whenever there is decline of Dharma and ascendance of Adharma, then, O scion of the Bharata race! I manifest (incarnate) Myself in a body.

परित्राणाय साधूनां विनाशाय च दुष्कृताम् ।
धर्मसंस्थापनार्थाय सम्भवामि युगे युगे ।।

Paritrāṇāya sādhūnāṁ
vināśāya ca duṣkṛtām /
dharma-saṁsthāpan'ārthāya
sambhavāmi yuge yuge // 8 //

For the protection of the good, for the destruction of the wicked, and for the establishment of Dharma, I am born from age to age.

जन्म कर्म च मे दिव्यमेवं यो वेत्ति तत्त्वतः ।
त्यक्त्वा देहं पुनर्जन्म नैति मामेति सोऽर्जुन ।।

Janma karma ca me divyam
evaṁ yo vetti tattvataḥ /
tyaktvā dehaṁ punar-janma
nai'ti mām eti so' rjuna // 9 //

O Arjuna! He who thus understands the truth about My embodiment and My deeds—he, on abandoning his present body, is not reborn; he attains to Me.

वीतरागभयक्रोधा मन्मया मामुपाश्रिताः ।
बहवो ज्ञानतपसा पूता मद्भावमागताः ।।

Vīta-rāga-bhaya-krodhā
manmayā mām upāśritāḥ /
bahavo jñāna-tapasā
pūtā mad-bhāvam
āgatāḥ // 10 //

Freed from passion, fear and anger, ever absorbed in My thought, and ever dependent on Me—many have attained to My state, being purified by the fire of knowledge and austerity.

ये यथा मां प्रपद्यन्ते तांस्तथैव भजाम्यहम् ।
मम वर्त्मानुवर्तन्ते मनुष्याः पार्थ सर्वशः ।।

Ye yathā māṁ prapadyante
tāṁs tath'aiva bhajāmy aham /
mama vartm'ānuvartante
manuṣyāḥ Pārtha
sarvaśaḥ // 11 //

O Partha! Whosoever worship Me through whatsoever path, I verily accept and bless them in that way. Men everywhere follow My path.

काङ्क्षन्तः कर्मणां सिद्धिं यजन्त इह देवताः ।
क्षिप्रं हि मानुषे लोके सिद्धिर्भवति कर्मजा ।।

Kāṅkṣantaḥ karmaṇāṁ siddhiṁ
yajanta iha devatāḥ /
kṣipraṁ hi mānuṣe loke
siddhir bhavati karmajā // 12 //

In this world those who entertain desire for the fruits of pious works, worship the deities. For, in this world of men such actions bear fruit quickly.

चातुर्वर्ण्यं मया सृष्टं गुणकर्मविभागशः ।
तस्य कर्तारमपि मां विद्ध्यकर्तारमव्ययम् ।।

Cāturvarṇyaṁ mayā sṛṣṭaṁ
guṇa-karma-vibhāgaśaḥ /
tasya kartāram api māṁ
viddhy akartāram
avyayam // *13* //

According to the aptitudes resulting from the dispositions of Nature (Guṇas) and from works, the social order of four fold division has been created by Me. Though I am their originator, know Me to be not an agent but the Spirit unchanging.

न मां कर्माणि लिम्पन्ति न मे कर्मफले स्पृहा ।
इति मां योऽभिजानाति कर्मभिर्न स बध्यते ॥

Na māṁ karmāṇi limpanti
na me karma-phale spṛhā /
ti māṁ yo' bhijānāti
karmabhir na sa badhyate // 14 //

Actions do not affect Me. Nor have I any desire for the fruits of action. Whoever knows Me to be so, is not bound by Karma.

कर्मणो ह्यपि बोद्धव्यं बोद्धव्यं च विकर्मणः ।
अकर्मणश्च बोद्धव्यं गहना कर्मणो गतिः ॥

Karmaṇo hy api boddhavyaṁ
boddhavyaṁ ca vikarmaṇaḥ /
akarmaṇaś ca boddhavyaṁ
gahanā karmaṇo gatiḥ // 17 //

The truth about the nature of 'beneficial work' has to be understood, as also of 'baneful work' and of 'non-work'. The way of work is difficult indeed to understand.

कर्मण्यकर्म यः पश्येदकर्मणि च कर्म यः ।
स बुद्धिमान्मनुष्येषु स युक्तः कृत्स्नकर्मकृत् ॥

Karmaṇy akarma yaḥ paśyed
akarmaṇi ca karma yaḥ /
sa buddhimān manuṣyeṣu
sa yuktaḥ kṛtsna-karma-
kṛt // 18 //

He who sees work in 'no work' and 'no work' in work, he is wise among men. Even while doing all work, he remains established in Yoga.

यस्य सर्वे समारम्भाः कामसङ्कल्पवर्जिताः ।
ज्ञानाग्निदग्धकर्माणं तमाहुः पण्डितं बुधाः ।।

Yasya sarve samārambhāḥ
kāma-saṅkalpa-varjitāḥ /
jñānāgni-dagdha-karmāṇaṁ
tam āhuḥ paṇḍitaṁ
budhāḥ // *19* //

Whose undertakings are devoid of self-centred objectives, whose works have been burnt up by the fire of knowledge—him the wisc call a sage.

त्यक्त्वा कर्मफलासङ्गं नित्यतृप्तो निराश्रयः ।
कर्मण्यभिप्रवृत्तोऽपि नैव किञ्चित्करोति सः ।।

Tyaktvā karma-phalāsaṅgaṁ
nitya tṛpto nirāśrayaḥ /
karmaṇy abhipravṛtto' pi
nai'va kiñcit karoti saḥ // 20 //

Without attachment to the fruits of action, ever-satisfied and free from calculations, he is verily doing nothing, even though engaged in actions.

निराशीर्यतचित्तात्मा त्यक्तसर्वपरिग्रहः ।
शारीरं केवलं कर्म कुर्वन्नाप्नोति किल्बिषम् ॥

Nirāśīr yata-citt'ātmā
tyaktasarva-parigrahaḥ /
śārīraṁ kevalaṁ karma
kurvan n'āpnoti kilbiṣam // *21* //

One who is free from desires, whose mind is well-controlled, and who is without any sense of ownership, incurs no sin from works, as his actions are merely physical.

यदृच्छालाभसन्तुष्टो द्वन्द्वातीतो विमत्सरः ।
समः सिद्धावसिद्धौ च कृत्वापि न निबध्यते ॥

Yadṛcchā-lābha-santuṣṭo
dvandv'ātīto vimatsaraḥ /
samaḥ siddhāv asiddhau ca
kṛtvā'pi na nibadhyate // 22 //

Satisfied with whatever comes without calculations, rising above the contrasting conditions of life, without any competitive spirit, and alike in success and in failure, a man, though working, incurs no sin.

गतसङ्गस्य मुक्तस्य ज्ञानावस्थितचेतसः ।
यज्ञायाचरतः कर्म समग्रं प्रविलीयते ।।

Gata-saṅgasya muktasya
jñān'āvasthita-cetasaḥ /
yajñāy'ācarataḥ karma
samagraṁ pravilīyate // 23 //

In the case of one who is without attachments and the sense of agency, and whose mind is fully established in the knowledge of God,—his actions, being done in dedication to the Lord, melt away with their very tendencies.

ब्रह्मार्पणं ब्रह्म हविर्ब्रह्माग्नौ ब्रह्मणा हुतम् ।
ब्रह्मैव तेन गन्तव्यं ब्रह्मकर्मसमाधिना ॥

Brahm'ārpaṇaṁ brahma havir-
brahm'āgnau brahmaṇā hutam /
brahm'āiva tena gantavyaṁ
brahma-karma-samādhinā // 24 //

To one of the above description, the ladle with which the offering is made and the oblations are Brahman; and the sacrificial rite (which is Brahman) is performed by the sacrificer who is Brahman, in the fire which too is Brahman. He who is thus absorbed in work as Brahman, attains to Brahman alone.

दैवमेवापरे यज्ञं योगिनः पर्युपासते ।
ब्रह्माग्नावपरे यज्ञं यज्ञेनैवोपजुह्वति ॥

Daivam ev'āpare yajñaṁ
yoginaḥ paryupāsate /
brahm'āgnau apare yajñaṁ
yajñen'aiv'opajuhvati // 25 //

Some Yogis perform sacrifices especially wanting to propitiate deities. Still others offer sacrifice (the Ātman) itself as oblation (Yajña) in the fire of Brahman.

श्रोत्रादीनीन्द्रियाण्यन्ये संयमाग्निषु जुह्वति ।
शब्दादीन्विषयानन्य इन्द्रियाग्निषु जुह्वति ॥

Śrotrādīnī'ndriyāṇy anye
saṁyam'āgniṣu juhvati /
śabdādīn viṣayān anya
indriy'āgniṣu juhvati // 26 //

Some offer their organs of knowledge like hearing as sacrifice in the fire of restraint, while others take in all their sense perceptions as oblations made in the fire of their respective senses.

सर्वाणीन्द्रियकर्माणि प्राणकर्माणि चापरे ।
आत्मसंयमयोगाग्नौ जुह्वति ज्ञानदीपिते ।।

Sarvāṇī'ndriya-karmāṇī
prāṇakarmāṇi cā'pare /
ātma-saṁyama yogāgnau
juhvati jñāna-dīpite // 27 //

Others offer all the functions of their senses and vital energy as sacrificial offerings in the fire of self-restraint kindled by knowledge.

द्रव्ययज्ञास्तपोयज्ञा योगयज्ञास्तथाऽपरे ।
स्वाध्यायज्ञानयज्ञाश्च यतयः संशितव्रताः ।।

Dravya-yajñās tapo-yajñā
yoga-yajñās tathā' pare /
svādhyāya-jñāna-yajñāś ca
yatayaḥ saṁśita-vratāḥ // 28 //

Likewise others, being of rigid vows and hard practice, offer their wealth, their austerities, their Yogic practices, and their daily study of the Vedas as sacrifice.

अपाने जुह्वति प्राणं प्राणेऽपानं तथाऽपरे ।
प्राणापानगती रुद्ध्वा प्राणायामपरायणाः ।।

Apāne juhvati prāṇaṁ
prāṇe' pāṇaṁ tathā' pare /
prāṇ'āpāna-gatī ruddhvā
prāṇāyāma-parāyaṇāḥ // 29 //

Others devoted to the practice of Prāṇāyāma, regulate the movement of Prāṇa and Apāna, and offer as oblation Prāṇa in Apāna, and likewise Apāna in Prāṇa.

अपरे नियताहाराः प्राणान्प्राणेषु जुह्वति ।
सर्वेऽप्येते यज्ञविदो यज्ञक्षपितकल्मषाः ।।

Apare niyat'āhārāḥ
prāṇān prāṇeṣu juhvati /
sarve' py ete yajña-vido
yajña-kṣapita-kalmaṣāḥ // 30 //

Some others, who observe regulation of food, make a sacrificial offering of the Prāṇa as the vital energy present in food stuffs, into the prāṇa as the vital energy enlivening the body. All these know the true nature of sacrifice and have all evil in them washed away by Yajña (sacrifice).

यज्ञशिष्टामृतभुजो यान्ति ब्रह्म सनातनम् ।
नायं लोकोऽस्त्ययज्ञस्य कुतोऽन्यः कुरुसत्तम ।।

Yajña-śiṣṭāmṛta-bhujo
yānti brahma sanātanam /
n'āyaṁ loko' sty ayajñasya
kuto' nyaḥ Kuru-sattama // 31 //

Those who partake of nectar, the sacramental remnants of sacrifice, attain to the eternal Brahman. O Thou the best of the Kurus! For one who sacrifices not, this world is lost, not to speak then of the hereaftor.

एवं बहुविधा यज्ञा वितता ब्रह्मणो मुखे ।
कर्मजान्विद्धि तान्सर्वानेवं ज्ञात्वा विमोक्ष्यसे ।।

Evaṁ bahuvidhā yajñā
vitatā brahmaṇo mukhe /
karmajān viddhi tān sarvān
evaṁ jñātvā vimokṣyase // 32 //

Thus many forms of sacrifice are set forth prominently in the Vedas (as paths to Brahman). All of them spring from work done by body, mind, and speech. Knowing this, you will attain liberation.

श्रेयान्द्रव्यमयाद्यज्ञाज्ज्ञानयज्ञः परन्तप ।
सर्वं कर्माखिलं पार्थ ज्ञाने परिसमाप्यते ।।

Śreyān dravyamayād yajñāt
jñāna-yajñaḥ Parantapa /
sarvaṁ karmā'khilaṁ Pārtha
jñāne parisamāpyate // 33 //

O scorcher of enemies! Sacrifice involving knowledge is superior to sacrifice with material objects; for, O son of Pṛthā, all works without exception culminate in knowledge.

तद्विद्धि प्रणिपातेन परिप्रश्नेन सेवया ।
उपदेक्ष्यन्ति ते ज्ञानं ज्ञानिनस्तत्त्वदर्शिनः ।।

Tad viddhi praṇipātena
paripraśnena sevayā /
upadekṣyanti te jñānaṁ
jñāninas tattva-darśinaḥ // 34 //

With reverential salutations do you approach them—the wise men who have known the Truth. Serve them, and question them repeatedly (with due respect, until your doubts are clarified). These wise men will impart the knowledge of this divine Truth to you.

यज्ज्ञात्वा न पुनर्मोहमेवं यास्यसि पाण्डव ।
येन भूतान्यशेषेण द्रक्ष्यस्यात्मन्यथो मयि ॥

Yaj jñātvā na punar moham
evaṁ yāsyasi Pāṇḍava /
yena bhūtāny aśeṣeṇa
drakṣyasy ātmany atho mayi // 35 //

They will impart to you that divine knowledge by knowing which you will not again fall into such delusion; for you will then see all beings in their entirety in the Self and also in Me.

अपि चेदसि पापेभ्यः सर्वेभ्यः पापकृत्तमः ।
सर्वं ज्ञानप्लवेनैव वृजिनं सन्तरिष्यसि ।।

Api ced asi pāpebhyaḥ
sarvebhyaḥ pāpa-kṛttamaḥ /
sarvaṁ jñāna-plaven'aiva
vṛjinaṁ santariṣyasi // 36 //

Even if you happen to be the worst of sinners, you will surely go across all sin by the raft of divine knowledge.

यथैधांसि समिद्धोऽग्निर्भस्मसात्कुरुतेऽर्जुन ।
ज्ञानाग्निः सर्वकर्माणि भस्मसात्कुरुते तथा ।।

Yath'aidhāṁsi samiddho' gnir
bhasmasāt kurute' rjuna /
jñānāgniḥ sarva-karmāṇi
bhasmasāt kurute tathā // 37 //

Just as a well-kindled fire reduces a heap of fire-wood to ashes, so does the fire of divine knowledge reduce all sins to ashes.

न हि ज्ञानेन सदृशं पवित्रमिह विद्यते ।
तत्स्वयं योगसंसिद्धः कालेनात्मनि विन्दति ।।

Na hi jñānena sadṛśaṁ
pavitram iha vidyate /
tat svayaṁ yoga-saṁsiddhaḥ
kālen'ātmani vindati // 38 //

Verily there is nothing so purifying as knowledge in this world. One who is perfect in Yoga discovers it in oneself in course of time.

श्रद्धावाँल्लभते ज्ञानं तत्परः संयतेन्द्रियः ।
ज्ञानं लब्ध्वा परां शान्तिमचिरेणाधिगच्छति ।।

Śraddhāvāṁl labhate jñānaṁ
tat-paraḥ saṁyat'endriyaḥ /
jñānaṁ labdhvā parāṁ śāntim
acireṇ'ādhigacchati // 39 //

A man of deep Faith (Śraddhā) obtains this divine knowledge, being full of zeal and devotion for it and endowed with mastery of the senses. Having obtained that knowledge, he is established in supreme peace very soon.

अज्ञश्चाश्रद्दधानश्च संशयात्मा विनश्यति ।
नायं लोकोऽस्ति न परो न सुखं संशयात्मनः ।।

Ajñaś c'āśraddadhānaś ca
saṁśay'ātmā vinaśyati /
n'āyaṁ loko' sti na paro
na sukhaṁ
saṁśay'ātmanaḥ // 40 //

An ignorant man without any positive faith, who knows only to doubt, goes to ruin. To such a doubting soul there is neither this world nor the world beyond. There is no happiness for him.

योगसन्न्यस्तकर्माणं ज्ञानसञ्छिन्नसंशयम् ।
आत्मवन्तं न कर्माणि निबध्नन्ति धनञ्जय ।।

Yoga-sannyasta-karmāṇaṁ
jñāna-sañcchinna-saṁśayam /
ātmavantaṁ na karmāṇi
nibadhnanti Dhanañjaya // *41* //

O Arjuna! Works do not bind one who has abandoned them through Yoga consisting in dedication and detachment, whose doubts have been dispelled by divine knowledge, and who is poised in the Self.

तस्मादज्ञानसम्भूतं हृत्स्थं ज्ञानासिनात्मनः ।
छित्त्वैनं संशयं योगमातिष्ठोत्तिष्ठ भारत ।।

Tasmād ajñāna-sambhūtaṁ
hṛt-sthaṁ jñān'āsinā'tmanaḥ /
chittv'ainaṁ saṁśayaṁ yogam
ātiṣṭh'ottiṣṭha Bhārata // 42 //

Therefore, cutting asunder the sceptical tendency of the heart by the sword of divine knowledge, betake yourself to Yoga (communion through sacrificial action) and arise, O scion of the Bharata race!

5. Yoga of Renunciation

'The Yogin who experiences the light within realises himself to be the Spirit.' (24)

Chapter 5

Yoga of Renunciation

अर्जुन उवाच —

सन्न्यासं कर्मणां कृष्ण पुनर्योगं च शंससि ।
यच्छ्रेय एतयोरेकं तन्मे ब्रूहि सुनिश्चितम् ।।

Arjuna uvāca:
Sannyāsaṁ karmaṇāṁ Kṛṣṇa
punar yogaṁ ca śaṁsasi /
yac chreya etayor ekaṁ
tan me brūhi suniścitam // 1 //

Arjuna said: O Kṛṣṇa! Thou praisest in one breath both abandonment of works and communion through their performance. Now tell me with certainty which of them leads to one's good.

श्रीभगवानुवाच —

सन्न्यासः कर्मयोगश्च निःश्रेयसकरावुभौ ।
तयोस्तु कर्मसन्न्यासात्कर्मयोगो विशिष्यते ।।

Śrī Bhagavān uvāca:

Sannyāsaḥ karma yogaś ca
niḥśreyasa-karāv ubhau /
tayos tu karma-sannyāsāt
karma-yogo viśiṣyate // 2 //

The Blessed Lord said:

Both abandonment of works and communion through works lead to liberation. But of them, communion through work excels abandonment of work.

ज्ञेयः स नित्यसन्न्यासी यो न द्वेष्टि न काङ्क्षति ।
निर्द्वन्द्वो हि महाबाहो सुखं बन्धात्प्रमुच्यते ॥

Jñeyaḥ sa nitya-sannyāsī
yo na dveṣṭi na kāṅkṣati /
nirdvandvo hi mahā-bāho
sukhaṁ bandhāt
pramucyate // 3 //

O mighty-armed one! Whoever hates not, nor desires, should be known as one established in renunciation. Indeed, one who is above such contraries is easily liberated from bondage.

साङ्ख्ययोगौ पृथग्बालाः प्रवदन्ति न पण्डिताः।
एकमप्यास्थितः सम्यगुभयोर्विन्दते फलम्।।

Sāṅkhya-yogau pṛthag bālāḥ
pravadanti na paṇḍitāḥ /
ekam apy āsthitaḥ samyag
ubhayor vindate phalam // 4 //

It is only the childish and not the wise that speak of Sāṅkhya (or Knowledge accompanied by abandonment of work) and Yoga (or communion through detached and dedicated work) as different. A person well-established in even one of these, attains the end that is the common goal of both. (That is, in the means they employ, they look different, but their end or ultimate purpose is identical.)

यत्साङ्ख्यैः प्राप्यते स्थानं तद्योगैरपि गम्यते ।
एकं साङ्ख्यं च योगं च यः पश्यति स पश्यति ॥

Yat sāṅkhyaih prāpyate sthānaṁ
tad yogair api gamyate /
ekaṁ sāṅkhyaṁ ca yogaṁ
ca yaḥ paśyati sa paśyati // 5 //

The state which one attains by Sāṁkhya, that same state is attained by Yoga too. He who sees both Sāṁkhya and Yoga as one, sees indeed.

सन्न्यासस्तु महाबाहो दुःखमाप्तुमयोगतः ।
योगयुक्तो मुनिर्ब्रह्म नचिरेणाधिगच्छति ।।

Sannyāsas tu mahā-bāho
duḥkham āptum ayogataḥ /
yoga-yukto munir brahma
nacireṇ'ādhigacchati // 6 //

O mighty-armed Arjuna! True abandonment of work (which the discipline of Sāṁkhya implies) is difficult to practise for one who is not accomplished in the Yoga discipline of detached work. But the sage accomplished in Yoga attains to Brahman in no long time.

योगयुक्तो विशुद्धात्मा विजितात्मा जितेन्द्रियः ।
सर्वभूतात्मभूतात्मा कुर्वन्नपि न लिप्यते ।।

Yoga-yukto viśuddh'ātmā
vijitātmā jit'endriyaḥ /
sarva-bhūtātma-bhūtātmā
kurvann api na lipyate // 7 //

One who is established in selfless and detached action, who is pure, whose mind and senses are under control, and whose self is identified with the self of all—he is never bound, though he be engaged in work.

नैव किञ्चित्करोमीति युक्तो मन्येत तत्त्ववित् ।
पश्यञ्शृण्वन्स्पृशञ्जिघ्रन्नश्नन्गच्छन्स्वपञ्श्वसन् ।।

प्रलपन्विसृजन्गृह्णन्नुन्मिषन्निमिषन्नपि ।
इन्द्रियाणीन्द्रियार्थेषु वर्तन्त इति धारयन् ।।

N'aiva kiñcit karomī'ti
yukto manyeta tattva-vit /
paśyan śṛṇvan spṛśan jighran
aśnan gacchan svapan
śvasan // 8 //

Pralapan visṛjan gṛhṇan
unmiṣan nimiṣann api /
indriyāṇī'ndriyārtheṣu
vartanta iti dhārayan // 9 //

I (the Self) do naught; only the senses are occupied with their objects—this should be the conviction of one who is detached in action and established in the truth (that he is the Ātman), even while seeing, hearing, touching, smelling, eating, walking, sleeping, breathing, conversing, evacuating, holding, and opening and closing the eyes.

ब्रह्मण्याधाय कर्माणि सङ्गं त्यक्त्वा करोति यः ।
लिप्यते न स पापेन पद्मपत्रमिवाम्भसा ।।

Brahmaṇy ādhāya karmāṇi
saṅgaṁ tyaktvā karoti yaḥ /
lipyate na sa pāpena
padma-patram iv'āmbhasā // ***10*** //

One who resigns all his actions to Brahma and works without any personal attachments, is not soiled by sin, as a lotus leaf is not wetted by water.

कायेन मनसा बुद्ध्या केवलैरिन्द्रियैरपि ।
योगिनः कर्म कुर्वन्ति सङ्गं त्यक्त्वात्मशुद्धये ॥

Kāyena manasā buddhyā
kevalair indriyair api /
yoginaḥ karma kurvanti
saṅgaṁ tyaktv'ātma-
śuddhaye // 11 //

For the attainment of mental purity, spiritual aspirants (Yogins) perform action devoid of attachment, with their body, mind, intellect or even merely with the senses.

युक्तः कर्मफलं त्यक्त्वा शान्तिमाप्नोति नैष्ठिकीम् ।
अयुक्तः कामकारेण फले सक्तो निबध्यते ॥

Yuktaḥ karma phalaṁ tyaktvā
śāntim āpnoti naiṣṭhikīm /
ayuktaḥ kāma-kāreṇa
phale sakto nibadhyate // 12 //

By abandoning the fruits of action a man of restrained mind attains to abiding peace. But the one with unrestrained mind, being prompted by desire for the fruits of action, gets bound.

सर्वकर्माणि मनसा सन्न्यस्यास्ते सुखं वशी ।
नवद्वारे पुरे देही नैव कुर्वन्न कारयन् ।।

Sarva-karmāṇi manasā
sannyasy'āste sukhaṁ vaśī /
nava-dvāre pure dehī
n'aiva kurvan na kārayan // 13 //

A self-controlled soul, having abandoned all work mentally (in the way described above), resides at ease (as a witness) in this corporeal mansion with nine gates, neither working nor causing work to be done.

न कर्तृत्वं न कर्माणि लोकस्य सृजति प्रभुः ।
न कर्मफलसंयोगं स्वभावस्तु प्रवर्तते ।।

Na kartṛtvaṁ na karmāṇi
lokasya sṛjati prabhuḥ /
na karma-phala-saṁyogaṁ
svabhāvas tu pravartate // *14* //

In regard to all beings in this world, the sovereign soul is not the cause of the sense of agency, nor of actions, nor of the fruition of actions. It is Nature that does all this.

नादत्ते कस्यचित्पापं न चैव सुकृतं विभुः ।
अज्ञानेनावृतं ज्ञानं तेन मुह्यन्ति जन्तवः ।।

N'ādatte kasyacit pāpaṁ
na c'aiva sukṛtaṁ vibhuḥ /
ajñānen'āvṛtaṁ jñānaṁ
tena muhyanti jantavaḥ // 15 //

The all-pervading Being does not accept the sins or merits of any one. Knowledge of the Divine Spirit is veiled by ignorance, and therefore beings are deluded.

ज्ञानेन तु तदज्ञानं येषां नाशितमात्मनः ।
तेषामादित्यवज्ज्ञानं प्रकाशयति तत्परम् ॥

Jñānena tu tad ajñānaṁ
yeṣāṁ nāśitam ātmanaḥ /
teṣām ādityavaj jñānaṁ
prakāśayati tat param // 16 //

But in the case of those whose ignorance has been destroyed by the knowledge of the Ātman, to them that knowledge reveals the supreme Truth, as the sun does the objects of the world.

तद्बुद्धयस्तदात्मानस्तन्निष्ठास्तत्परायणाः ।
गच्छन्त्यपुनरावृत्तिं ज्ञाननिर्धूतकल्मषाः ॥

Tad-buddhayas tad-ātmānas
tan-niṣṭhās tat-parāyaṇāḥ /
gacchanty apunar-āvṛttiṁ
jñāna-nirdhūta-kalmaṣāḥ // 17 //

Those who think of That always, who are ever at one with That, who are deeply devoted to That, and who look upon That as their goal, get purified of their sins by divine knowledge and go to the state from which there is no return to worldly life.

विद्याविनयसम्पन्ने ब्राह्मणे गवि हस्तिनि ।
शुनि चैव श्वपाके च पण्डिताः समदर्शिनः ॥

Vidyā-vinaya sampanne
brāhmaṇe gavi hastini /
śuni c'aiva śvapāke ca
paṇḍitāḥ sama-darśinaḥ // 18 //

Enlightened men are those who see the same (i.e. the Ātman) in a Brāhmana with learning and humility, in a cow, in an elephant, and even in a dog or in an eater of dog-meat (outcaste).

इहैव तैर्जितः सर्गो येषां साम्ये स्थितं मनः ।
निर्दोषं हि समं ब्रह्म तस्माद् ब्रह्मणि ते स्थिताः ॥

Ih'aiva tair jitaḥ sargo
yeṣāṁ sāmye sthitaṁ manaḥ /
nirdoṣaṁ hi samaṁ brahma
tasmād brahmaṇi te
sthitāḥ // 19 //

Even here in this embodied state, the cycle of births and deaths has been overcome by those who have this vision of sameness in all. Verily, Brahman is the Unsullied and the Pure. Therefore are those seers of sameness said to be established in Brahman.

न प्रहृष्येत्प्रियं प्राप्य नोद्विजेत्प्राप्य चाप्रियम् ।
स्थिरबुद्धिरसम्मूढो ब्रह्मविद् ब्रह्मणि स्थितः ।।

Na prahṛṣyet priyaṁ prāpya
n'odivijet prāpya cā'priyam /
sthira-buddhir asammūḍho
brahma-vid brahmaṇi
sthitaḥ // 20 //

Unperturbed and undeluded a knower of Brahman, who is established in Him, neither rejoices at pleasant experiences nor gets agitated at unpleasant ones.

बाह्यस्पर्शेष्वसक्तात्मा विन्दत्यात्मनि यत्सुखम् ।
स ब्रह्मयोगयुक्तात्मा सुखमक्षयमश्नुते ।।

Bāhya-sparśeṣu asakt'ātmā
vindaty ātmani yat sukham /
sa brahma-yoga-yuktātmā
sukham akṣayam aśnute // 21 //

An aspirant who is unattached to the contactual experiences of the external world, gains the joy that is in the Self within. He enjoys unending bliss with his mind absorbed in communion with Brahman.

ये हि संस्पर्शजा भोगा दुःखयोनय एव ते ।
आद्यन्तवन्तः कौन्तेय न तेषु रमते बुधः ।।

Ye hi saṁsparśa-jā bhogā
duḥkha-yonaya eva te /
ādy-anta vantaḥ Kaunteya
na teṣu ramate budhaḥ // 22 //

Whatever enjoyments are there born of sense contact, they are sources of suffering only. For, they are with a beginning and an end. A wise man finds no delight in them.

शक्नोतीहैव यः सोढुं प्राक्शरीरविमोक्षणात् ।
कामक्रोधोद्भवं वेगं स युक्तः स सुखी नरः ।।

Śaknotī h'aiva yaḥ soḍhuṁ
prāk śarīra-vimokṣaṇāt /
kāma-krodh'odbhavaṁ vegaṁ
sa yuktaḥ sa sukhī naraḥ // 23 //

Here, even while in the body, whoever is able to withstand the agitation caused by lust and anger, he is the self-controlled one, he is the happy man.

योऽन्तःसुखोऽन्तरारामस्तथान्तर्ज्योतिरेव यः ।
स योगी ब्रह्मनिर्वाणं ब्रह्मभूतोऽधिगच्छति ।।

Yo' ntaḥ-sukho' ntar-ārāmas
tathāntar-jyotir eva yaḥ /
sa yogī brahma-nirvāṇaṁ
brahma-bhūto' dhigacchati // 24 //

The Yogin whose happiness is within, whose resting place is within, who likewise experiences the light within—he realises himself to be the Spirit and attains to beatitude in Brahman.

लभन्ते ब्रह्मनिर्वाणमृषयः क्षीणकल्मषाः ।
छिन्नद्वैधा यतात्मानः सर्वभूतहिते रताः ।।

Labhante brahma-nirvāṇaṁ
ṛṣayaḥ kṣīṇa-kalmaṣāḥ /
chinna dvaidhā yat'ātmānaḥ
sarva-bhūta-hite ratāḥ // 25 //

Verily, they attain to beatitude in Brahman who are sinless, whose doubts have been destroyed, whose self is under their control and who rejoice in the good of all.

कामक्रोधवियुक्तानां यतीनां यतचेतसाम् ।
अभितो ब्रह्मनिर्वाणं वर्तते विदितात्मनाम् ।।

Kāma-krodha-viyuktānāṁ
yatīnāṁ yata-cetasām /
abhito brahma-nirvāṇaṁ
vartate vidit'ātmanām // 26 //

To those self-controlled ones (ascetics) who are free from lust and anger, who have controlled their minds and who have known their real nature as the spirit—the attainment of beatitude in Brahman is near at hand.

स्पर्शान्कृत्वा बहिर्बाह्यांश्चक्षुश्चैवान्तरे भ्रुवोः ।
प्राणापानौ समौ कृत्वा नासाभ्यन्तरचारिणौ ।।

यतेन्द्रियमनोबुद्धिर्मुनिर्मोक्षपरायणः ।
विगतेच्छाभयक्रोधो यः सदा मुक्त एव सः ।।

Sparśān kṛtvā bahir bāhyāṁś
cakṣuś c'aiv'āntare bhruvoḥ /
prāṇ'āpanau samau kṛtvā
nās'ābhyantara cāriṇau // 27 //

Yat'endriya-mano-buddhir
munir mokṣa parāyaṇaḥ /
vigat'ecchā-bhaya-krodho
yaḥ sadā mukta eva saḥ // 28 //

Excluding all sense perceptions; fixing the look between the eye brows: steadying the flow of Prāṇa (out-going breath) and Apāna (incoming breath) through the nostrils; controlling the senses, mind and intellect; devoid of desires, fear and anger; and aspiring for liberation alone—a meditative sage is liberated for ever.

भोक्तारं यज्ञतपसां सर्वलोकमहेश्वरम् ।
सुहृदं सर्वभूतानां ज्ञात्वा मां शान्तिमृच्छति ।।

Bhoktāraṁ yajña-tapasāṁ
sarva-loka-maheśvaram /
suhṛdaṁ sarva-bhūtānāṁ
jñātvā māṁ śāntim
ṛcchati // 29 //

Knowing Me, the recipient of all worship and austere practices, the Supreme Lord of all the worlds, and the friend of all beings, man attains to eternal peace.

6. Yoga of Meditation

'Yogi's mind is like the flame of a lamp sheltered from wind which does not flicker.' (19)

Chapter 6

Yoga of Meditation

श्रीभगवानुवाच—

अनाश्रितः कर्मफलं कार्यं कर्म करोति यः ।
स सन्न्यासी च योगी च न निरग्निर्न चाक्रियः ।।

Śrī Bhagavān uvāca:
Anāśritaḥ karma-phalaṁ
kāryaṁ karma karoti yaḥ /
sa sannyāsī ca yogī ca
na niragnir na c'ākriyaḥ // 1 //

The Blessed Lord Said: It is the man who performs his duties without dependence on the fruits that deserves to be called a Sannyāsin (renouncer) and a Yogin, not the one who keeps no fire or aviods works.

यं सन्न्यासमिति प्राहुर्योगं तं विद्धि पाण्डव ।
न ह्यसन्न्यस्तसङ्कल्पो योगी भवति कश्चन ॥

Yaṁ sannyāsam iti prāhur
yogaṁ taṁ viddhi Pāṇḍava /
na hy asannyasta-saṅkalpo
yogī bhavati kaścana // 2 //

O son of Pāṇḍu! What is called Sannyāsa or renunciation know that to be identical with Yoga or disciplines of selfless action. For, whoever has not abandoned subtle hankerings and self centred objectives, can never become a Yogi, or a practitioner of spiritual communion through works.

आरुरुक्षोर्मुनेर्योगं कर्म कारणमुच्यते ।
योगारूढस्य तस्यैव शमः कारणमुच्यते ॥

Ārurukṣor muner yogaṁ
karma kāraṇam ucyate /
yog'ārūḍhasya tasy'aiva
śamaḥ kāraṇam ucyate // 3 //

For one who desires to ascend the path leading to the heights of spiritual communion (Yoga), detached work is the means. For one who has ascended it, quiescence is verily the means.

यदा हि नेन्द्रियार्थेषु न कर्मस्वनुषज्जते ।
सर्वसङ्कल्पसन्न्यासी योगारूढस्तदोच्यते ॥

Yadā hi n'endriy'ārtheṣu
na karmasv anuṣajjate /
sarva-saṅkalpa sannyāsī
yog'ārūḍhas tad'ocyate // 4 //

When one ceases to be attached to sense objects and to one's actions, then that one, who has thus abandoned all subtle hankerings and self-centred objectives, is said to have ascended the heights of spiritual communion (Yoga).

उद्धरेदात्मनात्मानं नात्मानमवसादयेत् ।
आत्मैव ह्यात्मनो बन्धुरात्मैव रिपुरात्मनः ।।

Uddhared ātmanā'tmānaṁ
n'ātmānam avasādayet /
ātm'aiva hy ātmano bandhur
atm'aiva ripur ātmanaḥ // 5 //

One should uplift one's lower self by the higher self. One should not depress or downgrade one's self. For the self verily is both the friend and the foe of the self.

बन्धुरात्मात्मनस्तस्य येनात्मैवात्मना जितः ।
अनात्मनस्तु शत्रुत्वे वर्तेतात्मैव शत्रुवत् ॥

Bandhur ātmā'tmanas tasya
yen'ātm'aiv'ātmanā jitaḥ /
anātmanas tu śatrutve
vartet'ātm'aiva śatruvat // 6 //

To him who has subdued the lower self by the higher self, the self acts like a friend. But to him who has lost his higher self by the dominance of the lower one, the self functions as the enemy, always hostile to him.

जितात्मनः प्रशान्तस्य परमात्मा समाहितः ।
शीतोष्णसुखदुःखेषु तथा मानापमानयोः ।।

Jit'ātmanaḥ praśāntasya
param'ātmā samāhitaḥ /
śīt'oṣṇa-sukha-duḥkheṣu
tathā mān'āpamānayoḥ // 7 //

In one who has conquered his mind, the Self remains steady and unperturbed in the experience of the pairs of opposites like heat and cold, pleasure and pain, honour and dishonour.

ज्ञानविज्ञानतृप्तात्मा कूटस्थो विजितेन्द्रियः ।
युक्त इत्युच्यते योगी समलोष्टाश्मकाञ्चनः ॥

Jñāna-vijñāna-trptātmā
kūṭa-stho vijit'endriyaḥ /
yukta ity ucyate yogī
sama-loṣṭ'āśma-kāñcanaḥ // 8 //

A Yogin whose spirit has attained contentment through knowledge and experience, who is unperturbed, who has subdued his senses, to whom a lump of earth and a bar of gold are alike—such a Yogi is said to have attained steadfastness in spiritual communion.

सुहृन्मित्रार्युदासीनमध्यस्थद्वेष्यबन्धुषु ।
साधुष्वपि च पापेषु समबुद्धिर्विशिष्यते ।।

Suhṛn-mitr'āry-udāsīna-
madhyastha-dveṣya-bandhuṣu /
sādhuṣv api ca pāpeṣu
sama-buddhir viśiṣyate // 9 //

Specially noteworthy in excellence is he who is even-minded in his outlook on friend and foe, on comrade and stranger, on the neutral, on the ally, on the good, and even on the evil ones.

योगी युञ्जीत सततमात्मानं रहसि स्थितः ।
एकाकी यतचित्तात्मा निराशीरपरिग्रहः ॥

Yogī yuñjīta satatam
ātmānaṁ rahasi sthitaḥ /
ekākī yata-citt'ātmā
nirāśīr aparigrahaḥ // 10 //

Let a Yogin constantly practise spiritual communion, residing alone in a solitary spot, desireless, possessionless, and disciplined in body and mind.

शुचौ देशे प्रतिष्ठाप्य स्थिरमासनमात्मनः ।
नात्युच्छ्रितं नातिनीचं चैलाजिनकुशोत्तरम् ।।

तत्रैकाग्रं मनः कृत्वा यतचित्तेन्द्रियक्रियः ।
उपविश्यासने युञ्ज्याद्योगमात्मविशुद्धये ।।

Śucau deśe pratiṣṭhāpya
sthiram āsanam ātmanaḥ /
n'ātyucchritaṁ n'ātinīcaṁ
cail'ājina-kuśottaram // 11 //

Tatr'aikāgraṁ manaḥ kṛtvā
yata-citt'endriya-kriyaḥ /
upaviśy'āsane yuñjyād
yogam ātma-viśuddhaye // 12 //

At a clean spot, which is neither too high nor too low, a seat should be made with Kuśa grass, spread over with a skin and a cloth. Firmly seated on it, the Yogi should practise spiritual communion, with mind concentrated and with the working of the imaginative faculty and the senses under control, for self-purification.

समं कायशिरोग्रीवं धारयन्नचलं स्थिरः ।
सम्प्रेक्ष्य नासिकाग्रं स्वं दिशश्चानवलोकयन् ।।

प्रशान्तात्मा विगतभीर्ब्रह्मचारिव्रते स्थितः ।
मनः संयम्य मच्चित्तो युक्त आसीत मत्परः ।।

Samaṁ kāya-śiro-grīvaṁ
dhārayann acalaṁ sthiraḥ /
samprekṣya nāsik'āgraṁ svaṁ
diśaś c'ānavalokayan // 13 //

Praśāntātmā vigatabhīr
brahmacāri-vrate sthitaḥ /
manaḥ saṁyamya maccitto
yukta āsita matparaḥ // 14 //

Holding the body, head and neck erect, motionless and firm, gazing at the tip of the nose and not round about, fearless, serene, restrained in mind, and established in the vow of continence, he should sit in spiritual communion with Me, looking upon Me as his highest and most precious end.

युञ्जन्नेवं सदात्मानं योगी नियतमानसः ।
शान्तिं निर्वाणपरमां मत्संस्थामधिगच्छति ।।

Yuñjann evaṁ sadā'tmānaṁ
yogī niyata-mānasaḥ /
śāntiṁ nirvāṇa-paramāṁ
mat-saṁsthām
adhigacchati // 15 //

With the mind restrained from going outward to objects and always uniting with the Supreme in spiritual communion, the Yogi attains to Peace, which is the summit of bliss and enduring establishment in My state.

नात्यश्नतस्तु योगोऽस्ति न चैकान्तमनश्नतः ।
न चातिस्वप्नशीलस्य जाग्रतो नैव चार्जुन ।।

N'ātyaśnatas tu yogo' sti
na c'aikāntam anaśnataḥ /
na c'āti-svapna-śīlasya
jāgrato n'aiva c'ārjuna // 16 //

O Arjuna! Success in Yoga is not for those who eat too much, nor for those who eat too little. It is not also for those given to too much sleeping, nor to those who keep vigil too long.

युक्ताहारविहारस्य युक्तचेष्टस्य कर्मसु ।
युक्तस्वप्नावबोधस्य योगो भवति दुःखहा ।।

Yukt'āhara-vihārasya
yukta-ceṣṭasya karmasu /
yukta-svapn'āvabodhasya
yogo bhavati
duḥkha-hā // 17 //

For one who is temperate in food and recreation, who is detached and self-restrained in work, who is regulated in sleep and in vigil—Yoga brings about the cessation of the travail of Samsāra.

यदा विनियतं चित्तमात्मन्येवावतिष्ठते ।
निःस्पृहः सर्वकामेभ्यो युक्त इत्युच्यते तदा ॥

Yadā viniyataṁ cittam
atmany ev'āvatiṣṭhate /
niḥspṛhaḥ sarva-kāmebhyo
yukta ity ucyate tadā // 18 //

When the disciplined mind is able to remain established in the Ātman alone, when it is free from longing for all objects of desire—then is it spoken of as having attained to spiritual communion.

यथा दीपो निवातस्थो नेङ्गते सोपमा स्मृता ।
योगिनो यतचित्तस्य युञ्जतो योगमात्मनः ॥

Yathā dīpo nivātastho
n'eṅgate s'opamā smṛtā /
yogino yata-cittasya
yuñjato yogam ātmanaḥ // 19 //

The flame of a lamp sheltered from wind does not flicker. This is the comparison used to describe a Yogi's mind that is well under control and united with the Ātman.

यत्रोपरमते चित्तं निरुद्धं योगसेवया ।
यत्र चैवात्मनात्मानं पश्यन्नात्मनि तुष्यति ।।

Yatr'oparamate cittaṁ
niruddhaṁ yoga-sevayā /
yatra c'aiv'ātmanā'tmānaṁ
paśyann ātmani tuṣyati // 20 //

That state in which the Chitta (mind stuff), with its movements restrained by the practice of Yoga, finds rest; in which is experienced the joy of the Spirit born of the higher mind intuiting the Spirit.

सुखमात्यन्तिकं यत्तद्बुद्धिग्राह्यमतीन्द्रियम् ।
वेत्ति यत्र न चैवायं स्थितश्चलति तत्त्वतः ।।

Sukham ātyantikaṁ yat tad
buddhi-grāhyam atīndriyam /
vetti yatra na c'aiv'āyaṁ
sthitaś calati tattvataḥ // 21 //

In which he (the Yogin) experiences that endless bliss which is beyond the ken of the senses but is intuited by the purified intellect; wherein established, one does not waver from the Truth:

यं लब्ध्वा चापरं लाभं मन्यते नाधिकं ततः ।
यस्मिन्स्थितो न दुःखेन गुरुणापि विचाल्यते ॥

Yaṁ labdhvā c'āparaṁ lābhaṁ
manyate n'ādhikaṁ tataḥ /
yasmin sthito na duḥkhena
guruṇā'pi vicālyate // 22 //

Having obtained which no other gain is considered as greater; remaining in which one is not shaken even by the heaviest of afflictions,

तं विद्याद् दुःखसंयोगवियोगं योगसञ्ज्ञितम् ।
स निश्चयेन योक्तव्यो योगोऽनिर्विण्णचेतसा ॥

Taṁ vidyād duḥkha-saṁyoga-
viyogaṁ yoga-sañjñitam /
sa niścayena yoktavyo
yogo' nirviṇṇa-cetasā // 23 //

Know that severence of connection with pain as what is designated as Yoga. It has to be practised tirelessly with determination.

सङ्कल्पप्रभवान्कामांस्त्यक्त्वा सर्वानशेषतः ।
मनसैवेन्द्रियग्रामं विनियम्य समन्ततः ।।

शनैः शनैरुपरमेद् बुद्ध्या धृतिगृहीतया ।
आत्मसंस्थं मनः कृत्वा न किञ्चिदपि चिन्तयेत् ।।

Saṅkalpa-prabhavān kāmāṁs
tyaktvā sarvān aśeṣataḥ /
manas'aiv'endriya-grāmaṁ
viniyamya samantataḥ // 24 //

Śanaiḥ-śanair uparamed
buddhyā dhṛti-gṛhītayā /
ātma-saṁsthaṁ manaḥ kṛtvā
na kiñcid api cintayet // 25 //

Abandoning imagination-born longings in their entirety, restraining all the senses with the mind on every side, and setting that mind firmly on the Self under the direction of a steadfast intellect, one should practise tranquillity little by little, and abstain from every kind of thought.

यतो यतो निश्चरति मनश्चञ्चलमस्थिरम् ।
ततस्ततो नियम्यैतदात्मन्येव वशं नयेत् ।।

Yato-yato niścarati
manaś cañcalam asthiram /
tatas-tato niyamy'aitad
ātmany eva vaśaṁ nayet // *26* //

From whatsoever reason this wavering and fickle mind wanders away, it should be curbed and brought to abide in the Self alone.

प्रशान्तमनसं ह्येनं योगिनं सुखमुत्तमम् ।
उपैति शान्तरजसं ब्रह्मभूतमकल्मषम् ।।

Praśānta-manasaṁ hy enaṁ
yoginaṁ sukham uttamam /
upaiti śānta-rajasaṁ
brahma-bhūtam
akalmaṣam // 27 //

Supreme Bliss wells up in a Yogi, who is tranquil in mind, whose passions are subdued, who is free from impurities and who is in the Brahmic state.

युञ्जन्नेवं सदात्मानं योगी विगतकल्मषः ।
सुखेन ब्रह्मसंस्पर्शमत्यन्तं सुखमश्नुते ॥

Yuñjann evaṁ sadā'tmānaṁ
yogī vigata-kalmaṣaḥ /
sukhena brahma-saṁsparśam
atyantaṁ sukham aśnute // 28 //

Thus, ever engaged in making the mind steadfast in spiritual communion and having all the impurities of the mind effaced thereby, the Yogin easily experiences the infinite Bliss of contact with Brahman.

सर्वभूतस्थमात्मानं सर्वभूतानि चात्मनि ।
ईक्षते योगयुक्तात्मा सर्वत्र समदर्शनः ।।

Sarva-bhūta-stham ātmānaṁ
sarva-bhūtāni c'atmani /
īkṣate yoga-yukt'ātmā
sarvatra sama-darśanaḥ // 29 //

The man of spiritual insight, established in same-sightedness, sees the Self as residing in all beings and all beings as resting in the Self.

यो मां पश्यति सर्वत्र सर्वं च मयि पश्यति ।
तस्याहं न प्रणश्यामि स च मे न प्रणश्यति ।।

Yo māṁ paśyati sarvatra
sarvaṁ ca mayi paśyati /
tasy'āhaṁ na praṇaśyāmi
sa ca me na praṇaśyati // 30 //

He who sees Me in all beings, and all beings in Me—to him I am never lost, nor he to Me.

सर्वभूतस्थितं यो मां भजत्येकत्वमास्थितः ।
सर्वथा वर्तमानोऽपि स योगी मयि वर्तते ।।

Sarva-bhūta-sthitaṁ yo māṁ
bhajaty ekatvam āsthitaḥ /
sarvathā vartamano' pi
sa yogī mayi vartate // *31* //

Established in the unity of all existence, a Yogin who serves Me present in all beings, verily abides in Me, whatever be his mode of life.

आत्मौपम्येन सर्वत्र समं पश्यति योऽर्जुन ।
सुखं वा यदि वा दुःखं स योगी परमो मतः ।।

Ātm'aupamyena sarvatra
samaṁ paśyati yo' rjuna /
sukhaṁ vā yadi vā duḥkhaṁ
sa yogī paramo mataḥ // 32 //

O Arjuna! In My view that Yogi is the best who, out of a sense of identity with others on account of the perception of the same Ātman in all, feels their joy and suffering as his own.

अर्जुन उवाच —
योऽयं योगस्त्वया प्रोक्तः साम्येन मधुसूदन ।
एतस्याहं न पश्यामि चञ्चलत्वात् स्थितिं स्थिराम् ।।

Arjuna uvāca:
Yo' yaṁ yogas tvayā proktaḥ
sāmyena Madhusūdana /
etasy'āhaṁ na paśyāmi
cañcalatvāt sthitiṁ
sthirām // 33 //

Arjuna said:

O Slayer of Madhu! Owing to the fickleness of the mind, I find no way of firm establishment in spiritual communion through equanimity as instructed by you.

चञ्चलं हि मनः कृष्ण प्रमाथि बलवद्दृढम् ।
तस्याहं निग्रहं मन्ये वायोरिव सुदुष्करम् ॥

Cañcalaṁ hi manaḥ Kṛṣṇa
pramāthi balavad dṛḍham /
tasy'āhaṁ nigrahaṁ manye
vāyor iva suduṣkaram // 34 //

O Kṛṣṇa! Verily, the mind is fickle, turbulent, powerful and unyielding. To control it, I think, is as difficult as controlling the wind itself.

श्रीभगवानुवाच —

असंशयं महाबाहो मनो दुर्निग्रहं चलम् ।
अभ्यासेन तु कौन्तेय वैराग्येण च गृह्यते ।।

Śrī Bhagavān uvāca:
Asaṁsayaṁ mahā-bāho,
mano durnigrahaṁ calam /
abhyāsena tu Kaunteya
vairāgyeṇa ca gṛhyate // *35* //

The Blessed Lord said:

O mighty armed one! Undoubtedly the mind is fickle and difficult to be checked. Yet, O son of Kuntī, it can be brought under control by dispassion and spiritual practice.

असंयतात्मना योगो दुष्प्राप इति मे मतिः ।
वश्यात्मना तु यतता शक्योऽवाप्तुमुपायतः ॥

Asaṁyat'ātmanā yogo
duṣprāpa iti me matiḥ /
vaśy'ātmanā tu yatatā
śakyo' vāptum upāyataḥ // 36 //

My view is that Yoga is difficult of attainment by men of uncontrolled mind. But for those who have their minds under control, it is possible to attain, if they strive with the proper means.

अर्जुन उवाच —

अयतिः श्रद्धयोपेतो योगाच्चलितमानसः ।
अप्राप्य योगसंसिद्धिं कां गतिं कृष्ण गच्छति ॥

Arjuna uvāca:

Ayatiḥ śraddhay'opeto
yogāc calita-mānasaḥ /
aprāpya yoga-saṁsiddhiṁ
kāṁ gatiṁ Kṛṣṇa
gacchati // 37 //

Arjuna said:

What, O Kṛṣṇa, is the fate of a man who, though endowed with a firm faith, is not steadfast in his practices owing to distractions, and therefore fails to reach spiritual perfection?

कच्चिन्नोभयविभ्रष्टश्छिन्नाभ्रमिव नश्यति ।
अप्रतिष्ठो महाबाहो विमूढो ब्रह्मणः पथि ।।

Kaccin n'obhaya-vibhraṣṭas
chinn'ābhram iva naśyati /
apratiṣṭho mahā-bāho
vimūḍho brahmaṇaḥ
pathi // 38 //

O mighty-armed Lord! Bewildered in the path of Brahman, supportless, does he not lose both this world and the next? Does he not perish like a rain-cloud rent asunder?

एतन्मे संशयं कृष्ण छेत्तुमर्हस्यशेषतः ।
त्वदन्यः संशयस्यास्य छेत्ता न ह्युपपद्यते ॥

Etan me saṁśayaṁ Kṛṣṇa
chettum arhasy aśeṣataḥ /
tvad-anyaḥ saṁśayasy'āsya
chettā na hy upapadyate // 39 //

O Kṛṣṇa! My doubt in this respect has yet to be cleared completely. Indeed! I find none better than Thee to be that doubt dispeller.

श्रीभगवानुवाच —

पार्थ नैवेह नामुत्र विनाशस्तस्य विद्यते ।
न हि कल्याणकृत्कश्चिद् दुर्गतिं तात गच्छति ।।

Śrī Bhagavān uvāca:
Pārtha n'aiveha n'āmutra
vināśas tasya vidyate /
na hi kalyāṇa-kṛt kaścid
durgatiṁ tāta gacchati // 40 //

The Blessed Lord Said:

O son of Pṛthā! He does not meet with downfall either here in this world or in the hereafter. Know for certain, O dear one, that one who treads the path of virtue never goes the way of evil ones.

प्राप्य पुण्यकृतां लोकानुषित्वा शाश्वतीः समाः ।
शुचीनां श्रीमतां गेहे योगभ्रष्टोऽभिजायते ।।

Prāpya puṇya-kṛtāṁ lokān
uṣitvā śāśvatīḥ samāḥ /
śucīnāṁ śrīmatāṁ gehe
yoga-bhraṣṭo' bhijāyate // 41 //

The fallen Yogi goes (after death) to the spheres of the righteous, and after having lived there for unnumbered years, is reborn in this world in a pure and prosperous family.

अथवा योगिनामेव कुले भवति धीमताम् ।
एतद्धि दुर्लभतरं लोके जन्म यदीदृशम् ।।

Athavā yogināṁ eva
kule bhavati dhīmatām /
etadd hi durlabhataraṁ
loke janma yad īdṛśam // 42 //

Or he is re-born in a family of men full of wisdom and spirituality. Re-birth under such conditions is passing hard to get in this world.

तत्र तं बुद्धिसंयोगं लभते पौर्वदेहिकम् ।
यतते च ततो भूयः संसिद्धौ कुरुनन्दन ।।

Tatra taṁ buddhi-saṁyogaṁ
labhate paurvadehikam /
yatate ca tato bhūyaḥ
saṁsiddhau Kuru-
nandana // 43 //

There, O scion of the clan of Kurus! he will regain the spiritual discernment of his previous birth, and then he will strive harder than ever for perfection.

पूर्वाभ्यासेन तेनैव ह्रियते ह्यवशोऽपि सः ।
जिज्ञासुरपि योगस्य शब्दब्रह्मातिवर्तते ।।

Purv'ābhyāsena ten'aiva
hriyate hy avaśo' pi saḥ /
jijñāsur api yogasya
śabda-brahm'ātivartate // 44 //

Even if helpless, he will be driven towards the path of Yoga by the force of his previous striving. For even a beginner in the path of Yoga goes above the stage requiring the aid of Vedic ritualism (not to speak then of one who has made some progress in Yoga).

प्रयत्नाद्यतमानस्तु योगी संशुद्धकिल्बिषः ।
अनेकजन्मसंसिद्धस्ततो याति परां गतिम् ।।

Prayatnād yatamānas tu
yogī saṁśuddha-kilbiṣaḥ /
aneka-janma-saṁsiddhas
tato yāti parāṁ gatim // 45 //

As for the Yogi striving diligently, he is cleansed of all his sins and gains spiritual perfection after passing through several embodiments. Finally he reaches the highest state (which consists in release from the bondage of the body).

तपस्विभ्योऽधिको योगी
ज्ञानिभ्योऽपि मतोऽधिकः ।
कर्मिभ्यश्चाधिको योगी
तस्माद्योगी भवार्जुन ।।

Tapasvibhyo' dhiko yogī
jñānibhyo' pi mato' dhikaḥ /
karmibhyaś c'ādhiko yogī
tasmād yogī bhav'ārjuna // 46 //

A Yogi (one practising meditation) is superior to a man of austerity; he is superior to a scholar; he is superior to a ritualist too. Therefore, O Arjuna, be you a Yogi.

योगिनामपि सर्वेषां मद्गतेनान्तरात्मना ।
श्रद्धावान्भजते यो मां स मे युक्ततमो मतः ।।

Yoginām api sarveṣāṁ
mad-gaten'āntarātmanā /
śraddhāvān bhajate yo māṁ
sa me yuktatamo mataḥ // 47 //

Of all the Yogins, he is the most attuned in spiritual communion, who worships Me with abiding faith and with his innermost self fused with Me.

7. Yoga of Knowledge

'Know me, O Pārtha! to be the eternal seed of all beings.' (10)

Chapter 7

Yoga of Knowledge

श्रीभगवानुवाच —

मय्यासक्तमनाः पार्थ योगं युञ्जन्मदाश्रयः ।
असंशयं समग्रं मां यथा ज्ञास्यसि तच्छृणु ।।

Śrī Bhagavān uvāca:
Mayy āsakta-manāḥ Pārtha
yogaṁ yuñjan mad-āśrayaḥ /
asaṁśayaṁ samagraṁ māṁ
yathā jñāsyasi tac chṛṇu // 1 //

The Blessed Lord said:

Hear now, O son of Pṛthā, how one resigned to Me and absorbed in love of Me, attains to full knowledge of Me through the practice of spiritual communion.

ज्ञानं तेऽहं सविज्ञानमिदं वक्ष्याम्यशेषतः ।
यज्ज्ञात्वा नेह भूयोऽन्यज्ज्ञातव्यमवशिष्यते ।।

Jñānaṁ te' haṁ savijñānam
idaṁ vakṣyāmy aśeṣataḥ /
yaj jñātvā n'eha bhūyo' nyaj-
jñātavyam avaśiṣyate // 2 //

I shall now declare to you in fullness that Knowledge along with Special Knowledge, (its higher development), by means of which there will remain nothing more for you to understand.

मनुष्याणां सहस्रेषु कश्चिद्यतति सिद्धये ।
यततामपि सिद्धानां कश्चिन्मां वेत्ति तत्त्वतः ॥

Manuṣyāṇāṁ sahasreṣu
kaścid yatati siddhaye /
yatatām api siddhānāṁ
kaścin māṁ vetti tattvataḥ // 3 //

Among thousands of men, there will just be one here or there striving for spiritual perfection. From among the aspirants so striving, one perchance knows Me in truth.

भूमिरापोऽनलो वायुः खं मनो बुद्धिरेव च ।
अहङ्कार इतीयं मे भिन्ना प्रकृतिरष्टधा ॥

Bhūmir āpo' nalo vāyuḥ
khaṁ mano buddhir eva ca /
ahaṅkāra itī'yaṁ me
bhinnā prakṛtir aṣṭadhā // 4 //

My Nature is divided into eight categories—earth, water, fire, air, sky, mind, understanding, and I-sense.

अपरेयमितस्त्वन्यां प्रकृतिं विद्धि मे पराम् ।
जीवभूतां महाबाहो ययेदं धार्यते जगत् ।।

Apar'eyam itas tv anyāṁ
prakṛtiṁ viddhi me parām /
jīva-bhūtāṁ mahā-bāho
yay'edaṁ dhāryate jagat // 5 //

This, O mighty armed, is My lower Nature. Know that, as different from it, is My higher Nature forming the source of all Jīvas and the support of the whole universe.

एतद्योनीनि भूतानि सर्वाणीत्युपधारय ।
अहं कृत्स्नस्य जगतः प्रभवः प्रलयस्तथा ॥

Etad-yonīni bhūtāni
sarvāṇī'ty upadhāraya /
ahaṁ kṛtsnasya jagataḥ
prabhavaḥ pralayas tathā // 6 //

Know that all beings have these two Natures of Mine as their source. I am the origin and the dissolution of this entire universe.

मत्तः परतरं नान्यत् किञ्चिदस्ति धनञ्जय ।
मयि सर्वमिदं प्रोतं सूत्रे मणिगणा इव ।।

Mattaḥ parataraṁ n'ānyat
kiñcid asti Dhanañjaya /
mayi sarvam idaṁ protaṁ
sūtre maṇi-gaṇā iva // 7 //

O Arjuna! There is no being higher than Me. As a row of pearls threaded on a string, all the worlds are held on Me.

रसोऽहमप्सु कौन्तेय प्रभाऽस्मि शशिसूर्ययोः ।
प्रणवः सर्ववेदेषु शब्दः खे पौरुषं नृषु ॥

Raso' ham apsu Kaunteya
prabhā' smi śaśi-sūryayoḥ /
praṇavaḥ sarva-vedeṣu
śabdaḥ khe pauruṣaṁ nṛṣu // 8 //

O son of Kuntī! In water I am taste; in sun and moon, their brilliance; in all the Vedas, the sound symbol Om; in the sky-element, sound; and in men, their manliness.

पुण्यो गन्धः पृथिव्यां च तेजश्चास्मि विभावसौ ।
जीवनं सर्वभूतेषु तपश्चास्मि तपस्विषु ।।

Puṇyo gandhaḥ pṛthivyāṁ ca
tejaś c'āsmi vibhāvasau /
jīvanaṁ sarva-bhūteṣu
tapaś c'āsmi tapasviṣu // 9 //

In the earth element I am sweet fragrance; in fire I am brilliance: in living beings I am the life-principle: and in austere men, I am austerity.

बीजं मां सर्वभूतानां विद्धि पार्थ सनातनम् ।
बुद्धिर्बुद्धिमतामस्मि तेजस्तेजस्विनामहम् ।।

Bījaṁ māṁ sarva-bhūtānāṁ
viddhi Pārtha sanātanam /
buddhir buddhimatām asmi
tejas tejasvinām aham // 10 //

Know me, O Pārtha! to be the eternal seed of all beings. In the wise I am their wisdom and in puissant men, their prowess.

बलं बलवतां चाहं कामरागविवर्जितम् ।
धर्माविरुद्धो भूतेषु कामोऽस्मि भरतर्षभ ।।

Balaṁ balavatāṁ cāhaṁ
kāma-rāga-vivarjitam
dharm'āviruddho bhūteṣu
kāmo' smi Bharata'rṣabha // 11 //

In the strong I am strength uncorrupted by desire and attachment, and in living beings I am desire not contrary to virtue.

ये चैव सात्त्विका भावा राजसास्तामसाश्च ये ।
मत्त एवेति तान्विद्धि न त्वहं तेषु ते मयि ।।

Ye c'aiva sāttvikā bhāvā
rājasās tāmasāś ca ye /
matta ev'eti tān viddhi
na tv ahaṁ teṣu te mayi // 12 //

Whatever manifestations there are of Sattva, Rajas and Tamas, they have all come from Me. They are in Me, not I in them.

त्रिभिर्गुणमयैर्भावैरेभिः सर्वमिदं जगत् ।
मोहितं नाभिजानाति मामेभ्यः परमव्ययम् ।।

Tribhir guṇamayair bhāvair
ebhiḥ sarvam idaṁ jagat /
mohitaṁ n'ābhijānāti
mām ebhyaḥ param
avyayam // 13 //

Deluded by the mental states accruing from the three Guṇas of Prakṛti, this world knows not Me, the Imperishable, transcending these Guṇas.

दैवी ह्येषा गुणमयी मम माया दुरत्यया ।
मामेव ये प्रपद्यन्ते मायामेतां तरन्ति ते ।।

Daivī hy eṣā guṇamayī
mama māyā duratyayā /
mām eva ye prapadyante
māyām etāṁ taranti te // 14 //

My divine Māyā (power) constituted of the three Guṇas is difficult to overcome. Whoever takes refuge in Me alone, in utter devotion, overcomes it.

न मां दुष्कृतिनो मूढाः प्रपद्यन्ते नराधमाः ।
माययाऽपहृतज्ञाना आसुरं भावमाश्रिताः ।।

Na māṁ duṣkṛtino mūḍhāḥ
prapadyante nar'ādhamāḥ /
māyayā pahṛta-jñānā
āsuraṁ bhāvam āśritāḥ // 15 //

The lowest type of men, evil, foolish and demoniac in nature, being deprived of right understanding by Māyā, never take refuge in Me with devotion.

चतुर्विधा भजन्ते मां जनाः सुकृतिनोऽर्जुन ।
आर्तो जिज्ञासुरर्थार्थी ज्ञानी च भरतर्षभ ।।

Catur-vidhā bhajante māṁ
janāḥ sukṛtino' rjuna /
ārto jijñāsur arth'ārthī
jñānī ca Bharata'rṣabha // 16 //

O Arjuna, the greatest of the Bharata race! Four kinds of pious men adore Me. They are the distressed one, the knowledge-seeker, the wealth-seeker, and the knower.

तेषां ज्ञानी नित्ययुक्त एकभक्तिर्विशिष्यते ।
प्रियो हि ज्ञानिनोऽत्यर्थमहं स च मम प्रियः ।।

Teṣāṁ jñānī nitya-yukta
eka-bhaktir viśiṣyate /
priyo hi jñānino' tyartham
ahaṁ sa ca mama priyaḥ // 17 //

Among them, the knower (or the man of wisdom), ever communing and single-minded in devotion, is the best. I am indeed supremely dear to such a knower, and he in turn is dear to Me.

उदाराः सर्व एवैते ज्ञानी त्वात्मैव मे मतम् ।
आस्थितः स हि युक्तात्मा मामेवानुत्तमां गतिम् ।।

Udārāḥ sarva ev'aite
jñānī tv ātm'aiva me matam /
āsthitaḥ sa hi yukt'ātmā
mām ev'ānuttamāṁ gatim // 18 //

While all of them are certainly noble, the knower I cherish as My very self—such is My view. For, ever in union with Me, he is established in the conviction that I am his highest goal.

बहूनां जन्मनामन्ते ज्ञानवान्मां प्रपद्यते ।
वासुदेवः सर्वमिति स महात्मा सुदुर्लभः ।।

Bahūnāṁ janmanām ante
jñānavān māṁ prapadyate /
Vāsudevaḥ sarvam iti
sa mah'ātmā
sudurlabhaḥ // 19 //

At the end of many births (of striving), the knowing one makes Me his refuge, realising that Vāsudeva is All. A great soul of that type is rare to find.

कामैस्तैस्तैर्हृतज्ञानाः प्रपद्यन्तेऽन्यदेवताः ।
तं तं नियममास्थाय प्रकृत्या नियताः स्वया ॥

Kāmais tais-tair hṛta-jñānāḥ
prapadyante' nya-devatāḥ /
taṁ taṁ niyamam āsthāya
prakṛtyā niyatāḥ svayā // 20 //

Influenced by their inherent nature and deprived of correct judgement by numerous desires, people adore other deities with various forms of worship pertaining to them.

यो यो यां यां तनुं भक्तः श्रद्धयाऽर्चितुमिच्छति ।
तस्य तस्याचलां श्रद्धां तामेव विदधाम्यहम् ॥

Yo yo yāṁ yāṁ tanuṁ bhaktaḥ
śraddhayā' rcitum icchati /
tasya-tasy'ācalāṁ śraddhāṁ
tām eva vidadhāmy aham // 21 //

Whichever devotee desires to adore whatever such Deity with faith, in all such votaries I make that particular faith unshakable.

स तया श्रद्धया युक्तस्तस्याराधनमीहते ।
लभते च ततः कामान्मयैव विहितान्हि तान् ।।

Sa tayā śraddhayā yuktas
tasy'ārādhanam īhate /
labhate ca tataḥ kāmān
may'aiva vihitān hi tān // 22 //

Endowed with that faith, a votary performs the worship of that particular deity and obtains the fruits thereof, these being granted by Me alone.

अन्तवत्तु फलं तेषां तद्भवत्यल्पमेधसाम् ।
देवान्देवयजो यान्ति मद्भक्ता यान्ति मामपि ।।

Antavat tu phalaṁ teṣaṁ
tad bhavaty alpa-medhasām /
devān deva-yajo yānti
mad-bhaktā yānti
mām api // 23 //

The results accruing to such small-minded people are finite only. Those who worship the Devas go to the Devas, but My devotees attain to Me.

अव्यक्तं व्यक्तिमापन्नं मन्यन्ते मामबुद्धयः ।
परं भावमजानन्तो ममाव्ययमनुत्तमम् ॥

Avyaktaṁ vyaktim āpannaṁ
manyante mām abuddhayaḥ /
paraṁ bhāvam ajānanto
mamā'vyayam anuttamam // 24 //

Without any insight into My transcendental nature, unique and immutable, men of little understanding look upon Me as a mere human individual, having come into manifestation from an unmanifested state.

नाहं प्रकाशः सर्वस्य योगमायासमावृतः ।
मूढोऽयं नाभिजानाति लोको मामजमव्ययम् ॥

N'ahaṁ prakāśaḥ sarvasya
yoga-māyā samāvṛtaḥ /
mūḍho' yaṁ n'ābhijānāti
loko mām ajam avyayam // 25 //

Veiled as I am in My Yoga-māyā (Divine Power), I am not revealed to all. This deluded world does not know Me, the unoriginated and the indestructible.

वेदाहं समतीतानि वर्तमानानि चार्जुन ।
भविष्याणि च भूतानि मां तु वेद न कश्चन ॥

Ved'āhaṁ samatītāni
vartamānāni c'ārjuna /
bhaviṣyāṇi ca bhutāni
māṁ tu veda na kaścana // 26 //

O Arjuna! I know all beings—past, present and future. But none knows me.

इच्छाद्वेषसमुत्थेन द्वन्द्वमोहेन भारत ।
सर्वभूतानि सम्मोहं सर्गे यान्ति परन्तप ।।

Icchā-dveṣa-samutthena
dvandva-mohena Bhārata /
sarva-bhutāni sammohaṁ
sarge yānti parantapa // 27 //

O scion of Bharata's house! From their very birth all beings are deluded by the bewitchment of the pairs of opposites like pleasure and pain, springing from the instinctive feelings of attraction and aversion for them.

येषां त्वन्तगतं पापं जनानां पुण्यकर्मणाम् ।
ते द्वन्द्वमोहनिर्मुक्ता भजन्ते मां दृढव्रताः ॥

Yeṣāṁ tv anta-gataṁ pāpaṁ
janānāṁ puṇya-karmaṇām /
te dvandva-moha-nirmuktā
bhajante māṁ
dṛḍha-vratāḥ // 28 //

But those men of virtuous deeds, in whom sinfulness has been effaced—they, freed from the bewilderment of sense life, worship Me with great steadfastness in their vows.

जरामरणमोक्षाय मामाश्रित्य यतन्ति ये ।
ते ब्रह्म तद्विदुः कृत्स्नमध्यात्मं कर्म चाखिलम् ॥

Jarā-maraṇa-mokṣāya
mām āśritya yatanti ye /
te brahma tad viduḥ kṛtsnam
adhyātmaṁ karma
c'ākhilam // 29 //

Those that strive for liberation from the travails of old age and death in complete trust and dependence on Me, shall know all about the Absolute, His spiritual manifestation and His works of spiritual import.

साधिभूताधिदैवं मां साधियज्ञं च ये विदुः ।
प्रयाणकालेऽपि च मां ते विदुर्युक्तचेतसः ॥

Sādhibhūt'ādhidaivaṁ māṁ
sādhiyajñaṁ ca ye viduḥ /
prayāṇa-kāle' pi ca māṁ
te vidur yukta-cetasaḥ // 30 //

Those who have grasped that I am the spiritual power that sustains all material manifestations, all divine expressions and all spiritual endeavours—they continue to know Me as such even at the time of death, their mind being ever absorbed in Me.

8. Way to Brahman

'A person attains whatever object he thinks of at the time of death.' (6)

Chapter 8

Way to Brahman

अर्जुन उवाच —

किं तद्ब्रह्म किमध्यात्मं किं कर्म पुरुषोत्तम ।
अधिभूतं च किं प्रोक्तमधिदैवं किमुच्यते ।।

Arjuna uvāca:
Kiṁ tad brahma kim adhyātmaṁ
kiṁ karma puruṣ'ottama /
adhibhūtaṁ ca kiṁ proktam
adhidaivaṁ kim ucyate? // 1 //

Arjuna said: O Supreme Lord! What is Brahman (the Absolute)? What is the Spirit (the Adhyātma)? What is work (Karma)? And what is that which underlies the material manifestations (Adhibhūta), and what, the divinities (Adhidaiva)?

अधियज्ञः कथं कोऽत्र देहेऽस्मिन्मधुसूदन ।
प्रयाणकाले च कथं ज्ञेयोऽसि नियतात्मभिः ।।

Adhiyajñaḥ kathaṁ ko' tra
dehe' smin Madhusūdana /
prayāṇa-kāle ca kathaṁ
jñeyo' si niyat'ātmabhiḥ // 2 //

O Slayer of Madhu! Who is the Adhiyajña (the spirit underlying sacrifices) that resides in this body, and how does he do so? How should a man of a self-restraint meditate on the Supreme Being at the time of death?

श्रीभगवानुवाच —

अक्षरं ब्रह्म परमं स्वभावोऽध्यात्ममुच्यते ।
भूतभावोद्भवकरो विसर्गः कर्मसञ्ज्ञितः ॥

Śrī Bhagavān uvāca:
Akṣaraṁ brahma paramaṁ
svabhāvo' dhyātmam ucyate /
bhūta-bhāvodbhava-karo
visargaḥ karma-samjñitaḥ // 3 //

The Blessed Lord said:

Brahman is Akṣara, the Immutable Being than whom there is none higher. Brahman's power manifested in every body as the transmigrating self (the Jīva), is the *Adhyātma.* The creative act (identified with sacrificial offering), which brings all beings into existence, is *Karma* (work).

अधिभूतं क्षरो भावः पुरुषश्चाधिदैवतम् ।
अधियज्ञोऽहमेवात्र देहे देहभृतां वर ।।

Adhibhūtaṁ kṣaro bhāvaḥ
puruṣaś'c'ādhidaivatam /
adhiyajño' ham ev'ātra
dehe deha-bhṛtāṁ vara // 4 //

O noble one! The perishable Nature is the material aspect (Adhibhūta). The cosmic soul is the basis of all divine manifestations (Adhidaivata); and I verily form the Adhiyajña, the one object of all worship which men perform with their body and mind.

अन्तकाले च मामेव स्मरन्मुक्त्वा कलेवरम् ।
यः प्रयाति स मद्भावं याति नास्त्यत्र संशयः ॥

Anta-kāle ca mām eva
smaran muktvā kalevaram /
yaḥ prayāti sa mad-bhāvaṁ
yāti n'āsty atra saṁśayaḥ // 5 //

Whoever thinks of Me alone even at the time of death, attains to My state on abandoning the body. There is no doubt about this.

यं यं वापि स्मरन्भावं त्यजत्यन्ते कलेवरम् ।
तं तमेवैति कौन्तेय सदा तद्भावभावितः ॥

Yaṁ yaṁ v'āpi smaran bhāvaṁ
tyajaty ante kalevaram /
taṁ tam ev'aiti Kaunteya
sadā tad-bhāva-bhāvitaḥ // 6 //

O son of Kuntī! Whatever object a person thinks of at the time of death, having been absorbed in its thought all through,—he attains to that object alone.

तस्मात्सर्वेषु कालेषु मामनुस्मर युध्य च ।
मय्यर्पितमनोबुद्धिर्मामेवैष्यस्यसंशयः ॥

Tasmāt sarveṣu kāleṣu
mām anusmara yudhya ca /
mayy arpita-mano-buddhir
mām ev'aiṣyasy asaṁśayaḥ // 7 //

Therefore fight, remembering Me always. One who has dedicated his mind and understanding to Me, shall come to Me alone, undoubtedly.

अभ्यासयोगयुक्तेन चेतसा नान्यगामिना ।
परमं पुरुषं दिव्यं याति पार्थानुचिन्तयन् ॥

Abhyāsa-yoga-yuktena
cetasā n'ānya-gāminā /
paramaṁ puruṣaṁ divyaṁ
yāti Pārth'ānucintayan // 8 //

Thinking of Me continuously, with a mind trained in the practice of spiritual communion and freed from the tendency to stray away to other objects, one attains to the Divine Spirit Supreme.

कविं पुराणमनुशासितार-
मणोरणीयांसमनुस्मरेद्यः ।
सर्वस्य धातारमचिन्त्यरूप-
मादित्यवर्णं तमसः परस्तात् ।।
प्रयाणकाले मनसाऽचलेन
भक्त्या युक्तो योगबलेन चैव ।
भ्रुवोर्मध्ये प्राणमावेश्य सम्यक्
स तं परं पुरुषमुपैति दिव्यम् ।।

Kaviṁ purāṇam anuśāsitāram
aṇor aṇīyāṁsam anusmared yaḥ /
sarvasya dhātāram acintya-rūpam
āditya-varṇaṁ tamasaḥ parastat /9/
Prayāṇa-kāle manasā' calena
bhaktyā yukto yoga-balena c'aiva /
bhruvor madhye prāṇam āveśya samyak
sa taṁ paraṁ puruṣam upaiti
divyam // 10 //

He who, with a mind steady and endued with devotion and strength born of spiritual practice, fixes his entire life-force between the eye-brows at the time of death, and contemplates on Him who is all-knowing, primeval, subtler than even an atom, sustainer and director of all, glorious like the sun, and beyond all darkness of inertia and ignorance—he verily attains to that Supreme Being.

यदक्षरं वेदविदो वदन्ति
विशन्ति यद्यतयो वीतरागाः ।
यदिच्छन्तो ब्रह्मचर्यं चरन्ति
तत्ते पदं सङ्ग्रहेण प्रवक्ष्ये ॥

Yad akṣaraṁ veda-vido vadanti
viśanti yad yatayo vīta-rāgāḥ /
yad icchanto brahmacaryaṁ caranti
tat te padaṁ saṅgraheṇa
pravakṣye // *11* //

That which Vedic scholars call the Imperishable (Akṣara), which Sannyāsins devoid of worldly attachments enter, desiring which men follow the life of continence and asceticism,—that state I shall declare to you in brief.

सर्वद्वाराणि संयम्य मनो हृदि निरुध्य च ।
मूर्ध्न्याधायात्मनः प्राणमास्थितो योगधारणाम् ।।

ओमित्येकाक्षरं ब्रह्म व्याहरन्मामनुस्मरन् ।
यः प्रयाति त्यजन्देहं स याति परमां गतिम् ।।

Sarva-dvārāṇi saṁyamya
mano hṛdi nirudhya ca /
mūrdhny ādhāy' ātmanaḥ prāṇam
āsthito yoga-dhāraṇām // 12 //

Om ity ek'ākṣaraṁ brahma
vyāharan mām anusmaran /
yaḥ prayāti tyajan dehaṁ
sa yāti paramāṁ gatim // 13 //

Established in spiritual communion by inhibiting all sensations, concentrating on the heart centre, and drawing up the vital energies to the head, one should meditate on Me along with the utterance of the single-syllabled mantra Om denoting Brahman. Departing from the body in this state, one attains liberation.

अनन्यचेताः सततं यो मां स्मरति नित्यशः ।
तस्याहं सुलभः पार्थ नित्ययुक्तस्य योगिनः ।।

Ananya-cetāḥ satataṁ
yo māṁ smarati nityaśaḥ /
tasy'āhaṁ sulabhaḥ Pārtha
nitya-yuktasya yoginaḥ // 14 //

He who, with a mind undistracted by other things, thinks of Me constantly every day—to the Yogi thus ever-attuned, I am easy of attainment, O son of Pṛthā!

मामुपेत्य पुनर्जन्म दुःखालयमशाश्वतम् ।
नाप्नुवन्ति महात्मानः संसिद्धिं परमां गताः ।।

Mām upetya punar-janma
duḥkh'ālayam aśāśvatam /
n'āpnuvanti mah'ātmānaḥ
saṁsiddhiṁ paramāṁ
gatāḥ // 15 //

No more is re-birth, no more this home of transience and misery, for those great-souled ones who have attained to supreme perfection by realising Me.

आब्रह्मभुवनाल्लोकाः पुनरावर्तिनोऽर्जुन ।
मामुपेत्य तु कौन्तेय पुनर्जन्म न विद्यते ।।

Ābrahma-bhuvanāl lokāḥ
punar-āvartino' rjuna /
mām upetya tu Kaunteya
punarjanma na vidyate // 16 //

All the worlds from the realm of Brahma down to the earth, are subject to re-birth. But, O Arjuna, one who has attained to Me is never reborn.

सहस्रयुगपर्यन्तमहर्यद्ब्रह्मणो विदुः ।
रात्रिं युगसहस्रान्तां तेऽहोरात्रविदो जनाः ।।

Sahasra-yuga-paryantam
ahar yad brahmaṇo viduḥ /
rātriṁ yuga-sahasr'āntāṁ
te' ho-rātra-vido janāḥ // 17 //

Those who have an understanding of Brahma's day time, which lasts for a thousand ages, and of his night time, which too is of equal length,—they indeed understand what a day is and what a night.

अव्यक्ताद्व्यक्तयः सर्वाः प्रभवन्त्यहरागमे ।
रात्र्यागमे प्रलीयन्ते तत्रैवाव्यक्तसञ्ज्ञके ।।

Avyaktād vyaktayaḥ sarvāḥ
prabhavanty aharāgame /
ratry-āgame pralīyante
tatr'aiv'ā'vyakta sañjñake // 18 //

At the dawn of the day of Brahma this whole universe comes into manifestation from the Unmanifest (Prakṛti). When the night begins, it dissolves in that Unmanifest itself.

भूतग्रामः स एवायं भूत्वा भूत्वा प्रलीयते ।
रात्र्यागमेऽवशः पार्थ प्रभवत्यहरागमे ॥

Bhūta-grāmaḥ sa ev'āyaṁ
bhūtvā bhūtvā pralīyate /
rātry-āgame' vaśaḥ Pārtha
prabhavaty ahar-āgame // 19 //

O son of Pṛthā! This vast collectivity of beings comes inexorably into manifestation again and again, dissolving at the commencement of night, and again coming forth at the dawn of day.

परस्तस्मात्तु भावोऽन्योऽव्यक्तोऽव्यक्तात्सनातनः ।
यः स सर्वेषु भूतेषु नश्यत्सु न विनश्यति ॥

Paras tasmāt tu bhāvo' nyo'
vyakto' vyaktāt sanātanaḥ /
yaḥ sa sarveṣu bhūteṣu
naśyatsu na vinaśyati // 20 //

Different from this unmanifested state is the supreme and eternal Unmanifested whose being remains unaffected even when everything is destroyed.

अव्यक्तोऽक्षर इत्युक्तस्तमाहुः परमां गतिम् ।
यं प्राप्य न निवर्तन्ते तद्धाम परमं मम ।।

Avyakto' kṣara ity uktas
tam āhuḥ paramāṁ gatim /
yaṁ prāpya na nivartante
tad dhāma paramaṁ
mama // 21 //

Know that state, which is called the Unmanifested and the Imperishable, to be the ultimate goal of all. That is My supreme abode. Attaining to that, man is not reborn.

पुरुषः स परः पार्थ भक्त्या लभ्यस्त्वनन्यया ।
यस्यान्तःस्थानि भूतानि येन सर्वमिदं ततम् ।।

Puruṣaḥ sa paraḥ Pārtha
bhaktyā labhyas tv ananyayā /
yasy'āntaḥsthāni bhūtāni
yena sarvam idaṁ tatam // 22 //

That Supreme Puruṣa, the abode of all beings and the indweller of them all, can be attained by unswerving and exclusive devotion to Him.

यत्र काले त्वनावृत्तिमावृत्तिं चैव योगिनः ।
प्रयाता यान्ति तं कालं वक्ष्यामि भरतर्षभ ।।

Yatra kāle tv anāvṛttiṁ
āvṛttiṁ c'aiva yoginaḥ /
prayātā yānti taṁ kālaṁ /
vakṣyāmi Bharata'rṣabha // 23 //

I shall now tell you, O noblest of Bharatas, of the circumstances, dying under which a Yogi never returns to this world and also of the time, dying when he is sure to return.

अग्निर्ज्योतिरहः शुक्लः षण्मासा उत्तरायणम् ।
तत्र प्रयाता गच्छन्ति ब्रह्म ब्रह्मविदो जनाः ।।

Agnir jyotir ahaḥ śuklaḥ
ṣaṇmāsā uttar'āyaṇam /
tatra prayātā gacchanti
brahma brahma-vido
janāḥ // 24 //

Fire, light, day time, bright fortnight, six months of the northern course of the sun—the knowers of Brahman who depart along this path, attain to Brahman.

धूमो रात्रिस्तथा कृष्णः षण्मासा दक्षिणायनम् ।
तत्र चान्द्रमसं ज्योतिर्योगी प्राप्य निवर्तते ।।

Dhūmo rātris tathā kṛṣṇaḥ
ṣaṇmāsā dakṣiṇ'āyanam /
tatra cāndramasaṁ jyotir
yogī prāpya nivartate // 25 //

Smoke, night and likewise the black fortnight and the six months of the southern course of the sun—the Yogi departing by this path attains to the lunar sphere and thence returns.

शुक्लकृष्णे गती ह्येते जगतः शाश्वते मते ।
एकया यात्यनावृत्तिमन्ययावर्तते पुनः ।।

Śukla-kṛṣṇe gatī hy ete
jagataḥ śāśvate mate /
ekayā yāty anāvṛttim
anyayā'vartate punaḥ // 26 //

Verily, these two paths—the bright and the dark—are accepted as everlasting verities. By the one, the aspirant gains Mokṣa, the state of non-return, while the other leads him to rebirth.

नैते सृती पार्थ जानन्योगी मुह्यति कश्चन ।
तस्मात्सर्वेषु कालेषु योगयुक्तो भवार्जुन ॥

N'aite sṛtī Pārtha jānan
yogī muhyati kaścana /
tasmāt sarveṣu kāleṣu
yogayukto bhav'ārjuna // 27 //

O son of Pṛthā! Whoever among Yogis know these two paths, they are never deluded. Therefore, O Arjuna, be steadfast in Yoga at all times.

वेदेषु यज्ञेषु तपःसु चैव
दानेषु यत्पुण्यफलं प्रदिष्टम् ।
अत्येति तत्सर्वमिदं विदित्वा
योगी परं स्थानमुपैति चाद्यम् ।।

Vedeṣu yajñeṣu tapaḥsu c'aiva
dāneṣu yatpuṇya-phalaṁ pradiṣṭam /
atyeti tat sarvam idaṁ viditvā
yogī paraṁ sthānam upaiti c'ādyam // 28 //

Knowing this, a Yogi transcends all the meritorious rewards that are prescribed for the study of the Vedas, for the performance of austerities, and for charities too, and attains to that primeval state, which is the Supreme Being.

9. Sovereign Secret

'Let your mind be absorbed in Me.
You shall come to Me alone.' (34)

Chapter 9

Sovereign Secret

श्रीभगवानुवाच —

इदं तु ते गुह्यतमं प्रवक्ष्याम्यनसूयवे ।
ज्ञानं विज्ञानसहितं यज्ज्ञात्वा मोक्ष्यसेऽशुभात् ।।

Śrī Bhagavān uvāca:
Idaṁ tu te guhyatamaṁ
pravakṣyāmy anasūyave /
jñānaṁ vijñāna-sahitaṁ
yaj jñātvā mokṣyase' śubhāt // 1 //

The Blessed Lord said:

I shall now declare to you, who are endowed with reverence, that profoundest of all mystic doctrines and the way to its experience, by which you will be free from the baneful life of Saṁsāra.

राजविद्या राजगुह्यं पवित्रमिदमुत्तमम् ।
प्रत्यक्षावगमं धर्म्यं सुसुखं कर्तुमव्ययम् ।।

Rāja-vidyā rāja-guhyaṁ
pavitram idam uttamam /
pratyakṣ'āvagamaṁ dharmyaṁ
susukhaṁ kartum avyayam //2//

It is a sovereign science, and a profound mystery. Supremely sanctifying, demonstrable by experience, and yielding imperishable results, it is also easy to perform and is in agreement with the moral law.

अश्रद्दधानाः पुरुषा धर्मस्यास्य परन्तप ।
अप्राप्य मां निवर्तन्ते मृत्युसंसारवर्त्मनि ।।

Aśraddadhānāḥ puruṣā
dharmasy'āsya parantapa /
aprāpya māṁ nivartante
mṛtyu-saṁsāra-vartmani // 3 //

Men without faith in this sacred doctrine (who continue to look upon the body as the self) fail to attain Me. They remain caught up in Saṁsāra, the eternally recurring cycle of births and deaths.

मया ततमिदं सर्वं जगदव्यक्तमूर्तिना ।
मत्स्थानि सर्वभूतानि न चाहं तेष्ववस्थितः ॥

Mayā tatam idaṁ sarvaṁ
jagad avyakta-mūrtinā /
mat-sthāni sarvabhūtāni
na c'āhaṁ teṣv avasthitaḥ // 4 //

All this world is pervaded by Me, the Unmanifested Being. All objects subsist in Me, but not I in them.

न च मत्स्थानि भूतानि पश्य मे योगमैश्वरम् ।
भूतभृन्न च भूतस्थो ममात्मा भूतभावनः ।।

Na ca matsthāni bhūtāni
paśya me yogam aiśvaram /
bhūta-bhṛn na ca bhūta-stho
mam'ātmā bhūta-bhāvanaḥ // 5 //

And yet objects do not abide in Me! Behold My mysterious Divine Power! Source and support of all objects, and yet not abiding in (i.e. not limited by) them!

यथाकाशस्थितो नित्यं वायुः सर्वत्रगो महान् ।
तथा सर्वाणि भूतानि मत्स्थानीत्युपधारय ॥

Yathākāśa-sthito nityaṁ
vāyuḥ sarvatra-go mahān /
tathā sarvāṇi bhūtāni
mat-sthānī'ty upadhāraya // 6 //

Know that, as the mighty atmosphere ever abides in space, so do all objects abide in Me (without restricting or limiting Me in the least).

सर्वभूतानि कौन्तेय प्रकृतिं यान्ति मामिकाम् ।
कल्पक्षये पुनस्तानि कल्पादौ विसृजाम्यहम् ।।

Sarva-bhūtāni Kaunteya
prakṛtiṁ yānti māmikām /
kalpa-kṣaye punas tāni
kalp'ādau visṛjāmy aham // 7 //

At the end of a cosmic cycle, O son of Kuntī! all beings resolve into Nature (Prakṛti), which is My own, and at the beginning of a new one (after the period of dissolution or Pralaya is over), I bring them out again.

प्रकृतिं स्वामवष्टभ्य विसृजामि पुनः पुनः ।
भूतग्राममिमं कृत्स्नमवशं प्रकृतेर्वशात् ।।

Prakṛtiṁ svām avaṣṭabhya
visṛjāmi punaḥ-punaḥ /
bhuta-grāmam imaṁ kṛtsnam
avaśaṁ prakṛter vaśāt // 8 //

Resorting to Prakṛti (Nature) which is My own Power, I send forth again and again this multitude of beings that are without any freedom, owing to Nature's sway over them.

न च मां तानि कर्माणि निबध्नन्ति धनञ्जय ।
उदासीनवदासीनमसक्तं तेषु कर्मसु ।।

Na ca māṁ tāni karmāṇi
nibadhnanti Dhanañjaya /
udāsīnavad āsīnam
asaktaṁ teṣu karmasu // 9 //

These activities do not in any way bind me, because I remain detached like one unconcerned in their midst.

मयाध्यक्षेण प्रकृतिः सूयते सचराचरम् ।
हेतुनानेन कौन्तेय जगद्विपरिवर्तते ।।

Mayā'dhyakṣeṇa prakṛtiḥ
sūyate sacar'ācaram /
hetunā'nena Kaunteya
jagad viparivartate // 10 //

Under My direction and control, Nature brings out this mighty universe of living and non-living beings. Thus does the wheel of this world revolve.

अवजानन्ति मां मूढा मानुषीं तनुमाश्रितम् ।
परं भावमजानन्तो मम भूतमहेश्वरम् ।।

Avajānanti māṁ mūḍhā
mānuṣīṁ tanum āśritam /
paraṁ bhāvam ajānanto
mama bhūta-mah'eśvaram // 11 //

Foolish men, without an understanding of My higher nature as the Supreme Lord of all that exists, disregard Me manifested in the human body.

मोघाशा मोघकर्माणो मोघज्ञाना विचेतसः ।
राक्षसीमासुरीं चैव प्रकृतिं मोहिनीं श्रिताः ।।

Mogh'āśā mogha-karmāṇo
mogha-jñānā vicetasaḥ /
rākṣasīm āsurīṁ c'aiva
prakṛtiṁ mohinīṁ śritāḥ // 12 //

Futile are the hopes, futile the works, and futile the knowledge of these men of perverted understanding who are deluded by their cruel, proud and passionate nature, characteristic of Rākṣasas and Asuras.

महात्मानस्तु मां पार्थ दैवीं प्रकृतिमाश्रिताः ।
भजन्त्यनन्यमनसो ज्ञात्वा भूतादिमव्ययम् ।।

Mah'ātmānas tu māṁ Pārtha
daivīṁ prakṛtim āśritāḥ /
bhajanty ananya-manaso
jñātvā bhūt'ādim
avyayam // 13 //

But the high-souled ones, endowed with virtues characteristic of Devas, understand Me to be the Immutable and the source of all beings, and adore Me with a mind undistracted by anything else.

सततं कीर्तयन्तो मां यतन्तश्च दृढव्रताः ।
नमस्यन्तश्च मां भक्त्या नित्ययुक्ता उपासते ॥

Satataṁ kīrtayanto māṁ
yatantaś ca dṛḍha-vratāḥ /
namasyantaś ca māṁ bhaktyā
nitya-yuktā upāsate // 14 //

Strenuous and steadfast in their vows, these ever-integrated devotees worship Me with devotion, always singing My glories and prostrating before Me.

ज्ञानयज्ञेन चाप्यन्ये यजन्तो मामुपासते ।
एकत्वेन पृथक्त्वेन बहुधा विश्वतोमुखम् ॥

Jñāna-yajñena c'āpy anye
yajanto mām upāsate /
ekatvena pṛthaktvena
bahudhā viśvato-
mukham // 15 //

Others, again, who offer wisdom sacrifice to Me, worship Me the All-incluive Whole (All-formed)—as the One, as the Distinct, and as the Immanent in all.

अहं क्रतुरहं यज्ञः स्वधाहमहमौषधम् ।
मन्त्रोऽहमहमेवाज्यमहमग्निरहं हुतम् ।।

Aham kratur aham yajñaḥ
svadhā'ham aham auṣadham /
mantro' ham aham ev'ājyam
aham agnir aham hutam // 16 //

I am the sacrifice(*kratu*), I am the worship (*yajña*), I am the ancestral offering (*svadhā*), I am the medicinal herb. Again I am the Vedic hymn, I am the sacrificial ingredients. I am the sacrificial fire, and I am the sacrificial oblation too.

पिताहमस्य जगतो माता धाता पितामहः ।
वेद्यं पवित्रमोङ्कार ऋक्साम यजुरेव च ।।

Pitā'ham asya jagato
mātā dhātā pitāmahaḥ /
vedyaṁ pavitram oṁ-kāra
ṛk sāma yajur eva ca // 17 //

To this world I am the father, the mother, the grandsire and the sustainer. I am the Holy One to be known, as also the syllable Om, the Ṛk, Sāma and Yajus.

गतिर्भर्ता प्रभुः साक्षी निवासः शरणं सुहृत् ।
प्रभवः प्रलयः स्थानं निधानं बीजमव्ययम् ॥

Gatir bhartā prabhuḥ sākṣī
nivāsaḥ śaraṇaṁ suhṛt /
prabhavaḥ pralayaḥ sthānaṁ
nidhānaṁ bījam avyayam // 18 //

The goal, the support, the Lord, and the consciousness witnessing—all this I am. I am again the abode, the refuge, and the friend of all, as also their origin, their dissolution, their ground, their treasure-house and their seed imperishable.

तपाम्यहमहं वर्षं निगृह्णाम्युत्सृजामि च ।
अमृतं चैव मृत्युश्च सदसच्चाहमर्जुन ।।

Tapāmy aham, ahaṁ varṣaṁ
nigṛhṇāmy utsṛjāmi ca /
amṛtaṁ c'aiva mṛtyuś ca
sad asac c'āham Arjuna // 19 //

I give heat, and I send forth as well as withhold rain. I am, O Arjuna! both immortality and death, both being and non-being.

त्रैविद्या मां सोमपाः पूतपापा
यज्ञैरिष्ट्वा स्वर्गतिं प्रार्थयन्ते ।
ते पुण्यमासाद्य सुरेन्द्रलोक-
मश्नन्ति दिव्यान्दिवि देवभोगान् ॥

Traividyā māṁ soma-pāḥ pūta-pāpā
yajñair iṣṭvā svar-gatiṁ
prārthayante /
te puṇyam āsādya sur'endra-lokam
aśnanti divyān divi deva-bhogān / 20 /

Men versed in the Vedas, cleansed of their sins by the performance of sacrifices attended with the drinking of consecrated Soma juice, pray for heavenly regions (as the reward for adoring Me with those rites). They go to the heaven of Indra, attainable by meritorious deeds, and enjoy heavenly felicities there.

ते तं भुक्त्वा स्वर्गलोकं विशालं
क्षीणे पुण्ये मर्त्यलोकं विशन्ति ।
एवं त्रयीधर्ममनुप्रपन्ना
गतागतं कामकामा लभन्ते ।।

Te taṁ bhuktva svargā-lokaṁ viśālaṁ
kṣīṇe puṇye martya-lokaṁ viśanti /
evaṁ trayī-dharmam aṇuprapannā
gatāgataṁ kāma-kāmā
labhante // 21 //

Having enjoyed the varied felicities of heaven for long, they come back to the world of human beings when their asset of meritorious deeds is exhausted. Thus, being desire-ridden, the followers of the Vedic sacrificial rites stagnate in Saṁsāra, the repetitive state of going and returning.

अनन्याश्चिन्तयन्तो मां ये जनाः पर्युपासते ।
तेषां नित्याभियुक्तानां योगक्षेमं वहाम्यहम् ॥

Ananyāś cintayanto māṁ
ye janāḥ paryupāsate /
teṣāṁ nity'ābhiyuktānāṁ
yoga-kṣemaṁ vahāmy
aham // 22 //

Whoever, being devoted to me solely, engage themselves always in contemplation and worship of Me—to such ever-steadfast devotees I ensure the procurement of all their wants (salvation) and the preservation of their assets (worldly interests).

येऽप्यन्यदेवताभक्ता यजन्ते श्रद्धयान्विताः ।
तेऽपि मामेव कौन्तेय यजन्त्यविधिपूर्वकम् ।।

Ye' py anya-devatā-bhaktā
yajante śraddhayā'nvitāḥ /
te' pi mām eva Kaunteya
yajanty avidhi-pūrvakam // 23 //

O son of Kuntī! Those devotees who worship even other deities with deep faith, they also are worshipping Me alone, though contrary to injunctions.

अहं हि सर्वयज्ञानां भोक्ता च प्रभुरेव च ।
न तु मामभिजानन्ति तत्त्वेनातश्च्यवन्ति ते ।।

Ahaṁ hi sarva-yajñānāṁ
bhoktā ca prabhur eva ca /
na tu mām abhijānanti
tattven'ātaś cyavanti te // 24 //

I am indeed the only enjoyer and the Lord of all sacrifices. But they (the worshippers of other deities) do not understand Me in My true nature (as the object of all worship). So they fall.

यान्ति देवव्रता देवान्पितॄन्यान्ति पितृव्रताः ।
भूतानि यान्ति भूतेज्या यान्ति मद्याजिनोऽपि माम् ॥

Yānti deva-vratā devān
pitṛn yānti pitṛ-vratāḥ /
bhūtāni yānti bhūt'ejyā
yānti mad-yājino' pi mām // 25 //

The votaries of the deities go to the deities; of the manes, to the manes; and of the spirits, to the spirits, while My worshippers come to Me.

पत्रं पुष्पं फलं तोयं यो मे भक्त्या प्रयच्छति ।
तदहं भक्त्युपहृतमश्नामि प्रयतात्मनः ।।

Patraṁ puṣpaṁ phalaṁ toyaṁ
yo me bhaktyā prayacchati /
tad ahaṁ bhakty-upahṛtam
aśnāmi prayat'ātmanaḥ // 26 //

Whoever makes an offering to Me with devotion, be it of leaf, flower, fruit or water—that devout offering by a pure-hearted man, I accept with joy.

यत्करोषि यदश्नासि यज्जुहोषि ददासि यत् ।
यत्तपस्यसि कौन्तेय तत्कुरुष्व मदर्पणम् ।।

Yat karoṣi yad aśnāsi
yaj juhoṣi dadāsi yat /
yat tapasyasi Kaunteya
tat kuruṣva mad-
arpaṇam // 27 //

O son of Kuntī! Whatever you do, whatever you eat, whatever you offer in sacrifice, whatever you give as charity, whatever austerity you perform—do that as offering unto Me.

शुभाशुभफलैरेवं मोक्ष्यसे कर्मबन्धनैः ।
सन्न्यासयोगयुक्तात्मा विमुक्तो मामुपैष्यसि ॥

Śubhāśubha-phalair evaṁ
mokṣyase karma-bandhanaiḥ /
sannyāsa-yoga yuktātmā
vimukto mām upaiṣyasi // 28 //

Thus shall you be freed from the bonds of Karma bearing good and evil fruits. With the heart firmly set on renunciation, you will attain liberation and thereby come to Me.

समोऽहं सर्वभूतेषु न मे द्वेष्योऽस्ति न प्रियः ।
ये भजन्ति तु मां भक्त्या मयि ते तेषु चाप्यहम् ।।

Samo' haṁ sarvabhūteṣu
na me dveṣyo' sti na priyaḥ /
ye bhajanti tu māṁ bhaktyā
mayi te teṣu c'āpy aham // 29 //

I am the same towards all beings. None is hateful, and none dear to Me. But those who worship Me with devotion dwell in Me, and I too dwell in them.

अपि चेत्सुदुराचारो भजते मामनन्यभाक् ।
साधुरेव स मन्तव्यः सम्यग्व्यवसितो हि सः ।।

Api cet sudurācāro
bhajate mām ananya-bhāk /
sādhur eva sa mantavyaḥ
samyag vyavasito hi saḥ // 30 //

Even a confirmed sinner, if he worships Me with unwavering faith and devotion, must verily be considered as righteous; for he has indeed taken the right resolve.

क्षिप्रं भवति धर्मात्मा शश्वच्छान्तिं निगच्छति ।
कौन्तेय प्रतिजानीहि न मे भक्तः प्रणश्यति ।।

Kṣipraṁ bhavati dharm'ātmā
śaśvac-chāntiṁ nigacchati /
Kaunteya pratijānīhi
na me bhaktaḥ praṇaśyati // 31 //

Soon will he become righteous and attain to lasting peace. No devotee of Mine will ever perish; you may swear to this effect, O Arjuna!

मां हि पार्थ व्यपाश्रित्य येऽपि स्युः पापयोनयः ।
स्त्रियो वैश्यास्तथा शूद्रास्तेऽपि यान्ति परां गतिम् ॥

Māṁ hi Pārtha vyapāśritya
ye' pi syuḥ pāpa-yonayaḥ /
striyo vaiśyās tathā śūdrās
te' pi yānti parāṁ gatim // 32 //

O son of Pṛithā! Taking refuge in Me, women, Vaiśyas, Śūdrās, and likewise even men of inferior birth, attain to the highest spiritual goal.

किं पुनर्ब्राह्मणाः पुण्या भक्ता राजर्षयस्तथा ।
अनित्यमसुखं लोकमिमं प्राप्य भजस्व माम् ।।

Kiṁ punar brāhmaṇāḥ puṇyā
bhakta rāja-rṣayas tathā /
anityam asukhaṁ lokam
imaṁ prāpya bhajasva
mām // 33 //

Then how much more so in the case of holy Brāhmaṇas and also of devoted royal sages! Having come into this impermanent and unhappy world, engage yourself in My worship.

मन्मना भव मद्भक्तो मद्याजी मां नमस्कुरु ।
मामेवैष्यसि युक्त्वैवमात्मानं मत्परायणः ।।

Man-manā bhava mad-bhakto
madyājī māṁ namas-kuru /
mām ev'aiṣyasi yuktv'aivam
ātmānaṁ mat-parāyaṇaḥ // 34 //

Let your mind be absorbed in Me. Be devoted to Me, sacrifice unto Me, and bow down to Me. Thus, having Me as your highest goal, and united with Me in mind, you shall come to Me alone.

10. Divine Glories

'Supporting this mighty universe with a fragment of My self, I remain transcendent.' (42)

Chapter 10

Divine Glories

श्रीभगवानुवाच —

भूय एव महाबाहो श्रृणु मे परमं वचः ।
यत्तेऽहं प्रीयमाणाय वक्ष्यामि हितकाम्यया ।।

Śrī Bhagavān uvāca:

Bhūya eva mahā-bāho
śṛṇu me paramaṁ vacaḥ /
yat te' haṁ prīyamāṇāya
vakṣyāmi hita-kāmyayā // 1 //

The Blessed Lord said:

Hear again, O mighty armed one, My words on the Supreme Truth. Desirous of your good, I want to declare it to you, who are so beloved of Me.

न मे विदुः सुरगणाः प्रभवं न महर्षयः ।
अहमादिर्हि देवानां महर्षीणां च सर्वशः ।।

Na me viduḥ sura-gaṇāḥ
prabhavaṁ na maharṣayaḥ /
aham ādir hi devānām
maharṣīṇāṁ ca sarvaśaḥ // 2 //

Neither the hosts of gods nor Maharṣhis (great sages) know my origin, for I am Myself the origin of all those gods and great sages.

यो मामजमनादिं च वेत्ति लोकमहेश्वरम् ।
असम्मूढः स मर्त्येषु सर्वपापैः प्रमुच्यते ॥

Yo mām ajam anādiṁ ca
vetti loka-mah'eśvaram /
asammūḍhaḥ sa martyeṣu
sarva-pāpaiḥ pramucyate // 3 //

He who knows Me as the beginningless, the unborn and the Master of the worlds—he among mortals becomes undeluded, and he is freed from all sins.

बुद्धिर्ज्ञानमसम्मोहः क्षमा सत्यं दमः शमः ।
सुखं दुःखं भवोऽभावो भयं चाभयमेव च ।।

अहिंसा समता तुष्टिस्तपो दानं यशोऽयशः ।
भवन्ति भावा भूतानां मत्त एव पृथग्विधाः ।।

Buddhir jñānam asammohaḥ
kṣamā satyaṁ damaḥ śamaḥ /
sukhaṁ duḥkaṁ bhavo' bhāvo
bhayaṁ c'ābhayam eva ca // 4 //

Ahiṁsā samatā tuṣṭis
tapo dānaṁ yaśo' yaśaḥ /
bhavanti bhāvā bhūtānāṁ
matta eva pṛthag-vidhāḥ // 5 //

Intelligence, knowledge, sanity, patience, truth, sense-control, mind-control, pleasure, pain, birth, death, fear and also fearlessness; non-injury, same-sightednsss, contentment, austerity, benevolence, fame and obloquy—all these diverse modes of the mind seen in all beings proceed from Me alone, their ultimate sanctioner.

महर्षयः सप्त पूर्वे चत्वारो मनवस्तथा ।
मद्भावा मानसा जाता येषां लोक इमाः प्रजाः ।।

Maharṣayaḥ sapta pūrve
catvāro manavas tathā /
mad-bhāvā mānasā jātā
yeṣāṁ loka imāḥ prajāḥ // 6 //

The seven great sages (beginning with Marīchī) as also the four earlier ones like Sanaka and the rest and the Manus likewise are My emanations, being projections of my thought. All this race of men is their progeny.

एतां विभूतिं योगं च मम यो वेत्ति तत्त्वतः ।
सोऽविकम्पेन योगेन युज्यते नात्र संशयः ।।

Etāṁ vibhūtiṁ yogaṁ ca
mama yo vetti tattvataḥ /
so' vikampena yogena
yujyate n'ātra saṁśayaḥ // 7 //

He who knows the truth about this manifestation of My Divine majesties and about My power, gets united with Me in steady and unfalterimg communion. There is no doubt about this.

अहं सर्वस्य प्रभवो मत्तः सर्वं प्रवर्तते ।
इति मत्वा भजन्ते मां बुधा भावसमन्विताः ॥

Ahaṁ sarvasya prabhavo
mattaḥ sarvaṁ pravartate /
iti matvā bhajante māṁ
budhā bhāva-samanvitāḥ // 8 //

I am the source of all things, from Me all these go forth—knowing thus the wise ones worship Me, being filled with ecstatic devotional fervour.

मच्चित्ता मद्गतप्राणा बोधयन्तः परस्परम् ।
कथयन्तश्च मां नित्यं तुष्यन्ति च रमन्ति च ।।

Mac-cittā mad-gata-prāṇā
bodhayantaḥ parasparam /
kathayantaś ca māṁ nityaṁ
tuṣyanti ca ramanti ca // 9 //

With their minds engrossed and their vital energies deeply involved in Me, they are ever contented and delighted by mutually conversing about Me and enlightening each other thereby.

तेषां सततयुक्तानां भजतां प्रीतिपूर्वकम् ।
ददामि बुद्धियोगं तं येन मामुपयान्ति ते ।।

Teṣāṁ satata-yuktānāṁ
bhajatāṁ prīti-pūrvakam /
dadāmi buddhi-yogaṁ taṁ
yena mām upayānti te // 10 //

To those who serve Me with delight and are ever steadfast in spiritual communion, I bestow intuitive understanding by means of which they come to Me.

तेषामेवानुकम्पार्थमहमज्ञानजं तमः ।
नाशयाम्यात्मभावस्थो ज्ञानदीपेन भास्वता ।।

Teṣām ev'ānukamp'ārtham
aham ajñāna-jaṁ tamaḥ /
nāśayāmy ātma-bhāva-stho
jñāna-dīpena bhāsvatā // 11 //

Out of sheer compassion for them, residing within as their innermost self, I destroy the darkness born of ignorance in them by the brilliant lamp of wisdom.

अर्जुन उवाच —

परं ब्रह्म परं धाम पवित्रं परमं भवान् ।
पुरुषं शाश्वतं दिव्यमादिदेवमजं विभुम् ।।

आहुस्त्वामृषयः सर्वे देवर्षिर्नारदस्तथा ।
असितो देवलो व्यासः स्वयं चैव ब्रवीषि मे ।।

Arjuna uvāca:
Paraṁ brahma paraṁ dhāma
pavitraṁ paramaṁ bhavān /
puruṣaṁ śāśvataṁ divyam
ādi-devam ajaṁ vibhum // 12 //

Āhus tvām ṛṣayaḥ sarve
deva'rṣir Nāradas tathā /
Asito Devalo Vyāsaḥ
svayaṁ c'aiva bravīṣi me // 13 //

Arjuna said:

Thou art the Supreme Brahman, the Supreme Abode, the utterly Holy. Thou art the eternal divine Person—the birthless and all-pervading Divinity supreme. All the Rishis proclaim this—the divine sage Nārada as also Asita, Devala and Vyāsa; Thou Thyself too dost tell Me the same.

सर्वमेतदृतं मन्ये यन्मां वदसि केशव ।
न हि ते भगवन्व्यक्तिं विदुर्देवा न दानवाः ॥

Sarvam etad ṛtaṁ manye
yan māṁ vadasi Keśava /
na hi te bhagavan vyaktiṁ
vidur devā na dānavāḥ // 14 //

O Keśava! Whatever Thou hast told me, I deem as true. Verily, O Lord, neither the Devas nor the Dānavas know what Thy manifestations are.

स्वयमेवात्मनात्मानं वेत्थ त्वं पुरुषोत्तम ।
भूतभावन भूतेश देवदेव जगत्पते ।।

Svayam ev'ātman'ātmānaṁ
vettha tvaṁ Puruṣottama /
bhūta-bhāvana bhūt'eśa
deva-deva jagat-pate // 15 //

O Thou the highest of all beings! O Creator of all! O Lord of all! O God of gods! O Ruler of the world! Thou art known only to Thyself through self-intuition.

वक्तुमर्हस्यशेषेण दिव्या ह्यात्मविभूतयः ।
याभिर्विभूतिभिर्लोकानिमांस्त्वं व्याप्य तिष्ठसि ।।

Vaktum arhasy aśeṣeṇa
divyā hy ātma-vibhūtayaḥ /
yābhir vibhūtibhir lokān
imāṁs tvaṁ vyāpya
tiṣṭhasi // *16* //

Deign to speak to me in entirety of those divine manifestations of Thy glory, whereby, pervading all these worlds, Thou abidest in them and beyond.

कथं विद्यामहं योगिंस्त्वां सदा परिचिन्तयन् ।
केषु केषु च भावेषु चिन्त्योऽसि भगवन्मया ।।

Kathaṁ vidyām ahaṁ yogiṁs
tvāṁ sadā paricintayan /
keṣu keṣu ca bhāveṣu
cintyo' si bhagavan mayā // 17 //

How am I to know Thee, O Yogin, through constant meditation? In what all aspects shouldst Thou be contemplated upon by me, O Lord?

विस्तरेणात्मनो योगं विभूतिं च जनार्दन ।
भूयः कथय तृप्तिर्हि शृण्वतो नास्ति मेऽमृतम् ।।

Vistareṇ'ātmano yogaṁ
vibhūtiṁ ca Janārdana /
bhūyaḥ kathaya tṛptir hi
śṛṇvato n'āsti me' mṛtam // 18 //

O Janārdana! Tell me again and again of Thy divine powers and majesties; for I am ever eager to hear more and more of Thy nectarine words.

श्रीभगवानुवाच —
हन्त ते कथयिष्यामि दिव्या ह्यात्मविभूतयः ।
प्राधान्यतः कुरुश्रेष्ठ नास्त्यन्तो विस्तरस्य मे ॥

Śrī Bhagavān uvāca:
Hanta te kathayiṣyāmi
divyā hy ātma-vibhūtayaḥ /
prādhānyataḥ Kuru-śreṣtha
n'āstyanto vistarasya me // 19 //

The Blessed Lord said:

Behold, O best of the Kurus! I shall declare unto you what My divine self-manifestations are; but I shall mention only the chief of them. For, there is no end to their details.

अहमात्मा गुडाकेश सर्वभूताशयस्थितः ।
अहमादिश्च मध्यं च भूतानामन्त एव च ॥

Aham ātmā Guḍākeśa
sarva-bhūt'āśaya-sthitaḥ /
aham ādiś ca madhyaṁ ca
bhūtānām anta eva ca // 20 //

O Arjuna! I am the Self residing in the heart of every being. I am their beginning, their life-span, and their end.

आदित्यानामहं विष्णुर्ज्योतिषां रविरंशुमान् ।
मरीचिर्मरुतामस्मि नक्षत्राणामहं शशी ॥

Ādityānām aham Viṣṇur
jyotiṣām ravir amśumān /
Marīcir Marutām asmi
nakṣatrāṇām aham śaśī // 21 //

Of the twelve Ādityas (suns), I am Viṣṇu; among the luminaries I am the radiant sun; among the seven Maruts (winds) I am Marīcī; and of the Nakṣatras (asterisms), I am the moon.

वेदानां सामवेदोऽस्मि देवानामस्मि वासवः ।
इन्द्रियाणां मनश्चास्मि भूतानामस्मि चेतना ।।

Vedānāṁ sāma-vedo' smi
devānām asmi Vāsavaḥ /
indriyāṇāṁ manaś c'āsmi
bhūtānām asmi cetanā // 22 //

Of the Vedas, I am the Sāma Veda; among the Devas, I am Indra; of the senses, I am the mind; and in living beings, I am intelligence.

रुद्राणां शङ्करश्चास्मि वित्तेशो यक्षरक्षसाम् ।
वसूनां पावकश्चास्मि मेरुः शिखरिणामहम् ।।

Rudrāṇāṁ Śaṅkaraś c'āsmi
vitt'eśo yakṣa-rakṣasām /
Vasūnāṁ pāvakaś c'āsmi
Meruḥ śikhariṇām aham // 23 //

Of the eleven Rudras, I am Śaṅkara; among the Demigods and Titans, I am Kubera; of the eight Vasus, I am Agni; among mountains, I am the Meru.

पुरोधसां च मुख्यं मां विद्धि पार्थ बृहस्पतिम् ।
सेनानीनामहं स्कन्दः सरसामस्मि सागरः ।।

Purodhasāṁ ca mukhyaṁ māṁ
viddhi Pārtha Bṛhaspatiṁ /
senānīnām ahaṁ Skandaḥ
sarasām asmi sāgaraḥ // 24 //

Among the priests, know me to be the chief of them—Bṛhaspati, the priest of the Devas, O Arjuna. Among the war-lords I am Skanda; among the water reservoirs, I am the ocean.

महर्षीणां भृगुरहं गिरामस्म्येकमक्षरम् ।
यज्ञानां जपयज्ञोऽस्मि स्थावराणां हिमालयः ॥

Maha'rṣīṇāṁ Bhṛgur ahaṁ
girām asmy ekam akṣaram /
yajñānāṁ japa-yajño' smi
sthāvarāṇāṁ Himālayaḥ // 25 //

Among the great sages, I am Bhṛgu; among utterances I am the mono-syllabled 'Om'; among holy offerings, I am the offering of Japa (silent repetition of Divine Names); among immovable objects, I am the mount Himalaya.

अश्वत्थः सर्ववृक्षाणां देवर्षीणां च नारदः ।
गन्धर्वाणां चित्ररथः सिद्धानां कपिलो मुनिः ।।

Aśvatthaḥ sarva-vṛkṣāṇāṁ
deva'rṣīṇāṁ ca Nāradaḥ /
gandharvāṇāṁ Citrarathaḥ
siddhānāṁ Kapilo muniḥ // 26 //

Among all trees, I am the holy fig-tree; among the divine sages, I am Nārada; among celestial artistes, I am Citraratha; among perfected souls, I am Kapila the sage.

उच्चैःश्रवसमश्वानां विद्धि माममृतोद्भवम् ।
ऐरावतं गजेन्द्राणां नराणां च नराधिपम् ॥

Uccaiḥśrvasam aśvānāṁ
viddhi mām amṛt'odbhavam /
Airāvataṁ gaj'endrāṇāṁ
narāṇāṁ ca nar'ādhipam // 27 //

Among horses know Me to be the nectar-born Uccaiśravas, among the lordly elephants, the white celestial elephant Airāvata; and among men, persons endowed with leadership.

आयुधानामहं वज्रं धेनूनामस्मि कामधुक् ।
प्रजनश्चास्मि कन्दर्पः सर्पाणामस्मि वासुकिः ॥

Āyudhānām ahaṁ vajraṁ
dhenūnām asmi kāma-dhuk /
prajanās' c'āsmi Kandarpaḥ
sarpāṇām asmi Vāsukiḥ // 28 //

Among weapons I am the thunderbolt; among cows, Kāmadhenu the celestial cow of plenty; among progenitors, Kāma the god of love; and among snakes, Vāsuki.

अनन्तश्चास्मि नागानां वरुणो यादसामहम् ।
पितॄणामर्यमा चास्मि यमः संयमतामहम् ।।

Anantaś c'āsmi nāgānāṁ
Varuṇo yādasām aham /
pitṛṇām Aryamā c'āsmi
Yamaḥ saṁyamatām
aham // 29 //

Among serpents I am Ananta; among water-dwellers I am Varuṇa; among the manes I am Aryamā; and among the enforcers of law I am Yama.

प्रह्लादश्चास्मि दैत्यानां कालः कलयतामहम् ।
मृगाणां च मृगेन्द्रोऽहं वैनतेयश्च पक्षिणाम् ।।

Prahlādaś c'āsmi daityānāṁ
kālaḥ kalayatām aham /
mṛgāṇāṁ ca mṛg'endro' haṁ
Vainateyaś ca pakṣiṇām // 30 //

Among Daityas I am Prahlāda; among calculators I am time; among animals I am the lion; and among birds I am Garuḍa.

पवनः पवतामस्मि रामः शस्त्रभृतामहम् ।
झषाणां मकरश्चास्मि स्रोतसामस्मि जाह्नवी ।।

Pavanaḥ pavatām asmi
Rāmaḥ śastra-bhṛtām aham /
jhaṣāṇāṁ makaraś c'āsmi
srotasām asmi Jāhnavī // 31 //

Among purifying agents I am the wind; among warriors I am Rāma; among the fish I am the shark; and among rivers I am the Ganga.

सर्गाणामादिरन्तश्च मध्यं चैवाहमर्जुन ।
अध्यात्मविद्या विद्यानां वादः प्रवदतामहम् ।।

Sargāṇām ādir antaś ca
madhyaṁ c'aiv'āham Arjuna /
adhyātma-vidyā vidyānāṁ
vādaḥ pravadatām aham // 32 //

O Arjuna! Of the created objects I am the beginning, middle and end; among the sciences, I am the science of the spirit; and in debators I am the power of correct reasoning.

अक्षराणामकारोऽस्मि द्वन्द्वः सामासिकस्य च ।
अहमेवाक्षयः कालो धाताहं विश्वतोमुखः ॥

Akṣarāṇām akāro' smi
dvandvaḥ sāmāsikasya ca /
aham ev'ākṣayaḥ kālo
dhātā'haṁ viśvato-
mukhaḥ // 33 //

Among letters I am the letter 'A', among compound word formations I am the copulative *(dvandva).* I am also the never-ending Time and the all-seeing Brahmā (the dispenser of the Karmas of all beings).

मृत्युः सर्वहरश्चाहमुद्भवश्च भविष्यताम् ।
कीर्तिः श्रीर्वाक्च नारीणां स्मृतिर्मेधा धृतिः क्षमा ।।

Mṛtyuḥ sarva-haraś c'āham
udbhavaś ca bhaviṣyatām /
kīrtiḥ śrīr vāk ca nārīṇāṁ
smṛtir medhā dhṛtiḥ
kṣamā // 34 //

I am the all-destroying Death, and I am the origin of all that are to come too. Among virtues considered as female I am fame, fortune, speech, memory, intelligence, constancy and patience.

वृष्णीनां वासुदेवोऽस्मि पाण्डवानां धनञ्जयः ।
मुनीनामप्यहं व्यासः कवीनामुशना कविः ॥

Vṛṣṇīnāṁ Vāsudevo' smi
Pāṇḍavānāṁ Dhanañjayaḥ /
munīnām apy ahaṁ Vyāsaḥ
Kavīnām Uśanā kaviḥ // 37 //

I am Vāsudeva among the Vṛṣṇis and Arjuna among the Pāṇḍavas. I am Vyāsa among sages, and Śukra among the far-sighted.

दण्डो दमयतामस्मि नीतिरस्मि जिगीषताम् ।
मौनं चैवास्मि गुह्यानां ज्ञानं ज्ञानवतामहम् ।।

Daṇḍo damayatām asmi
nītir asmi jigīṣatām /
maunaṁ c'aiv'āsmi guhyānāṁ
jñānaṁ jñānavatām
aham // 38 //

I am the rod of chastisement in the disciplinarians; I am the wise policy in those seeking success; I am silence in the arts of secrecy; and I am wisdom in the wise.

यच्चापि सर्वभूतानां बीजं तदहमर्जुन ।
न तदस्ति विना यत्स्यान्मया भूतं चराचरम् ।।

Yac c'āpi sarva-bhūtānāṁ
bījaṁ tad aham Arjuna /
na tad asti vinā yat syān
mayā bhūtaṁ car'ācaram //39//

Of all beings I am the seed, O Arjuna. Whatever exists in this world, living or non-living, none of them can be, if I were not.

नान्तोऽस्ति मम दिव्यानां विभूतीनां परन्तप ।
एष तूद्देशतः प्रोक्तो विभूतेर्विस्तरो मया ।।

Nā'nto' sti mama divyānāṁ
vibhūtīnāṁ parantapa /
eṣa tū'ddeśataḥ prokto
vibhūter vistaro mayā // 40 //

O great warrior! There is no end to my divine manifestations. What I have expounded forms only a few of them by way of examples.

यद्यद्विभूतिमत्सत्त्वं श्रीमदूर्जितमेव वा ।
तत्तदेवावगच्छ त्वं मम तेजोंऽशसम्भवम् ।।

Yad-yad vibhūtimat sattvaṁ
śrīmad ūrjitam eva vā /
tat-tad evā'vagaccha tvaṁ
mama tejo' ṁśa-sambhavam //41//

Whatever there is endowed with extraordinary glory, attractiveness and vigour, know all that to be born of a fragment of My power.

अथवा बहुनैतेन किं ज्ञातेन तवार्जुन ।
विष्टभ्याहमिदं कृत्स्नमेकांशेन स्थितो जगत् ।।

Athavā bahun'aitena
kiṁ jñātena tavā'rjuna /
viṣṭabhy'āham idaṁ kṛtsnam
ek' āṁśena sthito jagat // 42 //

But then, of what avail is this detailed understanding of my manifestations to you, O Arjuna! Supporting this mighty universe with but one single fragment of My self, I remain unchanged and transcendent.

11. The Cosmic Form

'Who Thou art with this awe-inspiring form? To Thee my salutation!' (31)

Chapter 11

The Cosmic Form

अर्जुन उवाच —

मदनुग्रहाय परमं गुह्यमध्यात्मसंज्ञितम् ।
यत्त्वयोक्तं वचस्तेन मोहोऽयं विगतो मम ।।

Arjuna uvāca:
Mad-anugrahāya paramaṁ
guhyam adhyātma saṁjñitam /
yat tvay'oktaṁ vacas tena
moho' yaṁ vigato mama // 1 //

Arjuna said: Thy instructions on the grand Mystery, the highest spiritual Truth, imparted to me out of Thy abounding grace, have dispelled my delusion.

भवाप्ययौ हि भूतानां श्रुतौ विस्तरशो मया ।
त्वत्तः कमलपत्राक्ष माहात्म्यमपि चाव्ययम् ।।

Bhav'āpyayau hi bhūtānāṁ
śrutau vistaraśo mayā /
tvattaḥ kamala-patr'ākṣa
māhātmyam api c'āvyayam // 2 //

O lotus-eyed One! From Thee I have heard at length about the origin and dissolution of creatures as also about Thy greatness that knows no decay.

एवमेतद्यथात्थ त्वमात्मानं परमेश्वर ।
द्रष्टुमिच्छामि ते रूपमैश्वरं पुरुषोत्तम ॥

Evam etad yath'āttha tvam
ātmānaṁ param'eśvara /
draṣṭum icchāmi te rūpam
aiśvaraṁ puruṣ'ottama // *3* //

Thou art, O Lord Supreme, even as what Thou hast declared Thyself to be. (I understand and accept it.) Yet I now desire to see that form of Thine as the Lord of all.

मन्यसे यदि तच्छक्यं मया द्रष्टुमिति प्रभो ।
योगेश्वर ततो मे त्वं दर्शयात्मानमव्ययम् ।।

Manyase yadi tac chakyaṁ
mayā draṣṭum iti prabho /
yog'eśvara tato me tvaṁ
darśay'ātmānam avyayam // 4 //

If, O Lord, Thou thinkest me worthy of experiencing that immutable form of Thine, then deign to reveal the same to me, O Thou Master of all Yoga!

श्रीभगवानुवाच —

पश्य मे पार्थ रूपाणि शतशोऽथ सहस्रशः ।
नानाविधानि दिव्यानि नानावर्णाकृतीनि च ।।

Śrī Bhagavān uvāca:

Paśya me Pārtha rūpāṇi
śataśo' tha sahasraśaḥ /
nānā-vidhāni divyāni
nānā-varṇ'ākṛtīni ca // 5 //

The Blessed Lord said:

Behold. O Pārtha, My manifold forms in their hundreds and thousands—all divine and all of varied hues and shapes.

पश्यादित्यान्वसून्रुद्रान् अश्विनौ मरुतस्तथा ।
बहून्यदृष्टपूर्वाणि पश्याश्चर्याणि भारत ।।

Paśy'ādityān Vasūn Rudrān
Aśvinau Marutas tathā /
bahūny adṛṣṭa-pūrvāṇi
paśy'āścaryāṇi Bhārata // 6 //

Behold the Ādityas and the Vasus, the Rudras and the Aśvins, and the Maruts likewise—behold these marvels unseen by any beforc, O scion of Bharata's clan!

इहैकस्थं जगत्कृत्स्नं पश्याद्य सचराचरम् ।
मम देहे गुडाकेश यच्चान्यद्द्रष्टुमिच्छसि ॥

Ih'aikastham jagat kṛtsnaṁ
paśy'ādya sacar'ācaram /
mama dehe Guḍākeśa
yac c'ānyad draṣṭum icchasi // 7 //

O conqueror of sleep! Behold here and now the whole of this universe of conscious and unconscious entities as also anything else you desire to experience—all abiding as a unity in My body.

न तु मां शक्यसे द्रष्टुमनेनैव स्वचक्षुषा ।
दिव्यं ददामि ते चक्षुः पश्य मे योगमैश्वरम् ।।

Na tu māṁ śakyase draṣṭum
anen'aiva sva-cakṣuṣā /
divyaṁ dadāmi te cakṣuḥ
paśya me yogam aiśvaram // 8 //

You cannot have an experience of Me merely with your physical eye. I therefore give you the power of divine vision. Behold with that My power as the Lord of all.

सञ्जय उवाच —

एवमुक्त्वा ततो राजन्महायोगेश्वरो हरिः ।
दर्शयामास पार्थाय परमं रूपमैश्वरम् ।।

Sañjaya uvāca:
Evam uktvā tato rājan
mahā-yog'eśvaro hariḥ /
darśayāmāsa Pārthāya
paramaṁ rūpam
aiśvaram // 9 //

Sañjaya said:

So saying, Hari, the Master of all spiritual powers, now revealed to Arjuna His transcendent form as the Lord of the universe.

अनेकवक्त्रनयनमनेकाद्भुतदर्शनम् ।
अनेकदिव्याभरणं दिव्यानेकोद्यतायुधम् ।।

Aneka-vaktra-nayanam
anek'ādbhuta-darśanam /
aneka-divy'ābharaṇaṁ
divy'ānek'odyat'āyudham // 10 //

Having countless faces and eyes; exhibiting countless features; provoking wonder; bedecked with countless celestial ornaments equipped with countless divine weapons held aloft;

दिव्यमाल्याम्बरधरं दिव्यगन्धानुलेपनम् ।
सर्वाश्चर्यमयं देवमनन्तं विश्वतोमुखम् ॥

Divya-māly'āmbara dharaṁ
divya-gandh'ānulepanam /
sarv'āścaryamayaṁ devam
anantaṁ viśvato-mukham // 11 //

Wearing heavenly garlands and vestments; anointed with celestial unguents and perfumes; replete with incredible, marvellous features—a divinity boundless and all-seeing.

दिवि सूर्यसहस्रस्य भवेद्युगपदुत्थिता ।
यदि भाः सदृशी सा स्याद्भासस्तस्य महात्मनः

Divi sūrya-sahasrasya
bhaved yugapad utthitā /
yadi bhāḥ sadṛśī sā syād
bhāsas tasya
mah'ātmanaḥ // 12 //

What brilliance there would have been if a thousand suns were to blaze forth all of a sudden in the sky—to that was comparable the splendour of that great Being.

तत्रैकस्थं जगत्कृत्स्नं प्रविभक्तमनेकधा ।
अपश्यद्देवदेवस्य शरीरे पाण्डवस्तदा ॥

Tatr'aika-sthaṁ jagat kṛtsnaṁ
pravibhaktam anekadhā /
apaśyad deva-devasya
śarīre Pāṇḍavas tadā // 13 //

There in the body of that God of all divinities, the son of Pāṇḍu then saw the whole universe—a multiplicity abiding unified in His being.

ततः स विस्मयाविष्टो हृष्टरोमा धनञ्जयः ।
प्रणम्य शिरसा देवं कृताञ्जलिरभाषत ।।

Tataḥ sa vismay'āviṣṭo
hṛṣṭa-romā Dhanañjayaḥ /
praṇamya śirasā devaṁ
kṛt'āñjalir abhāṣata // 14 //

Thereupon Arjuna, struck with amazement and his hairs standing on end, bowed down before the Lord and said with hands folded in salutation.

अर्जुन उवाच—
पश्यामि देवांस्तव देव देहे
सर्वांस्तथा भूतविशेषसङ्घान् ।
ब्रह्माणमीशं कमलासनस्थ-
मृषींश्च सर्वानुरगांश्च दिव्यान् ।।

Arjuna uvāca:
Paśyāmi devāṁs tava deva dehe
sarvāṁs tathā bhūta-viśeṣa-saṅghān /
brahmāṇam īśaṁ kamal'āsana-stham
ṛṣīṁś ca sarvān uragāṁś ca
divyān // 15 //

Arjuna said:

In Thy form I see, O Lord, all the Devas and all the varied hosts of other beings—the divine Rishis. the celestial serpents and likewise Brahmā the Lord of creation, seated on his lotus throne.

अनेकबाहूदरवक्त्रनेत्रं
पश्यामि त्वां सर्वतोऽनन्तरूपम् ।
नान्तं न मध्यं न पुनस्तवादिं
पश्यामि विश्वेश्वर विश्वरूप ॥

Aneka-bāhū'dara-vaktranetraṁ
paśyāmi tvāṁ sarvato' nanta-rūpam
n'āntaṁ na madhyaṁ na punas tav'ādiṁ
paśyāmi viśveśvara viśva-rūpa // 16 //

I see Thee in Thy all encompassing form everywhere—with myriad arms, myriad trunks, myriad mouths, myriad eyes. O Lord of all! O the All-formed! I see not Thy beginning, Thy middle, or Thy end.

किरीटिनं गदिनं चक्रिणं च
तेजोराशिं सर्वतो दीप्तिमन्तम् ।
पश्यामि त्वां दुर्निरीक्ष्यं समन्ता-
द्दीप्तानलार्कद्युतिमप्रमेयम् ।।

Kirīṭinaṁ gadinaṁ cakriṇaṁ ca
tejo-rāśiṁ sarvato dīptimantam /
paśyāmi tvāṁ durnirīkṣyaṁ samantād
dīpt'ānalārka-dyu tim aprameyam // 17 //

I see Thee, boundless Being, diademed and armed with mace and discus, shining everywhere as a mass of light, and difficult to look at, like the blazing fire or the incandescent sun.

त्वमक्षरं परमं वेदितव्यं
त्वमस्य विश्वस्य परं निधानम् ।
त्वमव्ययः शाश्वतधर्मगोप्ता
सनातनस्त्वं पुरुषो मतो मे ॥

Tvam akṣaraṁ paramaṁ vedita-vyaṁ
tvam asya viśvasya paraṁ nidhānam /
tvam avyayaḥ śāśvata-dharma-goptā
sanātanas tvaṁ puruṣo mato
me // 18 //

In my view Thou art the Supreme Imperishable Being to be realised—the world's ultimate refuge and the guardian of eternal law, most ancient and perennial.

अनादिमध्यान्तमनन्तवीर्य-
मनन्तबाहुं शशिसूर्यनेत्रम् ।
पश्यामि त्वां दीप्तहुताशवक्त्रं
स्वतेजसा विश्वमिदं तपन्तम् ।।

Anādi-madhy'āntam ananta-vīryam
ananta-bāhuṁ śaśi-sūrya-netram /
paśyāmitvāṁ dīpta-hutāśa-vaktraṁ
sva-tejasā viśvam idaṁ
tapantam // 19 //

I see Thee—beginningless, middleless and endless; infinite in puissance; of boundless energy active everywhere; having the sun and the moon for eyes; with a face luminous like a flaming fire; and with spiritual radiance energising everything.

द्यावापृथिव्योरिदमन्तरं हि
व्याप्तं त्वयैकेन दिशश्च सर्वाः ।
दृष्ट्वाद्भुतं रूपमुग्रं तवेदं
लोकत्रयं प्रव्यथितं महात्मन् ।।

Dyāvā-pṛthivyor idam antaraṁ hi
vyāptaṁ tvay'aikena diśaś ca sarvāḥ
dṛṣṭvā'dbhutaṁ rūpam ugraṁ tav' edaṁ
loka-trayaṁ pravyathitaṁ mah'ātman // 20 //

O High-souled One! All the three worlds tremble with fear at the sight of this wondrous, awe inspiring form of Thine the one existence that fills all space betwixt heaven and earth and all the quarters as well.

अमी हि त्वां सुरसङ्घा विशन्ति
केचिद्भीताः प्राञ्जलयो गृणन्ति ।
स्वस्तीत्युक्त्वा महर्षिसिद्धसङ्घाः
स्तुवन्ति त्वां स्तुतिभिः पुष्कलाभिः ।।

Amī hi tvāṁ sura-saṅghā viśanti
kecid bhītāḥ prāñjalayo gṛṇanti /
svastī'ty uktvā maha'rṣi-siddha-saṅghāḥ
stuvanti tvāṁ stutibhiḥ puṣkalābhiḥ // 21 //

Verily, these bands of Devas enter into Thee, while others, awe-struck, stand with hands joined in salutation. Hosts of sages and celestial singers cry 'Hail' unto Thee, and extol Thee with hymns of abounding praise.

रुद्रादित्या वसवो ये च साध्याः
विश्वेऽश्विनौ मरुतश्चोष्मपाश्च ।
गन्धर्वयक्षासुरसिद्धसङ्घा
वीक्षन्ते त्वां विस्मिताश्चैव सर्वे ॥

Rudrādityā Vasavo ye ca Sādhyā
Viśve' śvinau Marutaś c'oṣmapāś ca
Gandharva-yakṣ'āsura-siddha-saṅghā
vīkṣante tvāṁ vismitāś c'aiva sarve // 22 //

And the Rudras, Ādityas, Vasus and Sādhyas; Viśvas, Aśvins, Maruts and Manes; and the hosts of Gandharvas, Yakṣas, Asuras and Siddhas—all view Thee in utter amazement.

रूपं महत्ते बहुवक्त्रनेत्रं
महाबाहो बहुबाहूरुपादम् ।
बहूदरं बहुदंष्ट्राकरालं
दृष्ट्वा लोकाः प्रव्यथितास्तथाहम् ।।

Rūpaṁ mahat te bahu vaktra-netraṁ
mahā bāho bahu-bāh'ūru-pādam /
bah'ūdaraṁ bahu-daṁṣṭrā-karālaṁ
dṛṣṭvā lokāḥ pravyathitās tathā' ham // 23 //

At the sight of Thy stupendous form, with faces, eyes, arms, trunks, thighs and legs in myriads, and Thy numerous fangs of forbidding appearance—the whole world, O mighty one, is trembling in awe, even as I.

नभःस्पृशं दीप्तमनेकवर्णं
व्यात्ताननं दीप्तविशालनेत्रम् ।
दृष्ट्वा हि त्वां प्रव्यथितान्तरात्मा
धृतिं न विन्दामि शमं च विष्णो ।।

Nabhaḥ-spṛśaṁ dīptam anekavarṇaṁ
vyātt'ānanaṁ dīpta-viśāla-netram /
dṛṣṭvā hi tvāṁ pravyathit'āntarātmā
dhṛtiṁ na vindāmi śamaṁ ca
Viṣṇo // 24 //

When I see Thy form reaching up to the skies and shining in varied hues, when I see Thy face with mouth wide open and eyes large and glowing bright, I feel shaken to the core of my being with awe. O All-pervading One! My strength is exhausted and my mind is without peace.

दंष्ट्राकरालानि च ते मुखानि
दृष्ट्वैव कालानलसन्निभानि ।
दिशो न जाने न लभे च शर्म
प्रसीद देवेश जगन्निवास ।।

Daṁṣṭrā-karālani ca te mukhāni
dṛṣṭv'aiva kāl'ānala-sannibhāni /
diśo na jāne na labhe ca śarma
prasīda dev'eśa jugan-nivāsa /25/

Even by beholding Thy faces, resembling the fire of cosmic destruction and striking terror with their fangs, I lose all sense of direction as also my presence of mind. O Thou the Lord of all and the home of the worlds! Be propitious unto me!

अमी च त्वां धृतराष्ट्रस्य पुत्राः
सर्वे सहैवावनिपालसङ्घैः ।
भीष्मो द्रोणः सूतपुत्रस्तथासौ
सहास्मदीयैरपि योधमुख्यैः ॥
वक्त्राणि ते त्वरमाणा विशन्ति
दंष्ट्राकरालानि भयानकानि ।
केचिद्विलग्ना दशनान्तरेषु
सन्दृश्यन्ते चूर्णितैरुत्तमाङ्गैः ॥

Amī ca tvāṁ Dhṛtarāṣṭrasya putrāḥ
sarve sah'ai'vā'vani-pāla-saṅghaiḥ
Bhīṣmo Droṇaḥ sūta-putras tathā' sau
sahā'smadīyair api yodha mukhyaiḥ /26/

Vaktrāṇi te tvaramāṇā viśanti
daṁṣṭrā-karālāni bhay'ānakāni /
kecid vilagnā dasan'āntareṣu
sandṛśyante cūrṇitair
uttamāṅgaiḥ / 27 /

All these hosts of kings, along with the sons of Dhṛtarāṣṭra, Bhīsma, Drona and yonder Karṇa, as also the principal warriors on our side—all are rushing headlong into Thy fearful mouth set with terrible fangs. Some are seen with their heads crushed and caught in the gaps of Thy teeth.

यथा नदीनां बहवोऽम्बुवेगाः
समुद्रमेवाभिमुखा द्रवन्ति ।
तथा तवामी नरलोकवीरा
विशन्ति वक्त्राण्यभिविज्वलन्ति ।।

Yathā nadīnāṁ bahavo' mbu-vegāḥ
samudram ev'ābhimukhā dravanti /
tathā tav'āmī nara-loka-vīrā
viśanti vaktrāṇy
abhivijvalanti // 28 //

As the swift-flowing waters of numerous rivers rush verily towards the sea, so these heroes among men are rushing into Thy flaming mouth.

यथा प्रदीप्तं ज्वलनं पतङ्गाः
विशन्ति नाशाय समृद्धवेगाः ।
तथैव नाशाय विशन्ति लोका-
स्तवापि वक्त्राणि समृद्धवेगाः ।।

Yathā pradīptaṁ jvalanaṁ pataṅgāḥ
viśanti nāśāya samṛddha-vegāḥ /
tath'aiva nāśāya viśanti lokās
tav'āpi vaktrāṇi
samṛddha-vegāḥ // 29 //

As moths swarm swiftly into a flaming fire and perish, so do these men rush headlong into Thy mouth to meet with sure destruction.

लेलिह्यसे ग्रसमानः समन्ता-
ल्लोकान्समग्रान्वदनैर्ज्वलद्भिः ।
तेजोभिरापूर्य जगत्समग्रं
भासस्तवोग्राः प्रतपन्ति विष्णो ।।

Lelihyase grasamānaḥ samantāt
lokān samagrān vadanairjvaladbhiḥ /
tejobhir āpūrya jagat samagraṁ
bhāsas tav'ogrāḥ pratapanti
Viṣṇo // 30 //

Thou lappest up all these worlds around, devouring them with Thy flaming mouth. Thy lustre, striking awe into the minds of all, fills this entire universe with its radiance and scorches it, O Viṣṇu!

आख्याहि मे को भवानुग्ररूपो
नमोऽस्तु ते देववर प्रसीद ।
विज्ञातुमिच्छामि भवन्तमाद्यं
न हि प्रजानामि तव प्रवृत्तिम् ॥

Ākhyāhi me ko bhavān ugra-rūpo
namo' stu te Deva-vara prasīda /
vijñātum icchāmi bhavantam ādyaṁ
nahiprajānāmi tava
pravṛttim // 31 //

Deign to tell me who Thou art with this awe-inspiring form. To Thee, O Supreme Lord, my salutation, and also my prayers for Thy grace. I wish to know more about Thee, the Primal Being, as also of Thy purpose here, of which I am in ignorance.

श्रीभगवानुवाच —

कालोऽस्मि लोकक्षयकृत्प्रवृद्धो
लोकान्समाहर्तुमिह प्रवृत्तः ।
ऋतेऽपि त्वां न भविष्यन्ति सर्वे
येऽवस्थिताः प्रत्यनीकेषु योधाः ॥

Śrī Bhagavān uvāca:
Kālo' smi loka-kṣaya-kṛt pravṛddho
lokān samāhartum iha pravṛttaḥ /
ṛte' pi tvāṁ na bhaviṣyanti sarve
ye' vasthitāḥ pratyanīkeṣu
yodhāḥ // 32 //

The Blessed Lord said: I am the mighty world destroying Time, engaged here in annihilating all beings. Even without you, not one of all the warriors arrayed in these rival armies shall survive.

तस्मात्त्वमुत्तिष्ठ यशो लभस्व
जित्वा शत्रून् भुङ्क्ष्व राज्यं समृद्धम् ।
मयैवैते निहताः पूर्वमेव
निमित्तमात्रं भव सव्यसाचिन् ॥

Tasmāt tvam uttiṣṭha yaso labhasva
jitvā śatrun bhuhkṣva rājyaṁ samṛddham /
may'aiv'aite nihatāḥ pūrvam eva
nimitta-mātraṁ bhava savyasācin // 33 //

Therefore arise! Win renown! And destroying your enemies, enjoy the prosperous kingdom. For, these warriors have already been slain by Me. Be you but an instrument thereof, O thou master-bowman, Arjuna.

द्रोणं च भीष्मं च जयद्रथं च
कर्णं तथान्यानपि योधवीरान् ।
मया हतांस्त्वं जहि मा व्यथिष्ठाः
युध्यस्व जेतासि रणे सपत्नान् ।।

Droṇaṁ ca bhīṣmaṁ ca Jayadrathaṁ ca
Karṇaṁ tathā'nyān api yodha-vīrān /
mayā hatāṁs tvaṁ jahi mā vyathiṣṭhāḥ
yudhyasva jetāsi raṇe
sapatnān // 34 //

Kill Droṇa and Bhīṣma, Jayadratha and Karṇa, as also these other heroic warriors, who are already doomed by Me. Fight on, and you shall conquer the enemies in battle.

सञ्जय उवाच —
एतच्छ्रुत्वा वचनं केशवस्य
कृताञ्जलिर्वेपमानः किरीटी ।
नमस्कृत्वा भूय एवाह कृष्णं
सगद्गदं भीतभीतः प्रणम्य ।।

Sañjaya uvāca:
Etac chrutvā vacanaṁ Keśavasya
kṛtāñjalir vepamānaḥ Kirīṭī /
namas-kṛtvā bhūya ev'āha Kṛṣṇaṁ
sagadgadaṁ bhīta-bhītaḥ
praṇamya // 35 //

Sañjaya said:
Hearing this declaration of Kṛṣṇa, Arjuna, with his frame trembling, saluted Him again and again with joined palms. Prostrating himself before Him in utter awe, Arjuna addressed Him in faltering voice.

अर्जुन उवाच —

स्थाने हृषीकेश तव प्रकीर्त्या
जगत्प्रहृष्यत्यनुरज्यते च ।
रक्षांसि भीतानि दिशो द्रवन्ति
सर्वे नमस्यन्ति च सिद्धसङ्घाः ॥

Arjuna uvāca:
Sthāne Hṛṣīkeśa tava prakīrtyā
jagat prahṛṣyaty anurajyate ca /
rakṣāṁsi bhītāni diśo dravanti
sarve namasyanti ca siddha-
saṅghāḥ // 36 //

Arjuna said:

Rightly do the worlds rejoice and delight in glorifying Thee. In Thy presence the Rākṣasas melt away in fear in all directions, while the hosts of Siddhas bow in adoration.

कस्माच्च ते न नमेरन्महात्मन्
गरीयसे ब्रह्मणोऽप्यादिकर्त्रे ।
अनन्त देवेश जगन्निवास
त्वमक्षरं सदसत्तत्परं यत् ।।

Kasmāc ca te na nameran mahātman
garīyase brahmaṇo' py ādi-kartre /
ananta dev'eśa jagan-nivāsa
tvam akṣaraṁ sad asat tat-paraṁ yat // 37 //

O High-souled one! Why should they not bow down to Thee who art the highest of all beings and the primal cause of even Brahmā the creator! O Infinite One! O Lord of all Gods and the Abode of all the worlds! Thou art that Imperishable Being who is both existence (effect condition) and non-existence (causal state) as also that which is beyond them both.

त्वमादिदेवः पुरुषः पुराण-
स्त्वमस्य विश्वस्य परं निधानम् ।
वेत्तासि वेद्यं च परं च धाम
त्वया ततं विश्वमनन्तरूप ॥

Tvam ādi-devaḥ puruṣaḥ purāṇas
tvam asya viśvasya paraṁ nidhānam /
vettā'si vedyaṁ ca paraṁ ca dhāma
tvayā tataṁ viśvam
anantarūpa // 38 //

Thou art the first of all divinities and the most ancient of all beings. Thou art the ultimate haven of rest and safety for the worlds. Thou art both the knower and the known as also the supreme Abode. O Thou of countless forms! By Thee the whole universe is pervaded.

वायुर्यमोऽग्निर्वरुणः शशाङ्कः
प्रजापतिस्त्वं प्रपितामहश्च ।
नमो नमस्तेऽस्तु सहस्रकृत्वः
पुनश्च भूयोऽपि नमो नमस्ते ।।

Vāyur Yamo' gnir Varuṇaḥ śaśāṅkaḥ
Prajāpatis tvaṁ prapitāmahaś ca /
namo namas te' stu sahasra-kṛtvaḥ
punaś ca bhūyo' pi namo
namas te // 39 //

Manifested as Vāyu the god of winds, as Yama the god of death, as Varuṇa the god of the seas, and as the moon with the hare-mark on the face—Thou art the Progenitor of all and the source of him as well. Hail, hail unto Thee a thousand times! Hail, and hail again and yet again.

नमः पुरस्तादथ पृष्ठतस्ते
नमोऽस्तु ते सर्वत एव सर्व ।
अनन्तवीर्यामितविक्रमस्त्वं
सर्वं समाप्नोषि ततोऽसि सर्वः ।।

Namaḥ purastād atha pṛṣṭhatas te
namo' stu te sarvata eva sarva /
ananta-vīry'āmita-vikramas tvaṁ
sarvaṁ samāpnoṣi tato' si
sarvaḥ // 40 //

Salutations unto Thee, the All-formed, from before, from behind and from all directions! Infinite in puissance and limitless in might, Thou pervadest everything and Thou art verily the All.

सखेति मत्वा प्रसभं यदुक्तं
हे कृष्ण हे यादव हे सखेति ।
अजानता महिमानं तवेदं
मया प्रमादात्प्रणयेन वापि ।।
यच्चावहासार्थमसत्कृतोऽसि
विहारशय्यासनभोजनेषु ।
एकोऽथवाप्यच्युत तत्समक्षं
तत्क्षामये त्वामहमप्रमेयम् ।।

Sakh'eti matvā prasabhaṁ yad uktaṁ
he Kṛṣṇa he Yādava he sakh'eti /
ajānatā mahimānaṁ tav'edaṁ
mayā pramādāt praṇayena vāpi / 41 /
Yac c'āvahās'ārtham asatkṛto' si
vihāra-śayy'āsana-bhojaneṣu /
eko' thavā'py acyuta tat-samakṣaṁ
tat kṣāmaye tvām aham
aprameyam / 42 /

O undecaying One! If, without knowing Thy greatness and taking Thee only to be a friend, I have, out of ignorance or love, alone or even in company, addressed Thee discourteously in fun, while playing, relaxing, sitting or feasting, with words such as, 'O Kṛṣṇa! O Yādava!'— I beseech Thee, O Boundless One, do pardon me for the same!

पितासि लोकस्य चराचरस्य
त्वमस्य पूज्यश्च गुरुर्गरीयान् ।
न त्वत्समोऽस्त्यभ्यधिकः कुतोऽन्यो
लोकत्रयेऽप्यप्रतिमप्रभाव ॥

Pitā'si lokasya car'ācarasya
tvam asya pūjyaś ca gurur-garīyān /
na tvat-samo' sty abhyadhikaḥ kuto' nyo
loka-traye' py apratima
prabhāva // 43 //

Thou art the father of the world—of all that is moving and unmoving. Thou art the object of its worship, the most venerable of its Teachers. In all the worlds there is not another equal to Thee, much less one greater, O Thou of incomparable puissance!

तस्मात्प्रणम्य प्रणिधाय कायं
प्रसादये त्वामहमीशमीड्यम् ।
पितेव पुत्रस्य सखेव सख्युः
प्रियः प्रियायार्हसि देव सोढुम् ॥

Tasmāt praṇamya praṇidhāya kāyaṁ
prasādaye tvām aham īsam īdyam /
pit'eva putrasya sakh'eva sakhyuḥ
priyaḥ priyāy'ārhasi deva sodhum // 44 //

Therefore greeting Thee with my body stretched in prostration, I beseech Thee, O worshipful Lord, to be gracious unto me. Bear with me as a father with a son, as a friend with a friend, and as a lover with his beloved.

अदृष्टपूर्वं हृषितोऽस्मि दृष्ट्वा
भयेन च प्रव्यथितं मनो मे ।
तदेव मे दर्शय देव रूपं
प्रसीद देवेश जगन्निवास ।।

Adṛṣṭa-pūrvaṁ hṛṣito' smi dṛṣṭvā
bhayena ca pravyathitaṁ mano me /
tad eva me darśaya deva rūpaṁ
prasīda dev'eśa
jagan-nivāsa // 45 //

Seeing this form unseen before, I am overjoyed but my mind is also perturbed with fear. Reveal to me that other familiar form of Thine and be gracious unto me, O Thou God of all gods, and Indwelling Spirit of the worlds.

किरीटिनं गदिनं चक्रहस्त-
मिच्छामि त्वां द्रष्टुमहं तथैव ।
तेनैव रूपेण चतुर्भुजेन
सहस्रबाहो भव विश्वमूर्ते ।।

Kirītinaṁ gadinaṁ cakra-hastam
icchāmi tvāṁ draṣṭum ahaṁ tath'aiva /
ten'aiva rūpeṇa catur-bhujena
sahasra bāho bhava
viśva-mūrte // 46 //

I desire to see Thee as before crowned with a diadem, and holding a mace and discus in hand. Deign to assume that four-armed shape, O Thou of a thousand arms and of universal form!

श्रीभगवानुवाच —
मया प्रसन्नेन तवार्जुनेदं
रूपं परं दर्शितमात्मयोगात् ।
तेजोमयं विश्वमनन्तमाद्यं
यन्मे त्वदन्येन न दृष्टपूर्वम् ।।

Śrī Bhagavān uvāca:
Mayā prasannena tav'ārjun'edaṁ
rūpaṁ paraṁ darśitam ātmayogāt /
tejomayaṁ viśvam anantam ādyaṁ
yan me tvad-anyena na
dṛṣṭapūrvam // 47 //

The Blessed Lord said:

Out of My grace, I have, by My divine power, revealed to you this transcendent form of Mine—infinite, primeval, radiant and all-inclusive. Never has it been seen by any one before except by you.

न वेदयज्ञाध्ययनैर्न दानै-
र्न च क्रियाभिर्न तपोभिरुग्रैः ।
एवंरूपः शक्य अहं नृलोके
द्रष्टुं त्वदन्येन कुरुप्रवीर ॥

Na veda-yajñ'ādhyayanair na dānair
na ca kriyābhir na tapobhir ugraiḥ /
evaṁ-rūpaḥ śakya ahaṁ nṛ-loke
draṣṭuṁ tvad-anyena
Kurupravīra // 48 //

Except by you (on whom My grace has been bestowed), none in this world of men could see Me in this Cosmic Form—be it by Vedic study, by sacrifice, by good works, by rituals, or by severe austerities.

मा ते व्यथा मा च विमूढभावो
दृष्ट्वा रूपं घोरमीदृङ्ममेदम् ।
व्यपेतभीः प्रीतमनाः पुनस्त्वं
तदेव मे रूपमिदं प्रपश्य ॥

Mā te vyathā mā ca vimūḍhabhāvo
dṛṣṭvā rūpaṁ ghoram īdṛṅ mam'edam /
vyapeta-bhīḥ prīta-manāḥ punas tvaṁ
tad eva me rūpam idaṁ prapaśya // 49 //

Fear not; nor be bewildered at seeing this awe-inspiring form of Mine. With fear assuaged and a heart full of joy, behold now this, My familiar form, again!

सञ्जय उवाच —
इत्यर्जुनं वासुदेवस्तथोक्त्वा
स्वकं रूपं दर्शयामास भूयः ।
आश्वासयामास च भीतमेनं
भूत्वा पुनः सौम्यवपुर्महात्मा ।।

Sañjaya uvāca:
Ity Arjunaṁ Vāsudevas tath'oktvā
svakaṁ rūpaṁ darśayāmāsa bhūyaḥ /
āśvāsayāmāsa ca bhītam enaṁ
bhūtvā punaḥ saumya-vapur
mah'ātmā // 50 //

Sañjaya said: Saying thus to Arjuna, Kṛṣṇa revealed again his own familiar form. Having thus assumed that gentle form, the Exalted One comforted the awe-struck Arjuna over again.

अर्जुन उवाच—

दृष्ट्वेदं मानुषं रूपं तव सौम्यं जनार्दन ।
इदानीमस्मि संवृत्तः सचेताः प्रकृतिं गतः ।।

Arjuna uvāca:

Dṛṣṭv'edaṁ mānuṣaṁ rūpaṁ
tava saumyaṁ Janārdana /
idānīm asmi saṁvṛttaḥ
sacetāḥ prakṛtiṁ gataḥ // 51 //

Arjuna said:

Seeing this gentle human form of Thine, O Janārdana, I am now composed and restored to my natural state of mind.

श्रीभगवानुवाच —

सुदुर्दर्शमिदं रूपं दृष्टवानसि यन्मम ।
देवा अप्यस्य रूपस्य नित्यं दर्शनकाङ्क्षिणः ॥

Śrī Bhagavān uvāca:
Sudurdarśam idaṁ rūpaṁ
dṛṣṭavān asi yan mama /
devā apy asya rūpasya
nityaṁ darśana-kāṅkṣiṇaḥ // 52 //

The Blessed Lord said:

This form of Mine which you have seen is extremely difficult to behold. Even Devas themselves are ever eager to see it.

नाहं वेदैर्न तपसा न दानेन न चेज्यया ।
शक्य एवंविधो द्रष्टुं दृष्टवानसि मां यथा ।।

N'āhaṁ vedair na tapasā
na dānena na c'ejyayā /
śakya evaṁ-vidho draṣṭuṁ
dṛṣṭavān asi māṁ yathā // 53 //

Neither by Vedic study, nor by austerities, nor by charities, nor by sacrifices could one behold Me in the way you have done.

भक्त्या त्वनन्यया शक्य अहमेवंविधोऽर्जुन ।
ज्ञातुं द्रष्टुं च तत्त्वेन प्रवेष्टुं च परन्तप ॥

Bhaktyā tv'ananyayā śakya
aham evaṁ-vidho' rjuna /
jñātuṁ draṣṭuṁ ca tattvena
praveṣṭuṁ ca parantapa // 54 //

But, O Arjuna, thou great warrior! Through unswerving devotion this form of Mine may be known in truth and in reality, may be experienced and entered into.

मत्कर्मकृन्मत्परमो मद्भक्तः सङ्गवर्जितः ।
निर्वैरः सर्वभूतेषु यः स मामेति पाण्डव ।।

Mat-karma-kṛn mat-paramo
mad-bhaktaḥ saṅga-varjitaḥ /
nirvairaḥ sarva-bhūteṣu
yaḥ sa mām eti Pāṇḍava // 55 //

Whoever works for Me, looking upon Me as the goal; whoever is My devotee, free from attachments and from antagonism to any being—such a man, O son of Pāṇḍu, shall enter into Me.

12. Loving Devotion

'Whosoever even seeks to follow the virtuous path to Immortality are dear to Me.' (20)

Chapter 12

Loving Devotion

अर्जुन उवाच —

एवं सततयुक्ता ये भक्तास्त्वां पर्युपासते ।
ये चाप्यक्षरमव्यक्तं तेषां के योगवित्तमाः ।।

Arjuna uvāca:
Evaṁ satata-yuktā ye
bhaktās tvāṁ paryupāsate /
ye c'āpy akṣaram avyaktaṁ
teṣāṁ ke yoga-vittamāḥ // 1 //

Arjuna said: There are Thy ever-steadfast devotees who love and worship Thee in the above way (as the Divine Person); there are again others who contemplate on Thee as the Imperishable Unmanifest (Impersonal Absolute)—which of these has a greater understanding of Yoga.

श्रीभगवानुवाच —

मय्यावेश्य मनो ये मां नित्ययुक्ता उपासते ।
श्रद्धया परयोपेतास्ते मे युक्ततमा मताः ॥

Śrī Bhagavān uvāca:
Mayy āveśya mano ye māṁ
nitya-yuktā upāsate /
śraddhayā paray'opetās
te me yukta-tamā matāḥ // 2 //

The Blessed Lord said:

Those I consider as the most perfect in Yoga, who, with their minds fixed intently on Me in steadfast love, worship Me with absolute faith.

ये त्वक्षरमनिर्देश्यमव्यक्तं पर्युपासते ।
सर्वत्रगमचिन्त्यं च कूटस्थमचलं ध्रुवम् ।।

सन्नियम्येन्द्रियग्रामं सर्वत्र समबुद्धयः ।
ते प्राप्नुवन्ति मामेव सर्वभूतहिते रताः ।।

Ye tv akṣaram anirdeśyam
avyaktaṁ paryupāsate /
sarvatra-gam acintyaṁ ca
kūṭa-stham acalaṁ
dhruvam // 3 //

Sanniyamy'endriya-grāmaṁ
sarvatra sama-buddhayaḥ
te prāpnuvanti mām eva
sarva-bhūta-hite ratāḥ // 4 //

Those who are devoted to the Imperishable (the Impersonal Absolute)—who is the firm support of the world and is also undefinable, unmanifested, transcendent, motionless, eternal and all-pervading,—even they reach Me alone, striving with their senses controlled, and with mind tranquillised and set on the welfare of all.

क्लेशोऽधिकतरस्तेषामव्यक्तासक्तचेतसाम् ।
अव्यक्ता हि गतिर्दुःखं देहवद्भिरवाप्यते ।।

Kleśo' dhikataras teṣāṁ
a vyakt'āsakta-cetasām
avyaktā hi gatir duḥkhaṁ
dehavadbhir avāpyate // 5 //

The obstacles facing those devoted to the Impersonal Absolute are far greater; for the way of any unclear ideal is difficult for an embodied being (the body-centred man) to understand or follow.

मय्येव मन आधत्स्व मयि बुद्धिं निवेशय ।
निवसिष्यसि मय्येव अत ऊर्ध्वं न संशयः ।।

Mayy eva mana ādhatsva
mayi buddhiṁ niveśaya /
nivasiṣyasi mayy eva
ata ūrdhvaṁ na saṁśayaḥ // 8 //

Fix your mind on Me alone; let your reason penetrate into Me; without doubt you will then abide in Me alone for ever more.

अथ चित्तं समाधातुं न शक्नोषि मयि स्थिरम् ।
अभ्यासयोगेन ततो मामिच्छाप्तुं धनञ्जय ॥

Atha cittaṁ samādhātuṁ
na śaknoṣi mayi sthiram /
abhyāsa-yogena tato
māṁ icch'āptuṁ
Dhanañjaya // 9 //

If you are unable to fix your mind steadily on Me (even at the start), then try to reach Me through the systematic practice of concentration.

अभ्यासेऽप्यसमर्थोऽसि मत्कर्मपरमो भव ।
मदर्थमपि कर्माणि कुर्वन्सिद्धिमवाप्स्यसि ।।

Abhyāse' py asamartho' si
mat-karma-paramo bhava /
mad-artham api karmāṇi
kurvan siddhim
avāpsyasi // 10 //

If you are not capable of practising systematic concentration, then devote yourself whole heartedly to works of service to Me (consisting in external worship and discharge of duties for My sake). Thus working for Me, man can attain to perfection.

अथैतदप्यशक्तोऽसि कर्तुं मद्योगमाश्रितः ।
सर्वकर्मफलत्यागं ततः कुरु यतात्मवान् ।।

Ath'aitad apy aśakto' si
kartuṁ mad-yogam āśritaḥ /
sarva-karma-phala-tyāgaṁ
tataḥ kuru yat'ātmavān // *11* //

If even this is too difficult for you to perform, then taking refuge in Me, and thus controlling the mind, give up the fruits of all your actions (recognising Me as their agent and enjoyer).

श्रेयो हि ज्ञानमभ्यासाज्ज्ञानाद्ध्यानं विशिष्यते ।
ध्यानात्कर्मफलत्यागस्त्यागाच्छान्तिरनन्तरम् ॥

Śreyo hi jñānam abhyāsāt
jñānād dhyānaṁ viśiṣyate /
dhyānāt karma-phala-tyāgas
tyāgāc chāntir anantaram // 12 //

Than (a mere formal) practice of disciplines, a clear intellectual understanding (of the doctrine) is better. Than such understanding, meditation is better. Even better than meditation is the abandonment of the fruits of action. For, such abandonment (of the fruits of works and sense of their agency) is immediately followed by peace.

अद्वेष्टा सर्वभूतानां मैत्रः करुण एव च ।
निर्ममो निरहङ्कारः समदुःखसुखः क्षमी ।।

सन्तुष्टः सततं योगी यतात्मा दृढनिश्चयः ।
मय्यर्पितमनोबुद्धिर्यो मद्भक्तः स मे प्रियः ।।

Adveṣṭā sarva-bhūtānāṁ
maitraḥ karuṇa eva ca /
nirmamo nirahaṅkāraḥ
sama duḥkhasukhaḥ
kṣamī // 13 //

santuṣṭaḥ satataṁ yogī
yat'ātmā dṛḍha niscayaḥ /
mayy arpita-mano-buddhir
yo mad-bhaktaḥ sa me
priyaḥ // 14 //

Friendly and compassionate to all and without any touch of hatred; devoid of possessiveness and arrogance; ever content and contemplative; alike in happiness and misery; self-controlled and firm in conviction; dedicated to Me with all his heart and all his soul—dear to Me is a man who is thus devoted.

यस्मान्नोद्विजते लोको लोकान्नोद्विजते च यः ।
हर्षामर्षभयोद्वेगैर्मुक्तो यः स च मे प्रियः ॥

Yasmān n'odvijate loko
lokān n'odvijate ca yaḥ /
harṣ'āmarṣa-bhay'odvegair
mukto yaḥ sa ca me
priyaḥ // 15 //

Who causes fear to none and whom none can frighten, who is thus free from the agitation of the moods caused by euphoria, anger, and excitement—such a person too is dear to Me.

अनपेक्षः शुचिर्दक्ष उदासीनो गतव्यथः ।
सर्वारम्भपरित्यागी यो मद्भक्तः स मे प्रियः ।।

Anapekṣaḥ śucir dakṣa
udāsīno gata-vyathaḥ /
sarvāram bha-parityāgī
yo mad-bhaktaḥ sa me
priyaḥ // 16 //

Desireless, pure, resourceful, unattached, unworried and without any sense of self-centred agency—a devotee thus endowed is dear to Me.

यो न हृष्यति न द्वेष्टि न शोचति न काङ्क्षति ।
शुभाशुभपरित्यागी भक्तिमान् यः स मे प्रियः ।।

Yo na hṛṣyati na dveṣṭi
na śocati na kāṅkṣati /
śubh'āśubha-parityāgī
bhaktimān yaḥ sa me
priyaḥ // 17 //

He who is free from elation, anger, sorrow, and craving, who neither seeks the pleasant nor shuns the unpleasant—dear to Me is the man who is thus devoted.

समः शत्रौ च मित्रे च तथा मानापमानयोः ।
शीतोष्णसुखदुःखेषु समः सङ्गविवर्जितः ।।

तुल्यनिन्दास्तुतिर्मौनी सन्तुष्टो येन केनचित् ।
अनिकेतः स्थिरमतिर्भक्तिमान्मे प्रियो नरः ।।

Samaḥ śatrau ca mitre ca
tathā mān'āpamānayoḥ /
śītoṣṇa-sukha-duḥkheṣu
samaḥ saṅga-vivarjitaḥ // 18 //

Tulya-nindā-stutir maunī
santuṣṭo yena kenacit /
aniketaḥ sthira-matir
bhaktimān me priyo
naraḥ // 19 //

Alike to friend and foe, alike in honour and insult, alike in heat and cold, alike in praise and blame—unattached, contented, homeless, and steady in mind—dear to Me is a man who is thus devoted.

ये तु धर्म्यामृतमिदं यथोक्तं पर्युपासते ।
श्रद्दधाना मत्परमा भक्तास्तेऽतीव मे प्रियाः ।।

Ye tu dharmy'āmṛtam idaṁ
yath'oktaṁ paryupāsate /
śraddadhānā mat-paramā
bhaktās te' tīva me
priyāḥ // 20 //

Whosoever even seeks to follow the virtuous path to Immortality thus set forth, with a mind full of faith and acceptance of Me as their supreme goal—exceedingly dear to Me are men who are thus devoted.

13. The Knower and the Known

'In the innermost recess of all beings is He established.' (17)

Chapter 13

The Knower and the Known

श्री भगवानुवाच —

इदं शरीरं कौन्तेय क्षेत्रमित्यभिधीयते ।
एतद्यो वेत्ति तं प्राहुः क्षेत्रज्ञ इति तद्विदः ॥

Śrī Bhagavān uvāca:
Idaṁ śarīraṁ Kaunteya
kṣetram ity abhidhīyate /
etad yo vetti taṁ prāhuḥ
*kṣetra-jña iti tad-vidaḥ // **1** //*

The Blessed Lord said:

This body, O son of Kuntī, is called the Kṣetra, the field (because the fruits of action are reaped in it). He who knows it (as his property) is the Kṣetrajña or the Spirit who knows the field. So say those versed in this subject.

क्षेत्रज्ञं चापि मां विद्धि सर्वक्षेत्रेषु भारत ।
क्षेत्रक्षेत्रज्ञयोर्ज्ञानं यत्तज्ज्ञानं मतं मम ॥

Kṣetra-jñaṁ c'āpi māṁ viddhi
sarva-kṣetreṣu Bhārata /
kṣetra-kṣetra-jñayor jñānaṁ
yat taj jñānaṁ mataṁ
mama // 2 //

Know Me, O scion of the Bhārata race, to be the Kṣetrajña (the Spirit) in all Kṣetras (bodies). The knowledge of the distinction between Kṣetra and Kṣetrajña alone is real knowledge according to Me.

तत्क्षेत्रं यच्च यादृक्च यद्विकारि यतश्च यत् ।
स च यो यत्प्रभावश्च तत्समासेन मे शृणु ।।

Tat kṣetraṁ yac ca yādṛk ca
yad-vikāri yataś ca yat /
sa ca yo yat-prabhāvaś ca
tat samāsena me śṛṇu // 3 //

Hear from Me in brief what the Kṣetra is, of what nature it is, what its modifications are, and from what causes what effects have sprung. Also know who the Kṣetrajña is and what his powers are.

ऋषिभिर्बहुधा गीतं छन्दोभिर्विविधैः पृथक् ।
ब्रह्मसूत्रपदैश्चैव हेतुमद्भिर्विनिश्चितैः ॥

Ṛṣibhir bahudhā gītaṁ
chandobhir vividhaiḥ pṛthak /
brahma-sūtra-padaiś c'aiva
hetumadbhir viniścitaiḥ // 4 //

In many and different ways have the Ṛṣis sung about this subject in metres of varying description. The well-reasoned and definitive aphorisms of the Brahma-sūtras too have discussed it.

महाभूतान्यहङ्कारो बुद्धिरव्यक्तमेव च ।
इन्द्रियाणि दशैकं च पञ्च चेन्द्रियगोचराः ॥

इच्छा द्वेषः सुखं दुःखं सङ्घातश्चेतना धृतिः ।
एतत्क्षेत्रं समासेन सविकारमुदाहृतम् ॥

Mahā-bhūtāny ahaṅkāro
buddhir avyaktam eva ca /
indriyāṇi daś'aikaṁ ca
pañca c'endriya-gocarāḥ // 5 //

Icchā dveṣaḥ sukhaṁ duḥkhaṁ
saṅghātaś cetanā dhṛtiḥ
etat kṣetraṁ samāsena
savikāram udāhṛtam // 6 //

The five great elements, the I-sense, the intellect, and the Unmanifested (Root Matter); the ten organs along with the mind as the eleventh, and the five objects of the senses; desire, hatred, pleasure and pain; the body, consciousness, and will—such is a brief description of the Kṣetra with all its modifications.

अमानित्वमदम्भित्वमहिंसा क्षान्तिरार्जवम् ।
आचार्योपासनं शौचं स्थैर्यमात्मविनिग्रहः ॥

Amānitvam adambhitvam
ahiṁsā kṣāntir ārjavam /
ācāry'opāsanaṁ śaucaṁ
sthairyam ātma-vinigrahaḥ // 7 //

Freedom from self-importance, unpretentiousness, non-violence, patience, straight-forwardness, service of the teacher, cleanliness, steadfastness, and self-control;

इन्द्रियार्थेषु वैराग्यमनहङ्कार एव च ।
जन्ममृत्युजराव्याधिदुःखदोषानुदर्शनम् ॥

Indriy'ārtheṣu vairāgyam
anahaṅkāra eva ca /
janma-mṛtyu-jarā-vyādhi-
duḥka-doṣ'ānudarśanam // 8 //

Abhorrence of sensuality, self-effacement and perception of evil and misery in birth, death, old age and sickness;

असक्तिरनभिष्वङ्गः पुत्रदारगृहादिषु ।
नित्यं च समचित्तत्वमिष्टानिष्टोपपत्तिषु ।।

Asaktir anabhiṣvaṅgaḥ
putra-dāra-gṛhādiṣu /
nityaṁ ca samacittatvam
iṣṭ'āniṣṭ'opapattiṣu // 9 //

Detachment from property and family members, non-identification with them and their fortunes, and constant evenness of mind in favourable and unfavourable situations;

मयि चानन्ययोगेन भक्तिरव्यभिचारिणी ।
विविक्तदेशसेवित्वमरतिर्जनसंसदि ॥

Mayi c'ānanya-yogena
bhaktir avyabhicāriṇī /
vivikta-deśa-sevitvam
aratir jana-saṁsadi // 10 //

Practice of unswerving devotion through contemplation on Me as one's 'own' (or on Me in non-separation), resort to solitude and abhorrence of vulgar company;

सर्वतःपाणिपादं तत्सर्वतोऽक्षिशिरोमुखम् ।
सर्वतःश्रुतिमल्लोके सर्वमावृत्य तिष्ठति ॥

Sarvataḥ pāṇi-pādaṁ tat
sarvato' kṣi-śiro-mukham /
sarvataḥ śrutimal loke
sarvam āvṛtya tiṣṭhati // 13 //

His hands and feet are everywhere. His eyes, ears and mouth grasp everything. His face is in all directions. He is the transcendent Spirit, enveloping all that exists.

सर्वेन्द्रियगुणाभासं सर्वेन्द्रियविवर्जितम् ।
असक्तं सर्वभृच्चैव निर्गुणं गुणभोक्तृ च ।।

Sarv'endriya-guṇ'ābhāsaṁ
sarv'endriya-vivarjitam /
asaktaṁ sarva-bhṛc c'aiva
nirguṇaṁ guṇa-bhoktṛ ca // 14 //

By His power the faculties of the senses function, but sense organs He has none. He is the support of all things, but they do not affect Him. He transcends Nature and its functions, but these constitute the objects for His enjoyment.

बहिरन्तश्च भूतानामचरं चरमेव च ।
सूक्ष्मत्वात्तदविज्ञेयं दूरस्थं चान्तिके च तत् ।।

Bahir antaś ca bhūtānām
acaraṁ caram eva ca /
sūkṣmatvāt tad avijñeyaṁ
dūrasthaṁ c'āntike ca tat // 15 //

He is within and without all beings. Though unmoving, He looks like one moving (because He is everywhere). He is both far and near—far to the ignorant, and near to the knowing ones. Owing to subtlety, He cannot be known like gross objects.

अविभक्तं च भूतेषु विभक्तमिव च स्थितम् ।
भूतभर्तृ च तज्ज्ञेयं ग्रसिष्णु प्रभविष्णु च ।।

Avibhaktaṁ ca bhūteṣu
vibhaktam iva ca sthitam /
bhūta-bhartṛ ca tat jñeyaṁ
grasiṣṇu prabhaviṣṇu ca // 16 //

He, (the Brahman) whom aspirants seek to know, is the impartible Whole, yet does He seem to dwell in all beings as if divided into many. He is the generator and supporter of all beings, and their devourer too.

ज्योतिषामपि तज्ज्योतिस्तमसः परमुच्यते ।
ज्ञानं ज्ञेयं ज्ञानगम्यं हृदि सर्वस्य विष्ठितम् ।।

Jyotiṣām api taj jyotis
tamasaḥ param ucyate /
jñānaṁ jñeyaṁ jñāna-gamyaṁ
hṛdi sarvasya viṣṭhitam // 17 //

The self-luminous light of consciousness revealing even all that is luminous, He is beyond obscuration by the darkness of ignorance. He, the light of knowledge, He, the quest of knowledge, He, the way to whom is knowledge—in the innermost recess of all beings is He established.

इति क्षेत्रं तथा ज्ञानं ज्ञेयं चोक्तं समासतः ।
मद्भक्त एतद्विज्ञाय मद्भावायोपपद्यते ।।

Iti kṣetraṁ tathā jñānaṁ
jñeyaṁ c'oktaṁ samāsataḥ /
mad-bhakta etad vijñāya
mad bhāvāy'opapadyate // 18 //

Thus has been briefly expounded what the Kṣetra (material Nature) is, as also what constitutes knowledge and the object of knowledge. My devotee who understands these verities becomes worthy of My state.

प्रकृतिं पुरुषं चैव विद्ध्यनादी उभावपि ।
विकारांश्च गुणांश्चैव विद्धि प्रकृतिसम्भवान् ।।

Prakṛtiṁ puruṣaṁ c'aiva
viddhy anādī ubhāvapi /
vikārāṁś ca guṇāṁś c'aiva
viddhi prakṛti-sambhavān // 19 //

Know both Prakṛti (Nature) and Puruṣa (Spirit) to be beginningless, eternal verities. Know also that all changeful objects and attributes (that constitute the world of daily experience) are sprung from Prakṛti.

कार्यकारणकर्तृत्वे हेतुः प्रकृतिरुच्यते ।
पुरुषः सुखदुःखानां भोक्तृत्वे हेतुरुच्यते ।।

Kārya-kāraṇa-kartṛtve
hetuḥ prakṛtir ucyate /
puruṣaḥ sukha-duḥkhānāṁ
bhoktṛtve hetur ucyate // 20 //

Prakṛti is the cause of the formation and functioning of the body and the senses, while it is the Puruṣa that experiences pleasure and pain, joy and sorrow.

पुरुषः प्रकृतिस्थो हि भुङ्क्ते प्रकृतिजान्गुणान् ।
कारणं गुणसङ्गोऽस्य सदसद्योनिजन्मसु ।।

Puruṣaḥ prakṛti-stho hi
bhuṅkte prakṛti-jān guṇān /
kāraṇaṁ guṇa-saṅgo' sya
sad-asad-yoni-janmasu // 21 //

Seated in bodies, which are the products of Prakṛti, the Puruṣa enjoys the objects and qualities born of Prakṛti. Attachment to these objects is the cause of the Spirit getting embodiments in evil or exalted wombs.

उपद्रष्टानुमन्ता च भर्ता भोक्ता महेश्वरः ।
परमात्मेति चाप्युक्तो देहेऽस्मिन्पुरुषः परः ।।

Upadraṣṭā'numantā ca
bhartā bhoktā mah'eśvaraḥ /
param'ātm'eti c'āpy ukto
dehe' smin puruṣaḥ
paraḥ // 22 //

In this body there is also the Transcendent and the Supreme Spirit, who is described as the Supreme Self and Sovereign Lord, the unconcerned Witness, the Sanctioner, the Supporter and the Enjoyer.

य एवं वेत्ति पुरुषं प्रकृतिं च गुणैः सह ।
सर्वथा वर्तमानोऽपि न स भूयोऽभिजायते ।।

Ya evaṁ vetti puruṣaṁ
prakṛtiṁ ca guṇaiḥ saha /
sarvathā vartamāno' pi
na sa bhūyo' bhijāyate // 23 //

Whoever thus knows the Puruṣa (Spirit) and Prakṛti (Nature) along with its effects, will never be born again, whatever be his mode of living.

ध्यानेनात्मनि पश्यन्ति केचिदात्मानमात्मना ।
अन्ये साङ्ख्येन योगेन कर्मयोगेन चापरे ।।

Dhyānen'ātmani paśyanti
kecid ātmānam ātmanā /
anye sāṅkhyena yogena
karma-yogena c'āpare // 24 //

There are some who perceive the Ātman within themselves by the practice of meditation with a purified mind. There are also others who approach Him through the discipline of knowledge or of work.

अन्ये त्वेवमजानन्तः श्रुत्वान्येभ्य उपासते ।
तेऽपि चातितरन्त्येव मृत्युं श्रुतिपरायणाः ॥

Anye tvevam ajānantaḥ
śrutvā nyebhya upāsate
te' pi c'ātitaranty eva
mṛtyuṁ śruti-parāyaṇāḥ // 25 //

There are still others, who, being unfit to follow the disciplines described before—for they lack the knowledge of the Yoga Sāstra and the Vedas—, adopt forms of worship (devotional disciplines) under instruction from teachers or elders. Full of faith in these instructions heard, and following them sincerely as their only refuge, they too certainly overcome the cycle of births and deaths.

यावत्सञ्जायते किञ्चित् सत्त्वं स्थावरजङ्गमम् ।
क्षेत्रक्षेत्रज्ञसंयोगात्तद्विद्धि भरतर्षभ ॥

Yāvat sañjāyate kiñcit
sattvaṁ sthāvara-jaṅgamam /
kṣetra-kṣetrajña saṁyogāt
tad viddhi Bharata'rṣabha // 26 //

O thou the best of the Bharata clan! Whatever there is born—whether moving or unmoving—it has come into being due to the union of Kṣetra (body) and Kṣetrajña (Spirit).

समं सर्वेषु भूतेषु तिष्ठन्तं परमेश्वरम् ।
विनश्यत्स्वविनश्यन्तं यः पश्यति स पश्यति ।।

Samaṁ sarveṣu bhūteṣu
tiṣṭhantaṁ param'eśvaram /
vinaśyatsu avinaśyantaṁ
yaḥ paśyati sa paśyati // 27 //

He really sees who perceives the Supreme Lord alike in everything—as the Imperishable Substance abiding amidst perishing phenomena.

समं पश्यन्हि सर्वत्र समवस्थितमीश्वरम् ।
न हिनस्त्यात्मनात्मानं ततो याति परां गतिम् ।।

Samaṁ paśyan hi sarvatra
samavasthitam īśvaram /
na hinasty ātmanā'tmānaṁ
tato yāti parāṁ gatim // 28 //

For, he who perceives the Lord's presence alike everywhere no longer works against his own spiritual well-being (by mistaking the ego for the true spiritual Self as men in ignorance do). He therefore attains to the Supreme Goal.

प्रकृत्यैव च कर्माणि क्रियमाणानि सर्वशः ।
यः पश्यति तथात्मानमकर्तारं स पश्यति ।।

Prakṛty'aiva ca karmāṇi
kriyamāṇāni sarvaśaḥ /
yaḥ paśyati tathā'tmānam
akartāraṁ sa paśyati // 29 //

He is the real seer who perceives that Prakṛti (i.e., one's body-mind born of Prakṛti) alone is doing all works and that the Ātman. the true spiritual Self, is the actionless witness.

यदा भूतपृथग्भावमेकस्थमनुपश्यति ।
तत एव च विस्तारं ब्रह्म सम्पद्यते तदा ।।

Yadā bhūta-pṛthag-bhāvam
eka-stham anupaśyati /
tata eva ca vistāraṁ
brahma sampadyate tadā // 30 //

When one perceives the manifold objects as centred in the One and as evolved from It as well—then he attains Brahman.

अनादित्वान्निर्गुणत्वात् परमात्मायमव्ययः ।
शरीरस्थोऽपि कौन्तेय न करोति न लिप्यते ।।

Anāditvān nirguṇatvāt
paramātmā'yam avyayaḥ /
śarīra-stho' pi Kaunteya
na karoti na lipyate // 31 //

That highest Self, being the immutable and unoriginated Spirit beyond Nature, is free from all action and stain, though dwelling in the body.

यथा सर्वगतं सौक्ष्म्यादाकाशं नोपलिप्यते ।
सर्वत्रावस्थितो देहे तथात्मा नोपलिप्यते ।।

Yathā sarva-gataṁ saukṣmyād
ākāsaṁ n'opalipyate /
sarvatr'āvasthito dehe
tathā'tmā n'opalipyate // 32 //

Just as the all-pervading Ākāsa. because of its subtlety, is not stained by anything, so this Ātman, though abiding in all bodies, is never affected by any impurity.

यथा प्रकाशयत्येकः कृत्स्नं लोकमिमं रविः ।
क्षेत्रं क्षेत्री तथा कृत्स्नं प्रकाशयति भारत ।।

Yathā prakāśayaty ekaḥ
kṛtsnaṁ lokam imaṁ raviḥ /
kṣetraṁ kṣetrī tathā kṛtsnaṁ
prakāśayati Bhārata // 33 //

Just as the single sun illumines the whole universe, so the (one) Indwelling Spirit enlivens all bodies (with self-consciousness).

क्षेत्रक्षेत्रज्ञयोरेवमन्तरं ज्ञानचक्षुषा ।
भूतप्रकृतिमोक्षं च ये विदुर्यान्ति ते परम् ।।

Kṣetra-kṣetrajñāyor evam
antaraṁ jñāna-cakṣuṣā /
bhūta-prakṛti-mokṣaṁ ca
ye vidur yānti te param // 34 //

Whoever perceives by spiritual insight the distinction between Kṣetra (Nature) and Kṣetrajña (Spirit) as also the freedom of the Spirit from the hold of Nature, they reach the Supreme.

14. The Three Guṇas

'Sattva, Rajas and Tamas born of Prakṛti, bind down the immortal soul to the body.' (5)

Chapter 14

The Three Guṇas

परं भूयः प्रवक्ष्यामि ज्ञानानां ज्ञानमुत्तमम् ।
यज्ज्ञात्वा मुनयः सर्वे परां सिद्धिमितो गताः ।।

Śrī Bhagavān uvāca:
Paraṁ bhūyaḥ pravakṣyāmi
jñānānāṁ jñānam uttamam /
yaj jñātvā munayaḥ sarve
parāṁ siddhim ito gatāḥ // 1 //

The Blessed Lord said:

I shall now expound to you again that knowledge relating to the Supreme Being, the most exalted of all forms of knowledge, by gaining which all sages passed from this state of bondage into the highest perfection.

इदं ज्ञानमुपाश्रित्य मम साधर्म्यमागताः ।
सर्गेऽपि नोपजायन्ते प्रलये न व्यथन्ति च ॥

Idaṁ jñānam upāśritya
mama sādharmyam āgatāḥ /
sarge' pi n'opajāyante
pralaye na vyathanti ca // 2 //

Those who have attained unity with My nature through this knowledge are not born again even at the beginning of a new creative cycle, nor are they subjected to the distress of dissolution.

मम योनिर्महद्ब्रह्म तस्मिन्गर्भं दधाम्यहम् ।
सम्भवः सर्वभूतानां ततो भवति भारत ।।

Mama yonir mahad brahma
tasmin garbhaṁ dadhāmy aham /
sambhavaḥ sarva-bhūtānāṁ
tato bhavati Bhārata // 3 //

The Great Nature Prakṛti is like a womb to Me. I deposit therein the germ of creation, the creative impulse, out of which everything comes into being.

तमस्त्वज्ञानजं विद्धि मोहनं सर्वदेहिनाम् ।
प्रमादालस्यनिद्राभिस्तन्निबध्नाति भारत ॥

Tamas tu ajñāna-jaṁ viddhi
mohanaṁ sarva-dehinām /
pramād'ālasya-nidrābhis
tan nibadhnāti Bhārata // 8 //

As for the Guṇa known as Tamas, it is ignorance-born and is productive of delusion in all beings. It binds the soul, O scion of the Bharata clan! with the obsession of a disposition characterised by negligence, indolence and sleepiness.

सत्त्वं सुखे सञ्जयति रजः कर्मणि भारत ।
ज्ञानमावृत्य तु तमः प्रमादे सञ्जयत्युत ।।

Sattvaṁ sukhe sañjayati
rajaḥ karmaṇi Bhārata /
jñānam āvṛtya tu tamaḥ
pramāde sañjayaty uta // 9 //

Sattva enslaves one to a mood of joy and happiness, and Rajas to one of activity, while Tamas, which veils up knowledge, fills one with negligence and laziness.

रजस्तमश्चाभिभूय सत्त्वं भवति भारत ।
रजः सत्त्वं तमश्चैव तमः सत्त्वं रजस्तथा ॥

Rajas tamaś c'ābhibhūya
sattvaṁ bhavati Bhārata /
rajaḥ sattvaṁ tamaś c'aiva
tamaḥ sattvaṁ
rajas tathā // *10* //

Overpowering Rajas and Tamas, Sattva prevails (sometimes); suppressing Sattva and Tamas, Rajas becomes dominant; and likewise dominating over Sattva and Rajas, Tamas holds the field.

सर्वद्वारेषु देहेऽस्मिन् प्रकाश उपजायते ।
ज्ञानं यदा तदा विद्याद् विवृद्धं सत्त्वमित्युत ।।

Sarva-dvāreṣu dehe' smin
prakāśa upajāyate /
jñānaṁ yadā tadā vidyād
vivṛddhaṁ sattvam ity uta // 11 //

When through all the senses, which are the portals of the body, knowledge, happiness and similar characteristics manifest, then indeed it should be understood that Sattva is dominant.

लोभः प्रवृत्तिरारम्भः कर्मणामशमः स्पृहा ।
रजस्येतानि जायन्ते विवृद्धे भरतर्षभ ।।

Lobhaḥ pravṛttir-āraṁbhaḥ
karmaṇām aśamaḥ spṛhā /
rajasy etāni jāyante
vivṛddhe Bharata'rṣabha // 12 //

Avarice, extroversion, ceaseless planning and execution of works, restlessness, desire for enjoyments—these arise when Rajas prevails.

अप्रकाशोऽप्रवृत्तिश्च प्रमादो मोह एव च ।
तमस्येतानि जायन्ते विवृद्धे कुरुनन्दन ॥

Aprakāśo' pravṛttiś ca
pramādo moha eva ca /
tamasy etāni jāyante
vivṛddhe Kuru-nandana // 13 //

When Tamas dominates, there is lack of intelligence, lack of effort, negligence and delusion.

यदा सत्त्वे प्रवृद्धे तु प्रलयं याति देहभृत् ।
तदोत्तमविदां लोकानमलान्प्रतिपद्यते ।।

Yadā sattve pravṛddhe tu
pralayaṁ yāti deha-bhṛt /
tadottama-vidāṁ lokān
amalān pratipadyate // 14 //

If one dies when Sattva is prevailing dominant, then one attains to the pure regions of the knowers of the Highest.

रजसि प्रलयं गत्वा कर्मसङ्गिषु जायते ।
तथा प्रलीनस्तमसि मूढयोनिषु जायते ।।

Rajasi pralayaṁ gatvā
karma-saṅgiṣu jāyate /
tathā pralīnas tamasi
mūḍha-yoniṣu jāyate // 15 //

Those who die when Rajas dominates are born among those attached to action (men); and likewise those dying in Tamas are born in the wombs of creatures without reason (animals).

कर्मणः सुकृतस्याहुः सात्त्विकं निर्मलं फलम् ।
रजसस्तु फलं दुःखमज्ञानं तमसः फलम् ।।

Karmaṇaḥ sukṛtasy'āhuḥ
sāttvikaṁ nirmalaṁ phalam /
rajasas tu phalaṁ duḥkham
ajñānaṁ tamasaḥ
phalam // 16 //

Virtuous actions promote spirituality and purity (Sattva), while the Rajas-dominated ones result in pain, and the Tamas dominated ones in ignorance.

सत्त्वात्सञ्जायते ज्ञानं रजसो लोभ एव च ।
प्रमादमोहौ तमसो भवतोऽज्ञानमेव च ।।

Sattvāt sañjāyate jñānaṁ
rajaso lobha eva ca /
pramāda-mohau tamaso
bhavato' jñānam eva ca // 17 //

From Sattva arises knowledge and from Rajas, avarice. Negligence, delusion and also ignorance are the products of Tamas.

ऊर्ध्वं गच्छन्ति सत्त्वस्था मध्ये तिष्ठन्ति राजसाः ।
जघन्यगुणवृत्तिस्था अधो गच्छन्ति तामसाः ॥

Urdhvaṁ gacchanti sattva sthā
madhye tiṣṭhanti rājasāḥ /
jaghanya guṇa vṛtti-sthā
adho gacchanti tāmasāḥ // 18 //

Those established in Sattva evolve to higher goals, while those abiding in Rajas remain in the mid-course. Steeped in evil tendencies, the Tamas-dominated ones degenerate.

नान्यं गुणेभ्यः कर्तारं यदा द्रष्टानुपश्यति ।
गुणेभ्यश्च परं वेत्ति मद्भावं सोऽधिगच्छति ।।

N'ānyaṁ guṇebhyaḥ kartāraṁ
yadā draṣṭā'nupaśyati /
guṇebhyaś ca paraṁ vetti
mad-bhāvaṁ
so' dhigacchati // 19 //

When the subject (Jīva) recognises the Guṇas alone as the agent in all actions, and himself as transcending the Guṇas—then he attains to My state.

गुणानेतानतीत्य त्रीन्देही देहसमुद्भवान् ।
जन्ममृत्युजरादुःखैर्विमुक्तोऽमृतमश्नुते ।।

Guṇān etān atītya trīn
dehī deha-samudbhavān /
janma-mṛtyu-jarā-duhkḥair
vimukto' mṛtam aśnute // 20 //

The embodied spirit (Jīva), having transcended the Guṇas from which the body has sprung, gains deliverance from the miseries of birth, death and old age, and attains to Immortality.

अर्जुन उवाच —

कैर्लिङ्गैस्त्रीन्गुणानेतानतीतो भवति प्रभो ।
किमाचारः कथं चैतांस्त्रीन्गुणानतिवर्तते ।।

Arjuna uvāca:
Kair liṅgais trīn guṇān etān
atīto bhavati prabho /
kim-ācāraḥ kathaṁ c'aitāṁs
trīn guṇān ativartate // 21 //

Arjuna said:

Lord! What are the marks of one who has transcended these three Guṇas? How does he behave? And how does he rise above them?

श्रीभगवानुवाच —

प्रकाशं च प्रवृत्तिं च मोहमेव च पाण्डव ।
न द्वेष्टि सम्प्रवृत्तानि न निवृत्तानि काङ्क्षति ।।

Śrī Bhagavān uvāea:
Prakāśaṁ ca pravṛttiṁ ca
moham eva ca Pāṇḍava /
na dveṣṭi sampravṛttāni
na nivṛttāni kāṅkṣati // 22 //

The Blessed Lord said:

O son of Pāṇḍu! He who shows no aversion to knowledge, activity, or delusion when any of them is dominant, nor longs for them when abscnt;

उदासीनवदासीनो गुणैर्यो न विचाल्यते ।
गुणा वर्तन्त इत्येव योऽवतिष्ठति नेङ्गते ॥

Udāsīnavad āsīno
guṇair yo na vicālyate /
guṇā vartanta ity eva
yo' vatiṣṭhati n'eṅgate // 23 //

Who remains like an unconcerned witness and is unperturbed by the Guṇa-born sense objects; who knows that it is only the Guṇa-born senses and mind that act and enjoy (and not his real self); who remains unwavering in all situations;

समदुःखसुखः स्वस्थः समलोष्टाश्मकाञ्चनः ।
तुल्यप्रियाप्रियो धीरस्तुल्यनिन्दात्मसंस्तुतिः ॥

Sama-duḥkha-sukhaḥ svasthaḥ
sama-loṣṭāśma kāñcanaḥ /
tulya-priy'āpriyo dhīras
tulyanind'ātma saṁstutiḥ // 24 //

Who is self-poised alike in pleasure and in pain; who makes no difference between stone, iron, and gold; who is the same towards the loving and the hating; who is unmoved by praise and blame alike;

मानापमानयोस्तुल्यस्तुल्यो मित्रारिपक्षयोः ।
सर्वारम्भपरित्यागी गुणातीतः स उच्यते ।।

Mānāpamānayos tulyas
tulyo mitr'āri-pakṣayoḥ /
sarv'ārambha-parityāgī
guṇ'ātītaḥ sa ucyate // 25 //

Who is alike in honour and in humiliation; who views a friend and a foe alike; who has abandoned all sense of agency—such a person is said to have transcended the Guṇas.

मां च योऽव्यभिचारेण भक्तियोगेन सेवते ।
स गुणान्समतीत्यैतान् ब्रह्मभूयाय कल्पते ॥

Māṁ ca yo' vyabhicāreṇa
bhakti-yogena sevate /
sa guṇān samatīty'aitān
brahma-bhūyāya kalpate // 26 //

He who serves Me through the communion of unswerving and exclusive devotion, transcends the Guṇas and attains fitness to become Brahman.

ब्रह्मणो हि प्रतिष्ठाहममृतस्याव्ययस्य च ।
शाश्वतस्य च धर्मस्य सुखस्यैकान्तिकस्य च ।।

Brahmaṇo hi pratiṣṭhā'ham
amṛtasy'āvyayasya ca /
śāśvatasya ca dharmasya
sukhasy'aikāntikasya ca // 27 //

Indeed, I (Kṛṣṇa, the God of love and grace, or the Pratyagātman the true Inner Self), am the basic support of Brahman—of the incorruptible state of Mokṣa, of the Eternal Law and of unending Bliss.

15. All-Pervading Divine Person

'The eternal Aśvattha's roots are in the Most High, branches in the lower regions.' (1)

Chapter 15

All-Pervading Divine Person

श्रीभगवानुवाच —

ऊर्ध्वमूलमधःशाखमश्वत्थं प्राहुरव्ययम् ।
छन्दांसि यस्य पर्णानि यस्तं वेद स वेदवित् ।।

Śrī Bhagavān uvāca:
Ūrdhva-mūlam adhaḥ-śākham
aśvatthaṁ prāhur avyayam /
chandāṁsi yasya parṇāni
yas taṁ veda sa veda-vit // 1 //

The Blessed Lord said:
The scriptures speak of the eternal Aśvattha, the World Tree, whose roots are in the Most High, branches in the lower regions, and leaves in Vedic hymns. He who knows it, understands the Veda really.

अधश्चोर्ध्वं प्रसृतास्तस्य शाखा
गुणप्रवृद्धा विषयप्रवालाः ।
अधश्च मूलान्यनुसन्ततानि
कर्मानुबन्धीनि मनुष्यलोके ।।

Adhaś c'ordhvaṁ prasṛtās tasya śākhā
guṇa-pravṛddhā viṣaya-pravālāḥ /
adhaś ca mūlāny anusantatāni
karm'ānubandhīni
manuṣya-loke // 2 //

Nourished by the Guṇas and covered with the budding foliage of sense objects, its branches spread into regions high and low. Stretching forth on the ground below in the world of men, are its secondary roots, entangling man in the bondage of action.

न रूपमस्येह तथोपलभ्यते
नान्तो न चादिर्न च सम्प्रतिष्ठा ।
अश्वत्थमेनं सुविरूढमूल-
मसङ्गशस्त्रेण दृढेन छित्त्वा ।।

ततः पदं तत्परिमार्गितव्यं
यस्मिन् गता न निवर्तन्ति भूयः ।
तमेव चाद्यं पुरुषं प्रपद्ये
यतः प्रवृत्तिः प्रसृता पुराणी ।।

Na rūpam asy'eha tath'opalabhyate
n'ānto na c'ādir na ca sam-pratiṣṭhā /
aśvattham enaṁ suvirūḍha-mūlam
asaṅga-śastreṇa dṛḍhena chittvā /3/

Tataḥ padaṁ tat parimārgitavyaṁ
yasmin gatā na nivartanti bhūyaḥ /
tam eva c'ādyaṁ puruṣaṁ prapadye
yataḥ pravṛttiḥ prasṛtā purāṇī /4/

For one involved in worldly life, the form of the World-Tree is not visible, nor its origin, nor its end, nor its foundation. Cutting asunder the firmly rooted Aśvattha (World-Tree) with the powerful axe of non-attachment, and saying, "I seek refuge in that Primeval Person from whom this eternal cosmic activity has streamed forth", man should seek that Status, attaining to which there is no more return to this life of Saṁsāra.

निर्मानमोहा जितसङ्गदोषा
अध्यात्मनित्या विनिवृत्तकामाः ।
द्वन्द्वैर्विमुक्ताः सुखदुःखसञ्ज्ञै-
र्गच्छन्त्यमूढाः पदमव्ययं तत् ॥

Nirmāna-mohā-jita-saṅga-doṣā
adhyātma-nityā vinivṛtta-kāmāḥ /
dvandvair vimuktāḥ sukha-duḥkha-sañjñair
gacchanty amūḍhāḥ padam avyayaṁ tat // 5 //

They who are free from pride and delusion, who have no attachments, who are ever absorbed in spritual pursuits, who are free from all worldly desires, who are unaffected by the varying situations of pleasurable and painful nature—suchpersons, freed from ignorance, attain to the Eternal State.

न तद्भासयते सूर्यो न शशाङ्को न पावकः ।
यद्गत्वा न निवर्तन्ते तद्धाम परमं मम ॥

Na tad bhāsayate sūryo
na śaśāṅko na pāvakaḥ /
yad gatvā na nivartante
tad dhāma paramaṁ
mama // *6* //

That the sun does not illumine, nor the moon, nor the fire; (for it is the Light of Pure Consciousness). Having attained It, the Spirit does not return again to the life of Saṁsāra. Such is My Supreme Abode.

ममैवांशो जीवलोके जीवभूतः सनातनः ।
मनःषष्ठानीन्द्रियाणि प्रकृतिस्थानि कर्षति ।।

Mam'aiv'āṁśo jīva-loke
jīva-bhūtaḥ sanātanaḥ /
manaḥ-ṣaṣṭhānī'ndriyāṇi
prakṛti-sthāni karṣati // 7 //

A fragment of Myself, immortal in nature, having become the embodied spirit in the world of the living, attracts to Himself the mind and the five senses born of Prakṛti.

शरीरं यदवाप्नोति यच्चाप्युत्क्रामतीश्वरः ।
गृहीत्वैतानि संयाति वायुर्गन्धानिवाशयात् ॥

Śarīraṁ yad avāpnoti
yac c'āpy utkrāmat'īśvaraḥ /
gṛhītv'aitāni saṁyāti
vāyur gandhān iv'āśayāt // 8 //

When he gets a new body or abandons an old one, the Jīva, the lord of the body, moves, carrying them (the mind and the senses) with him, as the wind carries smells from their seats (in flowers and the like).

श्रोत्रं चक्षुः स्पर्शनं च रसनं घ्राणमेव च ।
अधिष्ठाय मनश्चायं विषयानुपसेवते ।।

Śrotraṁ cakṣuḥ sparśanaṁ ca
rasanaṁ ghrāṇam eva ca /
adhiṣṭhāya manaś c'āyaṁ
viṣayān upasevate // 9 //

In identification with the senses like hearing, sight, touch, taste and smell, this Jīva experiences their respective objects.

उत्क्रामन्तं स्थितं वापि भुञ्जानं वा गुणान्वितम् ।
विमूढा नानुपश्यन्ति पश्यन्ति ज्ञानचक्षुषः ।।

Utkrāmantaṁ sthitaṁ vā'pi
bhuñjānaṁ vā gun'ānvitam /
vimūḍhā n'ānupaśyanti
paśyanti jñāna-cakṣuṣaḥ // 10 //

The deluded do not recognise the Spirit (Jīva) when, in identification with the Guṇas, he tenates or leaves a body, or when he experiences objects through it; but those endowed with the eye of wisdom do.

यतन्तो योगिनश्चैनं पश्यन्त्यात्मन्यवस्थितम् ।
यतन्तोऽप्यकृतात्मानो नैनं पश्यन्त्यचेतसः ॥

Yatanto yoginaś c'ainaṁ
paśyanty ātmany avasthitam /
yatanto' py akṛt'ātmāno
n'ainaṁ paśyanty acetasaḥ // *11* //

The striving contemplatives perceive the Ātman within themselves, but not the impure and the unregenerate, though they be striving.

यदादित्यगतं तेजो जगद्भासयतेऽखिलम् ।
यच्चन्द्रमसि यच्चाग्नौ तत्तेजो विद्धि मामकम् ।।

Yad āditya-gataṁ tejo
jagad bhāsayate' khilam /
yac candramasi yac c'āgnau
tat tejo viddhi māmakam // 12 //

That light of the sun which illumines the whole universe, which is present in the moon and in fire likewise—know that splendour to be Mine.

गामाविश्य च भूतानि धारयाम्यहमोजसा ।
पुष्णामि चौषधीः सर्वाः सोमो भूत्वा रसात्मकः ॥

Gām āviśya ca bhūtāni
dhārayāmy aham ojasā /
puṣṇāmi c'auṣadhīḥ sarvāḥ
somo bhūtvā ras'ātmakaḥ // 13 //

Entering the earth by My spiritual energy, I sustain all beings residing in it. As the watery moon, I nourish all herbs.

अहं वैश्वानरो भूत्वा प्राणिनां देहमाश्रितः ।
प्राणापानसमायुक्तः पचाम्यन्नं चतुर्विधम् ।।

Ahaṁ vaiśvānaro bhūtvā
prāṇināṁ deham āśritaḥ /
prāṇ'āpāna-samāyuktaḥ
pacāmy annaṁ
catur-vidham // 14 //

Based in the body of living beings, I manifest as the digestive Fire, Vaiśvānara, and in combination with the vital energies known as Prāṇa and Apāna, digest the four kinds of food taken by them.

सर्वस्य चाहं हृदि सन्निविष्टो
मत्तः स्मृतिर्ज्ञानमपोहनं च ।
वेदैश्च सर्वैरहमेव वेद्यो
वेदान्तकृद्वेदविदेव चाहम् ।।

Sarvasya c'āhaṁ hṛdi sannivisto
mattah smṛtirjñānam apohanaṁ ca /
vedaiś ca sarvair aham eva vedyo
vedānta-kṛd veda-vid eva
c'āham // 15 //

I abide in the hearts of all. By My will both the dawn and effacement of memory (of past births) and of supersensuous knowledge take place. The original teacher of the Vedanta I am, as also the knower of all Vedas.

द्वाविमौ पुरुषौ लोके क्षरश्चाक्षर एव च ।
क्षरः सर्वाणि भूतानि कूटस्थोऽक्षर उच्यते ॥

Dvāv imau puruṣau loke
kṣaraś c'ākṣara eva ca /
kṣaraḥ sarvāṇi bhūtani
kūta-stho' kṣara ucyate // 16 //

It is well known that there are two types of Puruṣas (spirits or categories)—the Kṣara or the Perishable and Akṣara, the Imperishable. The Kṣara consists of all the Jīvas in embodiment who are subject to change, while the Akṣara consists of the collectivity of liberated Jīvas who remain aloof from changeful matter and are unaffected by it; (or in the alternative, the Creative Power Māyā-śakti, which is the source of all falsity and the cause of endless Saṁsāra).

उत्तमः पुरुषस्त्वन्यः परमात्मेत्युदाहृतः ।
यो लोकत्रयमाविश्य बिभर्त्यव्यय ईश्वरः ॥

Uttamaḥ puruṣas tu anyaḥ
param'ātm'ety udāhṛtaḥ /
yo loka-trayam āviśya
bibharty avyaya īśvaraḥ // 17 //

But there is yet another Puruṣa, known as the Supreme Being or the Puruṣottama, who is the highest of spirits, and who pervades all the three worlds and sustains them.

यस्मात्क्षरमतीतोऽहमक्षरादपि चोत्तमः ।
अतोऽस्मि लोके वेदे च प्रथितः पुरुषोत्तमः ।।

Yasmāt kṣaram atīto' ham
akṣarād api c'ottamaḥ /
ato' smi loke vede ca
prathitaḥ puruṣ'ottamaḥ // 18 //

As I transcend the Perishable and am also superior to the Imperishable, I am well-known as the Puruṣottama (the Supreme Being) in both the Vedic and secular literature.

यो मामेवमसम्मूढो जानाति पुरुषोत्तमम् ।
स सर्वविद्भजति मां सर्वभावेन भारत ॥

Yo mām evam asammūḍho
jānāti puruṣ'ottamam /
sa sarvavid bhajati māṁ
sarva bhāvena Bhārata // 19 //

He who knows Me in this way as the Puruṣottama, he understands the true nature of this Totality, and he loves and adores Me with his whole being.

इति गुह्यतमं शास्त्रमिदमुक्तं मयाऽनघ ।
एतद्बुद्ध्वा बुद्धिमान्स्यात्कृतकृत्यश्च भारत ।।

Iti guhyatamaṁ śāstram
idam uktaṁ mayā' nagha /
etad buddhvā buddhimān syāt
kṛta-kṛtyaś ca Bhārata // 20 //

O sinless one! This spiritual doctrine, the most profound of all in the sacred lore, has now been revealed by Me. A true understanding of it makes a man really wise and established in a sense of total fulfilment.

16. Divine and Demoniac Types

'In this world there are two types of creation, the divine and the demoniac.' (6)

Chapter 16

Divine and Demoniac Types

श्रीभगवानुवाच —

अभयं सत्त्वसंशुद्धिर्ज्ञानयोगव्यवस्थितिः ।
दानं दमश्च यज्ञश्च स्वाध्यायस्तप आर्जवम् ।।

Śrī Bhagavān uvāca:
Abhayaṁ sattva-saṁśuddhir
jñāna-yoga-vyavasthitiḥ /
dānaṁ damaś ca yajñas ca
svādhyāyas tapa ārjavam // 1 //

The Blessed Lord said:

Fearlessness, purity of heart, steadfastness in knowledge and devotion, benevolence, control of the senses, worship, study of scriptures, austerity, uprightness;

अहिंसा सत्यमक्रोधस्त्यागः शान्तिरपैशुनम् ।
दया भूतेष्वलोलुप्त्वं मार्दवं ह्रीरचापलम् ।।

Ahiṁsā satyam akrodhas
tyāgaḥ śāntir apaiśunam /
dayā bhūteṣu aloluptvaṁ
mārdavaṁ hṛīr acāpalam // 2 //

Non-violence, truthfulness, freedom from anger, renunciation, tranquillity, aversion to slander, compassion to living beings, freedom from sensuality, gentleness, modesty, steadfastness;

तेजः क्षमा धृतिः शौचमद्रोहो नातिमानिता ।
भवन्ति सम्पदं दैवीमभिजातस्य भारत ।।

Tejaḥ kṣamā dhṛtiḥ śaucam
adroho n'ātimānitā /
bhavanti sampadaṁ daivīm
abhijātasya Bhārata // 3 //

Vigour, patience, fortitude, harmlessness, freedom from vanity—all these, O scion of the Bharatas, are present in those born to a divine heritage.

दम्भो दर्पोऽभिमानश्च क्रोधः पारुष्यमेव च ।
अज्ञानं चाभिजातस्य पार्थ सम्पदमासुरीम् ॥

Dambho darpo' bhimānaś ca
krodhaḥ pāruṣyam eva ca /
ajñānaṁ c'ābhijātasya
Pārtha sampadam āsurīm // 4 //

O son of Pṛthā! Pretentiousness, arrogance, overweening pride, wrath, rudeness, as also insensitiveness to spiritual values—all these are found in those born to a demoniac heritage.

दैवी सम्पद्विमोक्षाय निबन्धायासुरी मता ।
मा शुचः सम्पदं दैवीमभिजातोऽसि पाण्डव ।।

Daivī sampad vimokṣāya
nibandhāy'āsurī matā /
mā śucaḥ sampadaṁ daivīm
abhijāto' si Pāṇḍava // 5 //

It is deemed that the divine heritage leads to liberation and the demoniac to bondage. Grieve not, O son of Pāṇḍu! You are born to a divine heritage.

द्वौ भूतसर्गौ लोकेऽस्मिन्दैव आसुर एव च ।
दैवो विस्तरशः प्रोक्त आसुरं पार्थ मे शृणु ।।

Dvau bhūta-sargau loke' smin
daiva āsura eva ca /
daivo vistaraśaḥ prokta
āsuraṁ Pārtha me śṛṇu // 6 //

In this world there are two types of creation, the divine and the demoniac. The divine heritage has already been described. Now hear from Me what constitutes the demoniac heritage, O son of Pṛthā.

प्रवृत्तिं च निवृत्तिं च जना न विदुरासुराः ।
न शौचं नापि चाचारो न सत्यं तेषु विद्यते ।।

Pravṛttiṁ ca nivṛttiṁ ca
janā na vidur āsurāḥ /
na śaucaṁ nā'pi c'ācāro
na satyaṁ teṣu vidyate // 7 //

Men of demoniac nature know not what should be done and what should be avoided. Neither purity, nor good conduct, nor truthfulness is found in them.

असत्यमप्रतिष्ठं ते जगदाहुरनीश्वरम् ।
अपरस्परसम्भूतं किमन्यत्कामहैतुकम् ॥

Asatyam apratiṣṭhaṁ te
jagad āhur anīśvaram /
aparaspara-sambhūtaṁ
kimanyat kāma-haitukam // 8 //

According to them nothing is ultimately real in this world. It is Godless and without any moral basis. Being born of sexual union, what else but lust can be said to be its cause?

एतां दृष्टिमवष्टभ्य नष्टात्मानोऽल्पबुद्धयः ।
प्रभवन्त्युग्रकर्माणः क्षयाय जगतोऽहिताः ॥

Etāṁ dṛṣṭim avaṣṭabhya
naṣṭ'ātmāno' lpa-buddhayaḥ /
prabhavanty ugra-karmāṇaḥ
kṣayāya jagato' hitāḥ // 9 //

Holding such views, these lost souls—these men of little understanding—given, as they are, to cruel deeds opposed to general well-being, appear as agents for the destruction of the world.

कामममाश्रित्य दुष्पूरं दम्भमानमदान्विताः ।
मोहाद्गृहीत्वाऽसद्ग्राहान्प्रवर्तन्तेऽशुचिव्रताः ॥

Kāmam āśritya duṣpūraṁ
dambha-māna-mad'ānvitāḥ /
mohād gṛhītvā' sad-grāhān
pravartant' śuci-vratāḥ // 10 //

Steeped i insatiable lust, motivated by ypocrisy, vanity, arrogance a avarice, given to corrupt an npure ways of life, they wo n pursuit of false values ent ined through delusion.

चिन्तामपरिमेयां च प्रलयान्तामुपाश्रिताः ।
कामोपभोगपरमा एतावदिति निश्चिताः ॥

Cintām aparimeyāṁ ca
pralay'āntām upāśritāḥ /
kām'opabhoga-paramā
etāvad iti niścitāḥ // 11 //

Obsessed w h numerous cares all thro h life, looking on sex indulg e as the highest aim, convi that there is no higher ose in life than this;

आशापाशशतैर्बद्धाः कामक्रोधपरायणाः ।
ईहन्ते कामभोगार्थमन्यायेनार्थसञ्चयान् ॥

Āśā-pāśa-śatair baddhāḥ
kāma-krodha-parāyaṇāḥ /
īhante kāma-bhog'ārtham
anyāyen'ārtha-sañcayān // 12 //

Bound with a hundred cords of hopes and expectations, and enslaved by lust and anger, they strive to accumulate wealth in improper ways for the fulfilment of their sensuous desires.

इदमद्य मया लब्धमिमं प्राप्स्ये मनोरथम् ।
इदमस्तीदमपि मे भविष्यति पुनर्धनम् ।।

Idam adya mayā labdham
imaṁ prāpsye manoratham /
idam ast'īdam api me
bhaviṣyati punar dhanam // 13 //

'Today I have gained this object, tomorrow I shall gain that object of desire too; I have this much wealth now, much more will be mine hereafter;

असौ मया हतः शत्रुर्हनिष्ये चापरानपि ।
ईश्वरोऽहमहं भोगी सिद्धोऽहं बलवान्सुखी ।।

Asau mayā hataḥ śatrur
haniṣye cā'parān api /
īśvaro' ham ahaṁ bhogī
siddho' haṁ balavān
sukhī // 14 //

'This enemy has been slain, the others too I will soon destroy; I am the master; everything is for my enjoyment; I am the successful man, the powerful man, the happy man;

आढ्योऽभिजनवानस्मि कोऽन्योऽस्ति सदृशो मया।
यक्ष्ये दास्यामि मोदिष्य इत्यज्ञानविमोहिताः।।

Āḍhyo' bhijanavān asmi
ko' nyo' sti sadṛśo mayā /
yakṣye dāsyāmi modiṣya
ity ajñāna-vimohitāḥ // *15* //

'I am wealthy and high-born; who is there like unto me? I will perform sacrifices, I will make charity, and I will rejoice'—deluded thus by ignorance;

अनेकचित्तविभ्रान्ता मोहजालसमावृताः ।
प्रसक्ताः कामभोगेषु पतन्ति नरकेऽशुचौ ।।

Aneka-citta-vibhrāntā
moha-jāla-samāvṛtāḥ /
prasaktāḥ kāma-bhogeṣu
patanti narake' śucau // *16* //

Gripped by numerous bewildering thoughts, entangled in the meshes of delusion, and ever given to sex indulgences, they are degraded into states that are loathsome and full of suffering.

आत्मसम्भाविताः स्तब्धा धनमानमदान्विताः ।
यजन्ते नामयज्ञैस्ते दम्भेनाविधिपूर्वकम् ।।

Ātma-sambhāvitāḥ stabdhā-
dhana-māna-mad'ānvitāḥ /
yajante nāma-yajñais te
dambhen'āvidhipūrvakam // 17 //

Vain-glorious, stubborn and intoxicated with the pride of wealth, they perform for mere show Yajñas that are so in name only, being done without the observance of the commandments of the scriptures.

अहङ्कारं बलं दर्पं कामं क्रोधं च संश्रिताः ।
मामात्मपरदेहेषु प्रद्विषन्तोऽभ्यसूयकाः ॥

Ahaṅkāraṁ balaṁ darpaṁ
kāmaṁ krodhaṁ ca saṁśritāḥ /
mām ātma-para-deheṣu
pradviṣanto' bhyasūyakāḥ // 18 //

Dominated by self-conceit, prone to the use of force, arrogant, lustful and choleric, these traducers of virtue violate Me, dwelling in them and also in others.

तानहं द्विषतः क्रूरान्संसारेषु नराधमान् ।
क्षिपाम्यजस्रमशुभानासुरीष्वेव योनिषु ।।

Tān ahaṁ dviṣataḥ krūrān
saṁsāreṣu nar'ādhamān /
kṣipāmy ajasram aśubhān
āsurīṣveva yoniṣu // 19 //

These vicious men, oppressive cruel and sinful as they are,—are always hurled down by Me into demoniac wombs in life after life in the transmigratory cycle.

आसुरीं योनिमापन्ना मूढा जन्मनि जन्मनि ।
मामप्राप्यैव कौन्तेय ततो यान्त्यधमां गतिम् ।।

Āsurīṁ yonim āpannā
mūḍhā janmani janmani /
mām aprāpy'aiva Kaunteya
tato vānty adhamāṁ
gatim // 20 //

O son of Kuntī! Falling into demoniac wombs, in life after life, they go to still lower states of degradation, without attaining Me.

त्रिविधं नरकस्येदं द्वारं नाशनमात्मनः ।
कामः क्रोधस्तथा लोभस्तस्मादेतत्त्रयं त्यजेत् ॥

Tri-vidhaṁ narakasy'edaṁ
dvāraṁ nāśanam ātmanaḥ /
kāmaḥ krodhas-tathā lobhas
tasmād etat trayaṁ tyajet // 21 //

Lust, anger and greed—this triad leads to the destruction of man's spiritual nature. They form the gateway to hell; they should be abandoned.

एतैर्विमुक्तः कौन्तेय तमोद्वारैस्त्रिभिर्नरः ।
आचरत्यात्मनः श्रेयस्ततो याति परां गतिम् ।।

Etair vimuktaḥ Kaunteya
tamo-dvārais tribhir naraḥ /
ācaraty ātmanaḥ śreyas
tato yāti paraṁ gatim // 22 //

If a man is free from these three, the gateways to hell, he can work out his own good and reach the highest goal.

यः शास्त्रविधिमुत्सृज्य वर्तते कामकारतः ।
न स सिद्धिमवाप्नोति न सुखं न परां गतिम् ।।

Yaḥ śāstra-vidhim utsṛjya
vartate kāma-kārataḥ /
na sa siddhim avāpnoti
na sukhaṁ na parāṁ
gatim // 23 //

He who abandons the commandments of the scriptures and lives as his desires prompt him, he attains neither spiritual perfection, nor worldly happiness nor liberation.

तस्माच्छास्त्रं प्रमाणं ते कार्याकार्यव्यवस्थितौ ।
ज्ञात्वा शास्त्रविधानोक्तं कर्म कर्तुमिहार्हसि ।।

Tasmāc chāstraṁ pramāṇaṁ te
kāry'ākārya-vyavasthitau /
jñātvā śāstra-vidhān'oktaṁ
karma kartum ihā'rhasi // 24 //

Therefore let the scriptures be yout norm in determining what should be done and what not. Understand the injunction of the scriptures first and then set yourself to work.

17. Three Aspects of Faith

'The Faith of everyone is according to his natural disposition.' (3)

Chapter 17

Three Aspects of Faith

अर्जुन उवाच —

ये शास्त्रविधिमुत्सृज्य यजन्ते श्रद्धयान्विताः ।
तेषां निष्ठा तु का कृष्ण सत्त्वमाहो रजस्तमः ॥

Arjuna uvāca:
Ye śāstra-vidhim utsṛjya
yajante śraddhayā'nvitāḥ /
teṣāṁ niṣṭhā tu kā Kṛṣṇa
sattvam āho rajas tamaḥ // 1 //

Arjuna said:

There are persons who offer worship full of Faith, but without observing scriptural injunctions while doing so -of what nature is their Faith? Is it born of Sattva, Rajas or Tamas?

श्रीभगवानुवाच —
त्रिविधा भवति श्रद्धा देहिनां सा स्वभावजा ।
सात्त्विकी राजसी चैव तामसी चेति तां शृणु ।।

Śrī Bhagavān uvāca:
Tri-vidhā bhavati śraddhā
dehināṁ sā svabhāva-jā /
sāttvikī rājasī c'aiva
tāmasī c'eti tāṁ ṣṛṇu // 2 //

The Blessed Lord said:

The Faith of embodied beings, which is rooted in their natural disposition (derived from the impressions of past births), is of three kinds—those of the nature of Sattva, of Rajas and of Tamas.

सत्त्वानुरूपा सर्वस्य श्रद्धा भवति भारत ।
श्रद्धामयोऽयं पुरुषो यो यच्छ्रद्धः स एव सः ॥

Sattv'ānurūpā sarvasya
śraddhā bhavati Bhārata /
śraddhāmayo' yaṁ puruṣo
yo yac-chraddaḥ sa eva saḥ // 3 //

O scion of the Bharata race! The Faith of everyone is according to his natural disposition (derived from past impressions). Man is constituted of his Faith. What his Faith is that verily he is.

यजन्ते सात्त्विका देवान्यक्षरक्षांसि राजसाः ।
प्रेतान्भूतगणांश्चान्ये यजन्ते तामसा जनाः ।।

Yajante sāttvikā devān
yakṣa-rakṣāṁsi rājasāḥ /
pretān bhūta-gaṇāṁś c'ānye
yajante tāmasā janāḥ // 4 //

Those endowed with the quality of Sattva worship the Devas; those with Rajas, the Yakṣas and the Rākṣasas; and those with Tamas, the spirits of dead ancestors and the elementals.

अशास्त्रविहितं घोरं तप्यन्ते ये तपो जनाः ।
दम्भाहङ्कारसंयुक्ताः कामरागबलान्विताः ।।

कर्शयन्तः शरीरस्थं भूतग्राममचेतसः ।
मां चैवान्तःशरीरस्थं तान्विद्ध्यासुरनिश्चयान् ।।

Aśāstra-vihitaṁ ghoraṁ
tapyante ye tapo janāḥ /
dambh'āhaṅkāra-saṁyuktāḥ
kāma-rāga-balānvitāḥ // 5 //

karṣayantaḥ śarīra-sthaṁ
bhūta-grāmam acetasaḥ /
māṁ c'aivā'ntaḥ-śarīra-sthaṁ
tān viddhy āsura-niścayān // 6 //

Vain, conceited and moved by powerful passions and attachments, they perform various terrible mortifications contrary to scriptural injunctions. Thus do these senseless men torture their own bodies and Me dwelling in them. Know such persons to be of demoniac resolve.

आहारस्त्वपि सर्वस्य त्रिविधो भवति प्रियः ।
यज्ञस्तपस्तथा दानं तेषां भेदमिमं शृणु ।।

Āhāras as ty api sarvasya
tri-vidho bhavati priyaḥ /
yajñas-tapas-tathā dānaṁ
teṣām bhedaṁ imaṁ ṣṛṇu // 7 //

Even the food dear to these three types is of three different kinds. The same is the case with worship, austerity and charity. Hear from Me about this distinction regarding them.

आयुःसत्त्वबलारोग्यसुखप्रीतिविवर्धनाः।
रस्याः स्निग्धाः स्थिरा हृद्या आहाराः सात्त्विकप्रियाः॥

Āyuḥ-sattva-bal'ārogya
sukha-prīti-vivardhanāḥ /
rasyāḥ snigdhāḥ sthirā hṛdyā
āhārāḥ sāttvika-priyāḥ // 8 //

Persons who are Sattvika by nature like foods that promote longevity, vitality, energy, health, happiness and cheerfulness, as also those that are juicy, soft, nourishing and agreeable.

कट्वम्ललवणात्युष्णतीक्ष्णरूक्षविदाहिनः ।
आहारा राजसस्येष्टा दुःखशोकामयप्रदाः ।।

Kaṭv-amla-lavaṇ'ātyuṣṇa
tīkṣṇa-rūkṣa-vidāhinaḥ /
āhārā rājasasy'eṣṭā
duḥkha-śok'āmaya-
pradāḥ // 9 //

Persons who are Rajasa by nature like foods that are bitter, sour, salty, excessively heating, pungent, burning and thirst-producing as also what bring on uneasiness, depression and disease.

यातयामं गतरसं पूति पर्युषितं च यत् ।
उच्छिष्टमपि चामेध्यं भोजनं तामसप्रियम् ।।

Yātayāmaṁ gatarasaṁ
pūti paryuṣitaṁ ca yat /
ucchiṣṭam api cā'medhyaṁ
bhojanaṁ tāmasa-priyam // 10 //

Persons who are Tamasa by nature like foods that are stale, tasteless, putrid, decayed and unclean, and constitute the leavings of others.

अफलाकाङ्क्षिभिर्यज्ञो विधिदृष्टो य इज्यते ।
यष्टव्यमेवेति मनः समाधाय स सात्त्विकः ॥

Aphal'ākāṅkṣibhir yajño
vidhī-dṛṣṭo ya ijyate /
yaṣṭavyam ev'eti manaḥ
samādhāya sa sāttvikaḥ // 11 //

That worship is of the nature of Sattva which is in accordance with scriptural injunctions, and which is performed by one not with an eye for its fruits but merely out of the feeling that it is one's duty to perform it.

अभिसन्धाय तु फलं दम्भार्थमपि चैव यत् ।
इज्यते भरतश्रेष्ठ तं यज्ञं विद्धि राजसम् ।।

Abhisandhāya tu phalaṁ
daṁbh'ārtham api c'aiva yat /
ijyate bharata-śreṣṭha
taṁ yajñaṁ viddhi rājasam // 12 //

O scion of the Bharata race! Know that worship to be of the nature of Rajas, which is performed with its fruits in mind and for vain display.

विधिहीनमसृष्टान्नं मन्त्रहीनमदक्षिणम् ।
श्रद्धाविरहितं यज्ञं तामसं परिचक्षते ।।

Vidhihīnam asṛṣṭ'ānnaṁ
mantra-hīnam adakṣiṇam /
śraddhā-virahitaṁ yajñaṁ
tāmasaṁ paricakṣate // 13 //

That worship is of the nature of Tamas which is not sanctioned by scriptures, which is without gift of food, without the chanting of holy Mantras, without sacramental presents and without sincere faith.

देवद्विजगुरुप्राज्ञपूजनं शौचमार्जवम् ।
ब्रह्मचर्यमहिंसा च शारीरं तप उच्यते ।।

Deva-dvija-guru-prājña
pūjanaṁ śaucam ārjavam /
brahmacaryam ahiṁsā ca
śārīraṁ tapa ucyate // 14 //

Service of the Devas, holy men, teachers, parents and wise persons, as also observance of cleanliness, uprightness, continence and non-injury—these constitute austerities pertaining to the body.

अनुद्वेगकरं वाक्यं सत्यं प्रियहितं च यत् ।
स्वाध्यायाभ्यसनं चैव वाङ्मयं तप उच्यते ॥

Anudvega-karaṁ vākyaṁ
satyaṁ priya-hitaṁ ca yat /
svādhyāy'ābhyasanaṁ c'aiva
vāṅmayaṁ tapa ucyate // 15 //

Speaking only words that are inoffensive, true, pleasant and beneficial, as also regular recitation of scriptures, constitute austerity pertaining to speech.

मनःप्रसादः सौम्यत्वं मौनमात्मविनिग्रहः ।
भावसंशुद्धिरित्येतत्तपो मानसमुच्यते ।।

Manaḥ-prasādaḥ saumyatvaṁ
maunam ātma-vinigrahaḥ /
bhāva-saṁśuddhir ity-etat
tapo mānasam ucyate // 16 //

Serenity of mind, gentleness, moderation in speech, self-control, and purity of heart—these are called austerity of the mind.

श्रद्धया परया तप्तं तपस्तत्त्रिविधं नरैः ।
अफलाकाङ्क्षिभिर्युक्तैः सात्त्विकं परिचक्षते ॥

Śraddhayā parayā taptaṁ
tapas tat trividhaṁ naraiḥ /
aphal'ākāṅkṣibhir-yuktaiḥ
sātvikaṁ paricakṣate // 17 //

This threefold austerity, performed with the highest faith, by men who are not motivated by expectations of reward and who are established in mental equipoise, is declared to be of the nature of Sattva.

सत्कारमानपूजार्थं तपो दम्भेन चैव यत् ।
क्रियते तदिह प्रोक्तं राजसं चलमध्रुवम् ॥

Satkāra-māna-pūj'ārthaṁ
tapo dambhena c'aiva yat /
kriyate tad iha proktaṁ
rājasaṁ calam adhṛuvam // 18 //

The austerity that is performed with much show and ostentation, and having in view recognition, praise and adoration as a pious man by others, is said to be of the nature of Rajas. It is unstable and leads to no permanent good.

मूढग्राहेणात्मनो यत्पीडया क्रियते तपः ।
परस्योत्सादनार्थं वा तत्तामसमुदाहृतम् ।।

Mūḍha-grāheṇ'ātmano yat
pīḍayā kriyate tapaḥ /
parasyotsādan'ārtham vā
tat tāmasam udāhṛtam // 19 //

The austerity performed through the practice of self-torture under the influence of perverse theories or done for the destruction of another, is spoken of as Tamasa by nature.

दातव्यमिति यद्दानं दीयतेऽनुपकारिणे ।
देशे काले च पात्रे च तद्दानं सात्त्विकं स्मृतम् ॥

Dātavyam iti yad dānaṁ
dīyate' nupakāriṇe /
deśe kāle ca pātre ca
tad dānaṁ sāttvikaṁ
smṛtam // 20 //

That gift which is made out of a sheer sense of duty, without expectation of any kind of return, at the proper time and place, to a fit recipient, is said to be of the nature of Sattva.

यत्तु प्रत्युपकारार्थं फलमुद्दिश्य वा पुनः ।
दीयते च परिक्लिष्टं तद्दानं राजसं स्मृतम् ।।

Yat tu pratyupakār'ārthaṁ
phalam uddiśya vā punaḥ /
dīyate ca parikliṣṭaṁ
tad dānaṁ rājasaṁ
smṛtam // 21 //

The gift which is given in consideration of some gift in return, or with some fruit to be reaped in future, or in a grudging mood—that is considered to be of the nature of Rajas.

अदेशकाले यद्दानमपात्रेभ्यश्च दीयते ।
असत्कृतमवज्ञातं तत्तामसमुदाहृतम् ।।

Adeśa-kāle yad dānam
apātrebhyaś ca dīyate /
asatkṛtam avajñātaṁ
tat tāmasam udāhṛtam // 22 //

The gift that is made at an improper time and place, to an unworthy recipient, unceremoniously and in a slighting manner—that is said to be of the nature of Tamas.

ॐ तत्सदिति निर्देशो ब्रह्मणस्त्रिविधः स्मृतः ।
ब्राह्मणास्तेन वेदाश्च यज्ञाश्च विहिताः पुरा ॥

Om tat sad iti nirdeśo
brahmaṇas-tri-vidhaḥ smṛtaḥ /
brāhmaṇās tena vedāś ca
yajñāś ca vihitāḥ purā // 23 //

Om Tat Sat—these are the three symbolic designations of Brahman. By these were ordained the Brāhmaṇas, the Vedas and the Yajñas in ancient times.

तस्मादोमित्युदाहृत्य यज्ञदानतपःक्रियाः ।
प्रवर्तन्ते विधानोक्ताः सततं ब्रह्मवादिनाम् ।।

Tasmād om ity udāhṛtya
yajña-dāna-tapaḥ-kriyāḥ /
pravartante vidhān'oktāḥ
satataṁ brahma-
vādinām // 24 //

Therefore the followers of the Vedas always start their ordained works like sacrifice, gift, and austerities with the utterance of Om.

तदित्यनभिसन्धाय फलं यज्ञतपःक्रियाः ।
दानक्रियाश्च विविधाः क्रियन्ते मोक्षकाङ्क्षिभिः ।।

Tad ity anabhisandhāya
phalaṁ yajña-tapaḥ-kriyāḥ /
dāna-kriyāś ca vividhāḥ
kriyante mokṣa-
kāṅkṣibhiḥ // 25 //

Various forms of sacrifices, austerities and charities arc performed without any desire for the fruits by seekers after liberation, along with the utterancc of the syallable Tat (That).

सद्भावे साधुभावे च सदित्येतत्प्रयुज्यते ।
प्रशस्ते कर्मणि तथा सच्छब्दः पार्थ युज्यते ।।

Sad-bhāve sādhu-bhāve ca
sad ity etat prayujyate /
praśaste karmaṇi tathā
sac-chabdaḥ Pārtha
yujyate // 26 //

O son of Pṛthā! The syllable Sat is used in the sense of reality and goodness. It is also used to indicate an auspicious rite or act.

यज्ञे तपसि दाने च स्थितिः सदिति चोच्यते ।
कर्म चैव तदर्थीयं सदित्येवाभिधीयते ।।

Yajñe tapasi dāne ca
sthitiḥ sad iti c'ocyate /
karma c'aiva tad-arthīyaṁ
sad ity ev'ābhidhīyate // 27 //

Steadfastness in sacrifice (or worship), in austerity and in charity is called Sat (good). Any action connected with these is also called Sat.

अश्रद्धया हुतं दत्तं तपस्तप्तं कृतं च यत् ।
असदित्युच्यते पार्थ न च तत्प्रेत्य नो इह ॥

Aśraddhayā hutaṁ dattaṁ
tapas taptaṁ kṛtaṁ ca yat /
asad ity ucyate Pārtha
na ca tat pretya no iha // 28 //

O son of Pṛthā! Whatever is performed as a sacrifice, charity, or austerity without Faith—in fact anything done without Faith—is declared to be Asat (not good). It is of no significance here or in the hereafter.

18. Liberation Through Renunciation

'By worshipping Him through the dedicated performance of one's duty, man attains to spiritual competency (Siddhi).' (46)

Chapter 18

Liberation Through Renunciation

अर्जुन उवाच —

सन्न्यासस्य महाबाहो तत्त्वमिच्छामि वेदितुम् ।
त्यागस्य च हृषीकेश पृथक्केशिनिषूदन ॥

Arjuna uvāca:
Sannyāsasyā mahā-bāho
tattvam icchāmi veditum /
tyāgasya ca Hṛṣīkeśa
pṛthak Keśi-niṣūdana // 1 //

Arjuna said:

O mighty-armed One, famed as the destroyer of Keśin and the conqueror of the senses! I desire to know the true nature of Sannyāsa, and as distinguished from it, of Tyāga too.

श्रीभगवानुवाच —
काम्यानां कर्मणां न्यासं सन्न्यासं कवयो विदुः ।
सर्वकर्मफलत्यागं प्राहुस्त्यागं विचक्षणाः ॥

Śrī Bhagavān uvāca:
Kāmyānāṁ karmaṇāṁ nyāsaṁ
sannyāsaṁ kavayo viduḥ /
sarva-karma-phala-tyāgaṁ
prāhus tyāgaṁ vicakṣaṇāḥ // 2 //

The Blessed Lord said:

Abandonment of all desire-prompted actions is Sannyāsa (renunciation) according to the wise. Men of discernment speak of the abandonment of the fruits of all actions as Tyāga (relinquishment).

त्याज्यं दोषवदित्येके कर्म प्राहुर्मनीषिणः ।
यज्ञदानतपःकर्म न त्याज्यमिति चापरे ।।

Tyājyaṁ doṣavad ity eke
karma prāhur manīṣiṇaḥ /
yajña-dāna-tapaḥ-karma
na tyājyam iti c'āpare // 3 //

Some wise men say that all action is to be abandoned as evil. Others maintain that good works like worship, charity and practice of austerity are not to be abandoned.

निश्चयं शृणु मे तत्र त्यागे भरतसत्तम ।
त्यागो हि पुरुषव्याघ्र त्रिविधः सम्प्रकीर्तितः ।।

Niścayaṁ sṛṇu me tatra
tyāge Bharata-sattama /
tyago hi puruṣa-vyāghra
tri-vidhaḥ samprakīrtitaḥ // 4 //

O the best of the Bharata race! Hear my conclusive view on this subject of Tyāga (relinquishment). It is said that there are three types of Tyāga.

यज्ञदानतपःकर्म न त्याज्यं कार्यमेव तत् ।
यज्ञो दानं तपश्चैव पावनानि मनीषिणाम् ।।

Yajña-dāna-tapaḥ-karma
na tyājyaṁ kāryam eva tat /
yajño dānaṁ tapaś-c'aiva
pāvanāni manīṣiṇām // 5 //

Works like sacrifice, charity and austerity should not be abandoned. They should be performed; for sacrifice, charity and austerity are indeed purifying for the wise.

एतान्यपि तु कर्माणि सङ्गं त्यक्त्वा फलानि च ।
कर्तव्यानीति मे पार्थ निश्चितं मतमुत्तमम् ।।

Etāny api tu karmāṇi
saṅgaṁ tyaktvā phalāni ca /
kartavyānī'ti me Pārtha
niścitaṁ matam uttamam // 6 //

O Son of Pṛthā! Even these works are to be performed without attachment and desire for their fruits. This is My settled and decisivo view.

नियतस्य तु सन्न्यासः कर्मणो नोपपद्यते ।
मोहात्तस्य परित्यागस्तामसः परिकीर्तितः ।।

Niyatasya tu sannyāsaḥ
karmaṇo n'opapadyate /
mohāt tasya parityāgas
tāmasaḥ parikīrtitaḥ // 7 //

It is not at all proper to renounce works that ought to be done as duty. Their abandonment out of delusion is considered to be of the nature of Tamas.

दुःखमित्येव यत्कर्म कायक्लेशभयात्त्यजेत् ।
स कृत्वा राजसं त्यागं नैव त्यागफलं लभेत् ॥

Duḥkham ity eva yat karma
kāya-kleśa-bhayāt tyajet /
sa kṛtvā rājasaṁ tyāgaṁ
n'aiva tyāga-phalaṁ labhet // 8 //

Those who give up work out of a dread of physical suffering, out of a feeling that it is painful, they, performing relinquishment of a Rājasa nature, do not obtain the results of true relinquishment.

कार्यमित्येव यत्कर्म नियतं क्रियतेऽर्जुन ।
सङ्गं त्यक्त्वा फलं चैव स त्यागः सात्त्विको मतः ।।

Kāryam ity eva yat karma
niyataṁ kriyate' rjuna /
Saṅgaṁ tyaktvā phalaṁ c'aiva
sa tyāgaḥ sāttviko mataḥ // 9 //

But, O Arjuna! That relinquishment is considered as Sāttvika which consists in giving up attachment and thoughts of returns in respect of works, and which is done with the feeling that it is an obligatory duty that must necessarily be performed.

न द्वेष्ट्यकुशलं कर्म कुशले नानुषज्जते ।
त्यागी सत्त्वसमाविष्टो मेधावी छिन्नसंशयः ।।

Na dveṣṭy akuśalaṁ karma
kuśale n'ānuṣajjate /
tyāgī sattva-samāviṣṭo
medhāvī chinna-
saṁśayaḥ // 10 //

The relinquisher (Tyāgī), if he is endowed with the qualities of Sattva, wisdom and conviction in regard to the spiritual ideal, never avoids duties merely because they are unpleasant, nor does he get attached to works that seem pleasant to him.

न हि देहभृता शक्यं त्यक्तुं कर्माण्यशेषतः ।
यस्तु कर्मफलत्यागी स त्यागीत्यभिधीयते ।।

Na hi deha bhṛtā śakyaṁ
tyaktuṁ karmāṇy aśeṣataḥ /
yas tu karma-phala-tyāgī
sa tyagī'ty abdhidhīyate // 11 //

It is not indeed possible for any embodied being (i.e., one with body-consciousness) to abandon works in entirety. So all that one can do is to abandon the fruits of action. One doing so is called a Tyāgī (a relinquisher).

अनिष्टमिष्टं मिश्रं च त्रिविधं कर्मणः फलम् ।
भवत्यत्यागिनां प्रेत्य न तु सन्न्यासिनां क्वचित् ॥

Aniṣṭam iṣṭaṁ miśraṁ ca
tri-vidhaṁ karmaṇaḥ phalam /
bhavaty atyāgināṁ pretya
na tu sannyāsināṁ kvacit // 12 //

Regarding those who have not relinquished their desires *(atyāgīnām)*, they reap after death the fruits of their actions performed with desire. They are of three sorts—'unpleasant' like degradation into animal life or stay in purgatory for the very wicked; 'pleasant' like attainment of heavenly felicities for the virtuous; and 'mixed' as in human birth, for those who have Karmas of both these types to their credit. But Sannyāsins (true renouncers) will have none of these.

पञ्चैतानि महाबाहो कारणानि निबोध मे ।
साङ्ख्ये कृतान्ते प्रोक्तानि सिद्धये सर्वकर्मणाम् ॥

Pañc'aitāni mahā-bāho
kāraṇāni nibodha me /
sāṅkhye kṛtānte proktāni
siddhaye sarva-
karmaṇām // 13 //

Learn from me, O mighty armed! about the five causal factors required for all actions as described in the Sāṁkhya, the philosophy of spiritual illumination, which is the ultimate purpose of all actions.

अधिष्ठानं तथा कर्ता करणं च पृथग्विधम् ।
विविधाश्च पृथक्चेष्टा दैवं चैवात्र पञ्चमम् ।।

Adhiṣṭhānaṁ tathā kartā
karaṇaṁ ca pṛthag-vidham /
vividhāś ca pṛthak-ceṣṭā
daivaṁ c'aiv'ātra
pañcamam // 14 //

One's body which is the seat of action, the ego claiming to be the actor, the several instruments of actions (like the senses, the mind etc.), the varied and the distinct types of movements involved, and finally the unknown factor (or the deities presiding over the senses) as the fifth—these are the five causal factors.

शरीरवाङ्मनोभिर्यत्कर्म प्रारभते नरः ।
न्याय्यं वा विपरीतं वा पञ्चैते तस्य हेतवः ।।

Śarīra-vāṅ-manobhir yat
karma prārabhate naraḥ /
nyāyyaṁ vā viparītaṁ vā
pañc'aite tasya hetavaḥ // 15 //

These are the five causal factors involved in all actions, good as also bad, which men undertake with this body, speech and mind.

तत्रैवं सति कर्तारमात्मानं केवलं तु यः ।
पश्यत्यकृतबुद्धित्वान्न स पश्यति दुर्मतिः ।।

Tatr'aivaṁ sad kartāram
ātmānaṁ kevalaṁ tu yaḥ /
paśyaty akṛta-buddhitvān
na sa paśyati durmatiḥ // 16 //

That being so, he whose imperfect understanding makes him think that the self alone (or the unlimited and unrelated Ātman) is the agent involved in work—he verily sees not, being perverted in outlook.

यस्य नाहङ्कृतो भावो बुद्धिर्यस्य न लिप्यते ।
हत्वापि स इमाँल्लोकान्न हन्ति न निबध्यते ।।

Yasya n'āhaṅkṛto bhāvo
buddhir yasya na lipyate /
hattvā'pi sa imāṁl lokān
na hanti na nibadhyate // 17 //

He who is ever established in the feeling 'I am not the agent' and whose mind is consequently unsullied by attachments—he kills not really, nor is he bound, even though he annihilates all these beings.

ज्ञानं ज्ञेयं परिज्ञाता त्रिविधा कर्मचोदना ।
करणं कर्म कर्तेति त्रिविधः कर्मसङ्ग्रहः ॥

Jñānaṁ jñeyaṁ parijñātā
tri-vidhā karma-codanā /
karaṇaṁ karma kart'eti
tri-vidhaḥ karma-
saṅgrahaḥ // 18 //

Knowledge, object of knowledge, and knower—these constitute the threefold incitement to action. And the three constituents of action are the instruments of action, the purpose of action, and the agent.

ज्ञानं कर्म च कर्ता च त्रिधैव गुणभेदतः ।
प्रोच्यते गुणसङ्ख्याने यथावच्छृणु तान्यपि ।।

Jñānaṁ karma ca kartā ca
tridh'aiva guṇa-bhedataḥ /
procyate guṇa-saṅkhyāne
yathāvac chṛṇu tāny-api // 19 //

In the philosophy dealing with the Guṇas and their evolutes, knowledge, action and agent are each divided into three according to the preponderance of each Guṇa in them. Hear of them also as they are.

सर्वभूतेषु येनैकं भावमव्ययमीक्षते ।
अविभक्तं विभक्तेषु तज्ज्ञानं विद्धि सात्त्विकम् ॥

Sarva-bhūteṣu yen'aikaṁ
bhāvam avyayam īkṣate /
avibhaktaṁ vibhakteṣu
taj jñānaṁ viddhi
sāttvikam // 20 //

That knowledge by which one is able to see a unitary unmodifiable Essence, undivided among the divided,—know that knowledge to be of the nature of Sattva.

पृथक्त्वेन तु यज्ज्ञानं नानाभावान्पृथग्विधान् ।
वेत्ति सर्वेषु भूतेषु तज्ज्ञानं विद्धि राजसम् ।।

Pṛthaktvena tu yaj jñānaṁ
nānā-bhāvān pṛthag-vidhān /
vetti sarveṣu bhuteṣu
taj jñānaṁ viddhi
rājasam // *21* //

That knowledge which apprehends all beings as a multiplicity with mutual distinction and in their separateness only, without any apprehension of an underlying unity—know that knowledge to be born of Rajas.

यत्तु कृत्स्नवदेकस्मिन्कार्ये सक्तमहैतुकम् ।
अतत्त्वार्थवदल्पं च तत्तामसमुदाहृतम् ॥

Yat tu kṛtsnavad ekasmin
kārye saktam ahaitukam /
atattv'ārthavad alpaṁ ca
tat tāmasam udāhṛtam // 22 //

That by which one dogmatically holds on to a part as if it were the whole (or looks on the body, an effect, as the whole man)—a view which is irrational, untrue and silly—that knowledge is said to be born of Tamas.

नियतं सङ्गरहितमरागद्वेषतः कृतम् ।
अफलप्रेप्सुना कर्म यत्तत्सात्त्विकमुच्यते ।।

Niyataṁ saṅga-rahitam
arāga-dveṣataḥ kṛtam /
aphala-prepsunā karma
yat tat sāttvikam ucyate // 23 //

Work of the nature of duty done by one without hankering for fruits, and without attachment, or passion or hate—such work is spoken of as born of Sattva.

यत्तु कामेप्सुना कर्म साहङ्कारेण वा पुनः ।
क्रियते बहुलायासं तद्राजसमुदाहृतम् ।।

Yat tu kām'epsunā karma
s'āhaṅkāreṇa vā punaḥ /
kriyate bahul'āyāsaṁ
tad rājasam udāhṛtam // 24 //

But work that is done by a person merely for the gratification of his desire, and with great strain and a feeling of self-importance is said to be born of Rajas.

अनुबन्धं क्षयं हिंसामनवेक्ष्य च पौरुषम् ।
मोहादारभ्यते कर्म यत्तत्तामसमुच्यते ।।

Anubandhaṁ kṣayaṁ hiṁsām
anapekṣya ca pauruṣam /
mohād ārabhyate karma
yat tat tāmasam ucyate // 25 //

And that work which is performed under delusion, without any regard to consequences, loss, injury to others, and to one's own capacity—is said to be born of Tamas.

मुक्तसङ्गोऽनहंवादी धृत्युत्साहसमन्वितः ।
सिद्ध्यसिद्ध्योर्निर्विकारः कर्ता सात्त्विक उच्यते ॥

Mukta-saṅgo' nahaṁ-vādī
dhṛty-utsāha samanvitaḥ /
siddhy-asiddhyor nirvikāraḥ
kartā sāttvika ucyate // 26 //

A 'doer' (an agent of an action) who is without any attachment and sense of pride and self-importance, who is endowed with steadiness and zeal, and who is unruffled in success and failure—such a doer is said to be of the nature of Sattva.

रागी कर्मफलप्रेप्सुर्लुब्धो हिंसात्मकोऽशुचिः ।
हर्षशोकान्वितः कर्ता राजसः परिकीर्तितः ।।

Rāgī karma-phala-prepsur
lubdho hiṁs'ātmako' śuciḥ /
harṣa-śok'ānvitaḥ kartā
rājasaḥ parikīrtitaḥ // 27 //

A 'doer' who is swayed by passion, who is keen on the fruits of his actions, who is covetous, cruel and impure at heart, and who is subject to elation and depression in success and failure—such a doer is said to be of the nature of Rajas.

अयुक्तः प्राकृतः स्तब्धः शठो नैष्कृतिकोऽलसः ।
विषादी दीर्घसूत्री च कर्ता तामस उच्यते ॥

Ayuktaḥ prākṛtaḥ stabdhaḥ
śaṭho naikṛtiko' lasaḥ /
viṣādī dīrgha-sūtrī ca
kartā tāmasa ucyate // 28 //

And a 'doer' who is unsteady, vulgar, arrogant, deceitful, malicious, indolent, despondent and procrastinating—such a doer is said to be of the nature of Tamas.

बुद्धेर्भेदं धृतेश्चैव गुणतस्त्रिविधं शृणु ।
प्रोच्यमानमशेषेण पृथक्त्वेन धनञ्जय ॥

Buddher bhedaṁ dhṛteś'caiva
guṇatas tri-vidhaṁ śṛṇu /
procyamānam aśeṣeṇa
pṛthaktvena Dhanañjaya // 29 //

Hear now, O Arjuna, of the threefold division of the intellect and of the power of determination on the basis of their constituent Guṇas—hear of them severally and in their totality.

प्रवृत्तिं च निवृत्तिं च कार्याकार्ये भयाभये ।
बन्धं मोक्षं च या वेत्ति बुद्धिः सा पार्थ सात्त्विकी ।।

Pravṛttiṁ ca nivṛttiṁ ca
kāry'ākārye bhay'ābhaye /
bandhaṁ mokṣaṁ ca yā vetti
buddhiḥ sā Pārtha
sāttvikī // 30 //

O son of Pṛthā! That intellect is said to be of the nature of Sattva which grasps the distinction between worldliness and renunciation, between the moral and the immoral, between what should be feared and what should not be, and between knowledge and freedom.

यया धर्ममधर्मं च कार्यं चाकार्यमेव च ।
अयथावत्प्रजानाति बुद्धिः सा पार्थ राजसी ॥

Yayā dharmam adharmaṁ ca
kāryaṁ c'ākāryam eva ca
ayathāvat prajānāti
buddhiḥ sā Pārtha rājasī // 31 //

O son of Pṛthā! That intellect is said to be of the nature of Rajas, which takes a distorted and confused view of the moral and the immoral, of what should be done and what should not be.

अधर्मं धर्ममिति या मन्यते तमसावृता ।
सर्वार्थान्विपरीतांश्च बुद्धिः सा पार्थ तामसी ॥

Adharmaṁ dharmam iti yā
manyate tamasā'vṛtā /
sarv'ārthān viparītāṁś ca
buddhiḥ sā Pārtha
tāmasī // 32 //

O son of Pṛthā! That intellect is of the nature of Tamas, which, covered by the darkness of ignorance, understands the immoral as the moral and thus reverses all values.

धृत्या यया धारयते मनःप्राणेन्द्रियक्रियाः ।
योगेनाव्यभिचारिण्या धृतिः सा पार्थ सात्त्विकी ।।

Dhṛtyā yayā dhārayate
manaḥ-prāṇ'endriya-kriyāḥ /
yogen'āvyabhicāriṇyā
dhṛtiḥ sā Pārtha sāttvikī // 33 //

O Son of Pṛthā! That power of determination is of the nature of Sattva, by which the mind, the vital energy and the senses are held in control through unswerving concentration.

यया तु धर्मकामार्थान्धृत्या धारयतेऽर्जुन ।
प्रसङ्गेन फलाकाङ्क्षी धृतिः सा पार्थ राजसी ॥

Yayā tu dharma-kām'ārthān
dhṛtyā dhārayate' rjuna /
prasaṅgena phal'ākāṅkṣī
dhṛtiḥ sā Pārtha rājasī // 34 //

That power of determination is of the nature of Rajas, by which one holds on to duty, pleasure and wealth with passionate attachment, motivated by the desire for their fruits.

यया स्वप्नं भयं शोकं विषादं मदमेव च ।
न विमुञ्चति दुर्मेधा धृतिः सा पार्थ तामसी ।।

Yayā svapnaṁ bhayaṁ śokaṁ
viṣādaṁ madam eva ca /
na vimuñcati durmedhā
dhṛtiḥ sā Pārtha tāmasī // 35 //

That power of determination is of the nature of Tamas, due to which one of perverted intelligence does not give up sloth, fear, grief, despondency and frenzy of sense indulgences.

सुखं त्विदानीं त्रिविधं शृणु मे भरतर्षभ ।
अभ्यासाद्रमते यत्र दुःखान्तं च निगच्छति ।।

यत्तदग्रे विषमिव परिणामेऽमृतोपमम् ।
तत्सुखं सात्त्विकं प्रोक्तमात्मबुद्धिप्रसादजम् ।।

Sukhaṁ tu idānīṁ tri-vidhaṁ
śṛṇu me Bharata'rṣabha /
abhyāsād ramate yatra
duḥkh'āntaṁ ca nigacchati // 36 //

Yat tad agre viṣam iva
pariṇāme' mṛt'opamam /
tat sukhaṁ sāttvikaṁ proktam
ātma-buddhi-prasāda-jam // 37 //

Hear from Me now about the three kinds of pleasures, O the greatest of the Bharata clan! That pleasure is said to be of the nature of Sattva which is gained by long practice of disciplines, which puts an end to all sorrows that man is heir to, which is like poison in the beginning but nectar-like at the end, and which springs from the serenity arising from the consciousness of the Ātman.

विषयेन्द्रियसंयोगाद्यत्तदग्रेऽमृतोपमम् ।
परिणामे विषमिव तत्सुखं राजसं स्मृतम् ॥

Viṣay'endriya-saṁyogād
yat tad agre' mṛt'opamam /
pariṇāme viṣam iva
tat sukhaṁ rājasaṁ
smṛtam // 38 //

That pleasure is declared to be of the nature of Rajas, which is born of the union of the senses with their objects, which seems nectar-like in the beginning but turns to be poison in the end.

यदग्रे चानुबन्धे च सुखं मोहनमात्मनः ।
निद्रालस्यप्रमादोत्थं तत्तामसमुदाहृतम् ।।

Yad agre c'ānubandhe ca
sukhaṁ mohanam ātmanaḥ /
nidr'ālasya-pramād'otthaṁ
tat tāmasam udāhṛtam // 39 //

That pleasure is of the nature of Tamas, which springs from sleepiness, sloth and heedlessness, and which is delusive in its effect on the spirit from beginning to end.

न तदस्ति पृथिव्यां वा दिवि देवेषु वा पुनः ।
सत्त्वं प्रकृतिजैर्मुक्तं यदेभिः स्यात्त्रिभिर्गुणैः ।।

Na tad asti pṛthivyāṁ vā
divi deveṣu vā punaḥ /
sattvaṁ prakṛtijair muktaṁ
yad ebhiḥ syāt tribhir
guṇaiḥ // 40 //

Nowhere, be it in this world or in the heavenly regions of the Devas, is there any being who is free from these three Guṇas of Nature (Prakṛti).

ब्राह्मणक्षत्रियविशां शूद्राणां च परन्तप ।
कर्माणि प्रविभक्तानि स्वभावप्रभवैर्गुणैः ।।

Brāhmaṇa-kṣatriya-viśāṁ
śūdrāṇāṁ ca parantapa /
karmāṇi pravibhaktāni
svabhāva-prabhavair
guṇaiḥ // 41 //

O great hero! The duties of Brāhmaṇas, Kṣatriyas, Vaiśyas and also of Sūdras have been divided according to the qualities born of their own nature.

शमो दमस्तपः शौचं क्षान्तिरार्जवमेव च ।
ज्ञानं विज्ञानमास्तिक्यं ब्रह्मकर्म स्वभावजम् ।।

Śamo damas tapaḥ śaucaṁ
kṣāntir ārjavam eva ca /
jñānaṁ vijñānam āstikyaṁ
brahma-karma svabhāva-
jam // 42 //

Serenity, control of the senses, austerity, purity, straightforwardness, knowledge, insight, and faith in the Supreme Being—these are a Brāhmaṇa's duties born of his own nature.

शौर्यं तेजो धृतिर्दाक्ष्यं युद्धे चाप्यपलायनम् ।
दानमीश्वरभावश्च क्षात्रं कर्म स्वभावजम् ।।

Śauryaṁ tejo dhṛtir dākṣyaṁ
yuddhe c'āpy apalāyanam /
dānam īsvara-bhāvaś ca
kṣātraṁ karma svabhāva-
jam // 43 //

Prowess, splendour of personality, infailing courage, resourcefulness, dauntlessness in battle, generosity, leadership—these are a Kṣatriya's duties born of his own nature.

कृषिगौरक्ष्यवाणिज्यं वैश्यकर्म स्वभावजम् ।
परिचर्यात्मकं कर्म शूद्रस्यापि स्वभावजम् ॥

Kṛṣi-gaurakṣya-vāṇijyam
vaiśya-karma svabhāva-jam /
paricary'ātmakaṁ karma
śūdrasy'āpi svabhāva-jam // 44 //

Agriculture, cattle-rearing and trade form the duty of the Vaiśya springing from his own nature, while the natural duty of a Śūdra consists in subordinate service under others.

स्वे स्वे कर्मण्यभिरतः संसिद्धिं लभते नरः ।
स्वकर्मनिरतः सिद्धिं यथा विन्दति तच्छृणु ।।

Sve sve karmaṇy abhirataḥ
saṁsiddhiṁ labhate naraḥ /
sva-karma-nirataḥ siddhiṁ
yathā vindati tacchṛṇu // 45 //

By being devoted to one's own natural duty, man attains to spiritual competency. Now hear how devotion to one's own natural duty generates spiritual competency.

यतः प्रवृत्तिर्भूतानां येन सर्वमिदं ततम् ।
स्वकर्मणा तमभ्यर्च्य सिद्धिं विन्दति मानवः ॥

Yataḥ pravṛttir bhūtānāṁ
yena sarvam idaṁ tatam /
sva-karmaṇā tam abhyarcya
siddhiṁ vindati mānavaḥ // 46 //

From whom all beings have emanated and by whom all this universe is pervaded—by worshipping Him through the dedicated performance of one's duty, man attains to spiritual competency (Siddhi).

श्रेयान्स्वधर्मो विगुणः परधर्मात्स्वनुष्ठितात् ।
स्वभावनियतं कर्म कुर्वन्नाप्नोति किल्बिषम् ॥

Śreyān sva-dharmo viguṇaḥ
para-dharmāt svanuṣṭhitāt /
svabhāva-niyataṁ karma
kurvan n'āpnoti kilbiṣam // 47 //

One's own duty, even if without excellence (i.e. inferior) in the scale of worldly values, is more meritorious spiritually than the apparently well-performed duty of another. For, no sin is incurred by one doing works ordained according to one's nature (that is, in consonance with one's own natural evolution).

सहजं कर्म कौन्तेय सदोषमपि न त्यजेत् ।
सर्वारम्भा हि दोषेण धूमेनाग्निरिवावृताः ।।

Sahajaṁ karma Kaunteya
sadoṣam api na tyajet /
sarv'ārambhā hi doṣeṇa
dhumen'āgnir iv'āvṛtāḥ // 48 //

O son of Kuntī! Do not abandon the duty that is natural to you, even if some imperfections are incidental to it. For there is no undertaking without some imperfections, even as there is no fire without a covering of smoke.

असक्तबुद्धिः सर्वत्र जितात्मा विगतस्पृहः ।
नैष्कर्म्यसिद्धिं परमां सन्न्यासेनाधिगच्छति ॥

Asakta-buddhiḥ sarvatra
jit'ātmā vigata-spṛhaḥ /
naiṣkarmya siddhiṁ paramāṁ
sannyāsen'ādhigacchati // 49 //

Completely non-attached, self-subdued, and desireless, an aspirant attains the supreme perfection of transcendence of work through renunciation.

सिद्धिं प्राप्तो यथा ब्रह्म तथाप्नोति निबोध मे ।
समासेनैव कौन्तेय निष्ठा ज्ञानस्य या परा ॥

Siddhiṁ prāpto yathā Brahma
tath'āpnoti nibodha me /
samāsen'aiva Kaunteya
niṣṭhā jñānasya yā parā // 50 //

Now hear from Me in brief how one, who is established in the perfection of transcendence of work, attains to Brahman, the highest consummation of knowledge.

बुद्ध्या विशुद्धया युक्तो धृत्यात्मानं नियम्य च ।
शब्दादीन्विषयांस्त्यक्त्वा रागद्वेषौ व्युदस्य च ।।
विविक्तसेवी लघ्वाशी यतवाक्कायमानसः ।
ध्यानयोगपरो नित्यं वैराग्यं समुपाश्रितः ।।
अहङ्कारं बलं दर्पं कामं क्रोधं परिग्रहम् ।
विमुच्य निर्ममः शान्तो ब्रह्मभूयाय कल्पते ।।

Buddhyā viśuddhayā yukto
dhṛtyā'tmānaṁ niyamya ca /
sabdādīn viṣayāṁs tyaktvā
rāga-dveṣau vyudasya ca // 51 //
Vivikta-sevī laghvāśī
yata-vāk-kāya-mānasaḥ /
dhyāna-yoga-paro nityaṁ
vairāgyaṁ samupāśritaḥ // 52 //
Ahaṅkāraṁ balaṁ darpaṁ
kāmaṁ krodhaṁ parigraham /

चेतसा सर्वकर्माणि मयि सन्न्यस्य मत्परः ।
बुद्धियोगमुपाश्रित्य मच्चित्तः सततं भव ॥

Cetasā sarva-karmāṇi
mayi sannyasya mat-paraḥ /
buddhi-yogam upāśritya
mac-cittaḥ satataṁ bhava // 57 //

Mentally resigning all actions to Me (in respect of their fruits and agency), devoting yourself intensely to Me, and ever practising the communion of intellectual love, be you ever established in the thought of Me.

मच्चित्तः सर्वदुर्गाणि मत्प्रसादात्तरिष्यसि ।
अथ चेत्त्वमहङ्कारान्न श्रोष्यसि विनङ्क्ष्यसि ॥

Mac-cittaḥ sarva-durgāṇi
mat-prasādāt tariṣyasi /
atha cet tvam ahaṅkārān
na śroṣyasi vinaṅkṣyasi // 58 //

If you are thus ever in communion with Me in mind, you will overcome every obstacle. But if, out of self-conceit, you do not listen to Me, destruction will be your fate.

यदहङ्कारमाश्रित्य न योत्स्य इति मन्यसे ।
मिथ्यैष व्यवसायस्ते प्रकृतिस्त्वां नियोक्ष्यति ॥

Yad ahaṅkāram āśritya
na yotsya iti manyase /
mithy'aiṣa vyavasāyas te
prakṛtis tvāṁ niyokṣyati // 59 //

Vain is your resolve not to fight, born as it is of self-conceit. Nature will compel you.

स्वभावजेन कौन्तेय निबद्धः स्वेन कर्मणा ।
कर्तुं नेच्छसि यन्मोहात्करिष्यस्यवशोऽपि तत् ॥

Svabhāva-jena Kaunteya
nibaddhaḥ svena karmaṇā /
kartuṁ n'ecchasi yan mohāt
kariṣyasy avaśo' pi tat // 60 //

O son of Kuntī! Duties which your natural tendencies have imposed upon you, but which out of delusion you refuse to do, even that you will have to perform by the compulsion of Nature.

ईश्वरः सर्वभूतानां हृद्देशेऽर्जुन तिष्ठति ।
भ्रामयन्सर्वभूतानि यन्त्रारूढानि मायया ॥

Iśvaraḥ sarva-bhūtānāṁ
hṛd-deśe' rjuna tiṣṭhati /
bhrāmayan sarva-bhūtāni
yantr'ārūḍhāni māyayā // 61 //

O Arjuna! The Lord dwells in the heart of all beings revolving them all by His mysterious Power Māyā, as if they were objects mounted on a machine.

तमेव शरणं गच्छ सर्वभावेन भारत ।
तत्प्रसादात्परां शान्तिं स्थानं प्राप्स्यसि शाश्वतम् ।।

Tam eva śaraṇaṁ gaccha
sarva-bhāvena Bhārata /
tat-prasādāt parāṁ śāntiṁ
sthānaṁ prāpsyasi
śāśvatam // 62 //

O scion of Bharata's clan! Seek refuge in Him, making a total surrender of your being—body, mind and soul. By His grace you shall attain to supreme peace and the everlasting abode.

इति ते ज्ञानमाख्यातं गुह्याद्गुह्यतरं मया ।
विमृश्यैतदशेषेण यथेच्छसि तथा कुरु ॥

Iti te jñānam ākhyātaṁ
guhyād guhyataraṁ mayā /
vimṛśy'aitad aśeṣeṇa
yath'ecchasi tathā kuru // 63 //

Thus have I imparted to you wisdom which is more secret (profound) than all that is secret (profound). Reflecting over this whole teaching, do as you think fit.

सर्वगुह्यतमं भूयः शृणु मे परमं वचः ।
इष्टोऽसि मे दृढमिति ततो वक्ष्यामि ते हितम् ॥

Sarva-guhyatamaṁ bhūyaḥ
śṛṇu me paramaṁ vacaḥ /
iṣṭo' si me dṛḍham iti
tato vakṣyāmi te hitam // 64 //

Listen again to My supreme word, the profoundest of all spiritual teachings. You are well beloved of Me; and so I shall tell you what is beneficial to you:

मन्मना भव मद्भक्तो मद्याजी मां नमस्कुरु ।
मामेवैष्यसि सत्यं ते प्रतिजाने प्रियोऽसि मे ।।

Man-manā bhava mad-bhakto
mad-yājī māṁ namas-kuru /
mām ev'aiṣyasi satyaṁ te
pratijāne priyo' si me // 65 //

Let your mind be engrossed in Me. Offer worship to Me. Be resigned to Me. Beloved as you are of me, I pledge in truth you shall come to Me alone.

सर्वधर्मान्परित्यज्य मामेकं शरणं व्रज ।
अहं त्वा सर्वपापेभ्यो मोक्षयिष्यामि मा शुचः ॥

Sarva-dharmān parityajya
mām ekam śaraṇam vraja /
ahaṁ tvā sarva-pāpebhyo
mokṣayiṣyāmi mā śucaḥ // 66 //

Abandoning (after sincere trial) dependence on all Dharmas (or human efforts at moral and spiritual upliftment),come to Me as the only Refuge. Grieve not; I will deliver you from all sins.

इदं ते नातपस्काय नाभक्ताय कदाचन ।
न चाशुश्रूषवे वाच्यं न च मां योऽभ्यसूयति ।।

Idaṁ te n'ātapaskāya
n'ābhaktāya kadācana /
na c'āśuśrūṣave vācyaṁ
na ca māṁ yo' bhyasūyati //67//

This should on no account be imparted to those who do not practise austere living, who have no devotion to Me, who cavil at Me, and are devoid of the discipline of service.

य इमं परमं गुह्यं मद्भक्तेष्वभिधास्यति ।
भक्तिं मयि परां कृत्वा मामेवैष्यत्यसंशयः ।।

Ya idam paramaṁ guhyaṁ
mad-bhakteṣv abhidhāsyati /
bhaktiṁ mayi parāṁ kṛtvā
mām ev'aiṣyaty asaṁśayaḥ // 68 //

He who teaches this supremely profound doctrine among men devoted to Me, having thereby offered to Me the highest form of loving service, shall undoubtedly come to Me alone.

न च तस्मान्मनुष्येषु कश्चिन्मे प्रियकृत्तमः ।
भविता न च मे तस्मादन्यः प्रियतरो भुवि ॥

Na ca tasmān manuṣyeṣu
kaścin me priya-kṛttamaḥ /
bhavitā na ca me tasmād
anyaḥ priyataro bhuvi // 69 //

No man can do anything more pleasing to Me than he, and nor shall any one on earth be dearer to Me than he.

अध्येष्यते च य इमं धर्म्यं संवादमावयोः ।
ज्ञानयज्ञेन तेनाहमिष्टः स्यामिति मे मतिः ।।

Adhyeṣyate ca ya imaṁ
dharmyaṁ saṁvādam āvayoḥ /
jñāna-yajñena ten'āham
iṣṭaḥ syām iti me matiḥ // 70 //

It is My view that he who studies this conversation between us should be regarded as adoring Me with a sacrifice of knowledge.

श्रद्धावाननसूयश्च शृणुयादपि यो नरः ।
सोऽपि मुक्तः शुभाँल्लोकान्प्राप्नुयात्पुण्यकर्मणाम् ।।

Śraddhāvān anasūyaś ca
sṛṇuyād api yo naraḥ /
so' pi muktaḥ śubhāṁl lokan
prāpnuyāt puṇya-
karmaṇām // 71 //

Even a man who listens to this holy conversation between us with deep faith and receptivity shall attain to liberation and the happy regions open to righteous men.

कच्चिदेतच्छ्रुतं पार्थ त्वयैकाग्रेण चेतसा ।
कच्चिदज्ञानसम्मोहः प्रनष्टस्ते धनञ्जय ।।

Kaccid etac chrutaṁ Pārtha
tvay'aik'āgreṇa cetasā /
kaccid ajñāna-sammohaḥ
praṇaṣṭas te Dhanañjaya // 72 //

Has this teaching been heard by you, O Arjuna, with a concentrated mind? Has all delusion born of ignorance been dispelled from you, O Dhanañjaya?

अर्जुन उवाच —
नष्टो मोहः स्मृतिर्लब्धा त्वत्प्रसादान्मयाच्युत ।
स्थितोऽस्मि गतसन्देहः करिष्ये वचनं तव ॥

Arjuna uvāca:
Naṣṭo mohaḥ smṛtir labdhā
tvat-prasādān mayā'cyuta /
sthito' smi gata-sandehaḥ
kariṣye vacanaṁ tava // 73 //

Arjuna said:

My delusion has been dispelled and my memory restored by Thy grace, O Undecaying Lord! I now stand firm, with all my doubts cleared, ready to execute Thy command.

सञ्जय उवाच —

इत्यहं वासुदेवस्य पार्थस्य च महात्मनः ।
संवादमिममश्रौषमद्भुतं रोमहर्षणम् ।।

Sañjaya uvāca:
Ity ahaṁ Vāsudevasya
Pārthasya ca mahātmanaḥ /
saṁvādam imam aśrauṣam
adbhutaṁ roma-
harṣaṇam // 74 //

Sañjaya said:

Thus have I heard, with my hair standing on end, this wonderful conversation between Kṛṣṇa and the high-souled son of Pṛthā.

व्यासप्रसादाच्छ्रुतवानेतद्गुह्यमहं परम् ।
योगं योगेश्वरात्कृष्णात्साक्षात्कथयतः स्वयम् ॥

Vyāsa-prasādāc chrutavān
etad guhyam ahaṁ param /
yogaṁ yog'eśvarāt kṛṣṇāt
sākṣāt kathayataḥ svayam //75//

Thus did I, by Vyāsa's grace, directly hear Kṛṣṇa, the Lord of Yoga, Himself teaching this Yoga, profound and supreme.

राजन्संस्मृत्य संस्मृत्य संवादमिममद्भुतम् ।
केशवार्जुनयोः पुण्यं हृष्यामि च मुहुर्मुहुः ।।

Rājan saṁsmṛtya-saṁsmṛtya
saṁvādam imam adbhutam /
Keśav'ārjunayoḥ puṇyaṁ
hṛṣyāmi ca muhur-muhuḥ // 76 //

Again and again, O King, does the memory of that sacred and astounding dialogue between Keśava and Arjuna come to my mind, causing no end of joy.

तच्च संस्मृत्य संस्मृत्य रूपमत्यद्भुतं हरेः ।
विस्मयो मे महान्राजन्हृष्यामि च पुनः पुनः ॥

Tac ca saṁsmṛtya-saṁsmṛtya
rūpam atyadbhutaṁ Hareḥ /
vismayo me mahān rājan
hṛṣyāmi ca punaḥ-punaḥ // 77 //

Again and again does that most wondrous form of Hari arise in my mind, generating great astonishment and endless thrills of joy.

यत्र योगेश्वरः कृष्णो यत्र पार्थो धनुर्धरः ।
तत्र श्रीर्विजयो भूतिर्ध्रुवा नीतिर्मतिर्मम ।।.

Yatra yog'eśvaraḥ Kṛṣṇo
yatra Pārtho dhanur-dharaḥ /
tatra śrīr vijaya bhūtir
dhrūvā nītir matir mama // 78 //

Wherever there is Kṛṣṇa, the Lord of Yoga, accompanied by Arjuna wielding the bow—there reign good fortune, victory, prosperity and sound policy. Such is my conviction.

Srī Kṛṣṇārpaṇam astu